P 2

CW00663214

Inside M

A Cornish Arthurian Reader
1000–2000

Amy Hale was born in Michigan and grew up in Florida. She is Lecturer in Contemporary Celtic Studies at the Institute of Cornish Studies. In 1998 she was awarded a doctorate for her research into Celtic identities in Cornwall. Recent publications have included chapters in *Celtic Geographies* and *Cornish Studies*, as well as reviews for *Folklore (Journal of the Folklore Society)*. She is co-editor of *New Directions in Celtic Studies*.

Alan M. Kent was born in St Austell. He is an author and academic. His recent publications include *The Literature of Cornwall: Continuity, Identity, Difference 1000–2000*, *Voices from West Barbary: An Anthology of Anglo-Cornish Poetry 1549–1928* and *Looking at the Mermaid: A Reader in Cornish Literature 900–1900*. He is presently completing a new verse adaptation of the *Ordinalia*.

Tim Saunders was born in Northumberland and was brought up in Cornwall. As well as writing poetry he is the author of a range of important articles, essays and translations. He is the editor of *The Wheel: An Anthology of Modern Cornish Poetry 1850–1980* and co-editor of *Looking at the Mermaid: A Reader in Cornish Literature 900–1900*. His book *The High Tide: Collected Poems in Cornish 1974–1999* was published in 1999. He is a bard of the Cornish Gorseth.

Amy Hale, Alan M. Kent
and Tim Saunders

Inside Merlin's Cave

A Cornish Arthurian Reader
1000–2000

edited by Amy Hale, Alan M. Kent
and Tim Saunders

Francis
Boutle
Publishers

First published by Francis Boutle Publishers
23 Arlington Way
London EC1R 1UY
(020) 7278 4497
email: merlin@francisboutle.demon.co.uk
www.francisboutle.demon.co.uk

Introduction, essays, translations and selection copyright © Amy
Hale, Alan M. Kent and Tim Saunders 2000

All rights reserved.
No part of this book may be reproduced, stored
in a retrieval system, or transmitted, in any form
or by any means, electronic, mechanical photocopying
or otherwise without the prior permission of the publishers.

ISBN 1 903427 04 5

Printed in Great Britain by Redwood Books

Acknowledgements

In our researches for this collection, we would like to thank the following people without whom it would have been difficult to have made this volume as comprehensive as it is: Charles Thomas, Brian Murdoch, Bernard Deacon, Garry Tregidga, Richard Jenkin, Ann Trevenen Jenkin, James Whetter, Les and Gill Goldman, Simon Trezise, Dan Parsons, Andrew C. Symons, Julyan Holmes, Terry Knight, Angela Broome and Roger Penhallurick of the Courtney Library, Royal Institution of Cornwall, Kim Cooper and the staff of the Cornish Studies Library, Redruth, Roger Toy and Don Hutchinson of King Arthur's Hall of Chivalry, Tintagel, the Victoria and Albert Museum, London, Peter Keelan of Salisbury Library, University of Wales, Cardiff, Christina Mackwell and the staff of the Lambeth Palace Library, London, the University of Cambridge Library, the staff of the Morrab Library, Penzance, Melissa Hardie and the Hypatia Trust. Finally, our continued thanks to Clive Boutle and David Russell of Francis Boutle Publishers. We would like to thank authors and their executors for permission to include their work, and in particular Donald R. Rawe and the Lodenek Press for permission to include the extract from *Geraint: Last of the Arthurians*. Every effort has been made to contact authors and we apologise to those we failed to trace. We would be happy to correct omissions in future editions.

Amy Hale, Alan M. Kent and Tim Saunders

Contents

10   List of illustrations
11   Introduction
13   King Arthur and literature in Cornwall
        – Alan M. Kent
20   King Arthur and modern Cornwall – Amy Hale
27   King Arthur and ideology – Tim Saunders

Cornish Arthurian Texts

35   **1** *From* Stone Inscriptions of Cornwall
        (500–800 AD)
35   **2** The Dialogue of Arthur and Eliud by Taliesin
        (c.550)
36   **3** *From* How Culhwch Won Olwen (c.1000)
37   **4** *From* The History of the Kings of Britain by
        Geoffrey of Monmouth (1136)
42   **5** Concerning the Miracles of St Mary of Laudun by
        Hermann of Tournai (1146)
42   **6** The Prophecy of Merlin by John of Cornwall
        (c.1150)
46   **7** *From* The Cornish Glosses of the Prophecy of
        Merlin by John of Cornwall (c.1150)
47   **8** *From* The Romance of Tristan by Béroul (c.1150)
49   **9** The Sicilian Coverlet (c.1400)
50   **10** *From* Arthur, a short sketch of his life and
        history in English verse by the Marquis of Bath
        (c.1428)
52   **11** *From* Le Morte D'Arthur by Thomas Malory
        (1485)
67   **12** *From* Beunans Meriasek by Radolphus Ton
        (1504)
67   **13** *From* Itinerary by John Leland (c.1540)
68   **14** *From* A Herring's Tail by Richard Carew (1598)
70   **15** *From* The Survey of Cornwall by Richard Carew
        (1602)
71   **16** *From* The Lives of the Saints by Nicholas
        Roscarrock (c.1620)

71   **17** *From* Merlin's Prophecies and Predictions by
     Thomas Heywood (1651)

72   **18** *From* The Dutchesse of Cornwall's progresse to
     see the Land's end & to visit the mount by Nicholas
     Boson (c.1665)

73   **19** The History of King Arthur, and his Progenitors
     by William Hals (c.1736)

81   **20** *From* Cornubia: A Poem in Five Cantos by
     George Woodley (1819)

82   **21** *From* The Fabulous History of Cornwall by
     Thomas Hogg (1827)

87   **22** The Sisters of Glen Nectan by Robert Stephen
     Hawker (c.1831)

88   **23** *From* Scilly and its Legends by H.J. Whitfeld
     (1852)

96   **24** *From* Idylls of the King by Alfred, Lord Tennyson
     (1856–74)

101 **25** The Quest of the Sangraal by Robert Stephen
     Hawker (1863)

113 **26** *From* Popular Romances of the West of
     England: The Drolls, Traditions, and Superstitions
     of Old Cornwall by Robert Hunt (1865)

120 **27** The Buried City by John Harris (1868)

121 **28** Dozmare Pool, Cornwall by John Brent (1880)

123 **29** *From* Tristram of Lyonesse by A.C. Swinburne
     (1882)

126 **30** *From* An Unsentimental Journey through
     Cornwall by Dinah Craik (1884)

127 **31** *From* Cornish Feasts and Folklore
     by Margaret A. Courtney (1890)

128 **32** *From* The Arthurian Legend
     by John Rhys (1890)

128 **33** Lyonesse by James Dryden Hosken (1902)

129 **34** *From* Some Possible Arthurian Place-Names in
     West Penwith by Henry Jenner (1912)

142 **35** *From* Legend Land by 'Lyonesse' (1922)

144 **36** The Famous Tragedy of the Queen of Cornwall
     at Tintagel in Lyonesse by Thomas Hardy (1923)

173 **37** The Coming of Arthur by John Baragwanath
     King (1925)

183 **38** Anglice, a Patriotic Song of our Motherland by
     Katharine Lee Jenner (1926)

184 **39** Tintagel Castle in History and Romance by
     Henry Jenner (1927)

191   **40** *From* Ceremonies of the Gorseth of the Bards of Cornwall (1928–present)

191   **41** *From* King Arthur's Territory by J. Hambley Rowe (1929)

193   **42** *From* King Arthur: His Symbolic Story in Verse by B.D. Vere (1930)

198   **43** An Balores/The Chough by Robert Morton Nance (1932)

202   **44** *From* Dawn in Lyonesse by Mary Ellen Chase (1938)

203   **45** *From* Trystan hag Ysolt/Tristan and Isolt by A.S.D. Smith (1951) and D.H. Watkins (1962)

213   **46** *From* Mines and Miners of Cornwall by A.K. Hamilton Jenkin (1970)

215   **47** *From* Geraint: Last of the Arthurians by Donald R. Rawe (1972)

216   **48** Arthur by Tim Saunders (1990)

217   **49** *From* Nativitas Christi/The Nativity by Alan M. Kent (2000)

219   Appendix: texts in Cornish

235   List of primary characters

236   Bibliography and sources

247   Notes

254   Further reading

List of illustrations

14   The Sicilian Coverlet (c. 1400)
23   Tintagel Haven by J.M.W. Turner (1818)
25   The Cornish Gorseth in 1933 at Roche Rock by Herbert Truman.
30   Tintagel Castle by J. Farington (1813)

Introduction

A visit to any of the numerous book and gift shops at Tintagel, or elsewhere in Cornwall, will reveal to the reader a host of books, pamphlets, posters, postcards, models, sculptures, toys and music inspired by Arthurian legend. Yet despite all the vast international outpouring of literature about Arthur there has not been a volume which collected writing, creative and critical, which placed Arthurian legend firmly in a Cornish context. A lacuna all the more surprising since Arthurian legend has numerous associations with Cornwall; Tintagel itself, Lyonesse, and the ancillary Arthurian corpus of Tristan and Isolde literature.

Cornwall is often viewed as marginal to the main story, as providing little more than a birthplace for Arthur at Tintagel. We hope that this volume will be a corrective, presenting texts which demonstrate the special continuum of Arthurian writings and scholarship within the Cornish context.

Our sweep has been wide. We have drawn on some sources common to many Arthurian anthologies, together with others long neglected, or even unknown. We pay attention to the continuum of Arthuriana concerning Cornwall in its links with wider global Arthurian interests, but highlight the legend's interaction with Cornish literature and culture. As interest in Cornish literature and history seems to be growing at a rapid pace, we hope that this is a timely collection of material, which will help to define and celebrate the Cornish imagining of Arthurian legend.

Our three introductory essays examine particular threads of the Arthur theme. Following the texts themselves, there is an appendix containing the original Cornish texts of translated material, contextual biographies, commentaries and references to sources, and notes. Older maps of Tintagel Island give no mention of Merlin's Cave, but in the nineteenth century with the accompanying rise in tourism and mining, the name came to be applied to the cave below the promontory. In an imaginative spirit we hope that you will enjoy exploring the spell-books, prophecies, manuscripts and books inside this literary Merlin's Cave.

Amy Hale
Alan M. Kent
Tim Saunders

King Arthur and literature in Cornwall

Two stories seem to have pervaded my childhood and they have both been with me ever since. The earliest, so far as I can remember, was King Arthur and the Knights of the Round Table, told to us (from which version I have no idea now) by Mrs Hacker at Foxhole Primary School. This narrative was then reinforced in my boyish mind by one of the many trips that Currian Tours of Nanpean would run each summer up to Tintagel on the north coast. This spot was everything that the china clay area was not, glamorous, beautiful, ancient and (I choose this adjective carefully) 'magical'. The fascination stayed with me and in the course of my work on Cornish and Anglo-Cornish literatures, and other literatures from across the globe, I have discovered a tremendous variety of versions, forms and re-tellings of the legends.

But I mentioned two stories. The second narrative was from an entirely different source, the St Austell cinema, for it was there in 1977 (I was ten) that I first saw George Lucas' epoch-defining space fantasy *Star Wars*. Not that I knew it at the time, but in this vision were all the hallmarks of Lucas' knowledge of Arthurian legend – Luke Skywalker (a kind of young Arthur), Obi-Wan Kenobi (a Merlin figure), the chivalric rescue of Princess Leia, and the fight against an oppressive Empire (Celts against Saxons).[1] There were also Jedi Knights wielding lightsabres which resembled swords. Fast forward to 1999 and Lucas begins to release a set of three prequels to the original *Star Wars* trilogy. The first, *The Phantom Menace*, more fully establishes the Jedi Knights as the guardians of peace and justice in the Galaxy, far, far away, a long time ago, and has a Round Table gathering known as the Jedi Council.

It is through the studies of mythology by Joseph Campbell that we are able to comprehend these two phenomena. In *The Hero with a Thousand Faces* (1949) Campbell demonstrates how despite infinite variations, the myths of the world actually show a limited number of responses to our life experience.[2] At the core of these responses is Campbell's astounding analysis of the composite hero and his journey to self-understanding and amelioration of the rest of the world. First of the stages is what Campbell terms 'departure', followed by 'initiation', then the 'return'. Alongside this, there is exploration of the transformation of the hero and place of myths in our society. It is often said that the authentic art of storytelling (and of the droll-telling of Cornwall) has died. But this is a misguided view. Luke Skywalker is

V&A Picture Library

The Sicilian Coverlet (c.1400), one of fourteen quilted silk panels depicting the early part of the Tristan narrative. It shows the popularity of Cornish narratives across Europe in the medieval period.

as much a figure consonant with Campbell's argument as King Arthur, Tristan or any of the Knights of the Round Table. This hero and this kind of myth continues to fascinate us today as it did our ancestors.

The development of Arthurian myth in literature has been examined by numerous scholars and that is ground I do not wish to retread here.[3] However, in order to better understand the relationship between the development of the wider European myth of Arthur and his Cornish context, it is perhaps worth considering some of the major trends and moments of production. That way the reader will be able to locate Cornish Arthurian material into the broader continuum.

Arthur can be identified as a single or perhaps multiple historical figure(s) who fought against invading Germanic peoples. To this extent, he may be read as a Celtic chieftain fighting for the last remaining unconquered pieces of territory, broadly Wales, Scotland, Cumbria and the south-west peninsula of the island of Britain. That he was successful can in part be measured by the fact that these areas long retained their older languages into the modern era,[4] and that a sense of 'difference' can still be discerned.[5] What happens after his death is a process of embellishment, whereby various writers took the story and retold the narrative to fit their particular cultural and political situation. This process has continued throughout the twentieth century and will no doubt continue well into the new millennium.

Initially, however, Arthur was a symbol of British/Celtic resistance against invasion and it is not surprising that we find our first evidence of literary imaginings of Arthur in medieval Welsh sources, though it is indeed probable that Cornish or south-western based writers were generating their own constructions which are now sadly lost.[6] Besides, though certain texts are now viewed as Welsh, they were actually written in lowland Scotland. Therefore it is an emergent Brythonic literature (which would at a later date sub-divide into Cornish, Breton and Welsh) which first starts to record the events of Arthur. Presumably, the earliest of these accounts would be the most accurate, since there was less embellishment, and perhaps more fact. Not surprisingly we have drawn on some of those sources here, wherever the 'Welsh' writer chose to incorporate Cornish material.

This period was followed by the first more romantic imaginings of Arthur, inspired in part, by Geoffrey of Monmouth's *History of the Kings of Britain*,[7] but also by other Prophetic Merlin texts,[8] and perhaps also by other lost manuscripts. Certainly, it is Geoffrey who is popularly viewed as making the link between Arthur and Tintagel. Geoffrey's account was enormously influential in its day and is really the text which initiates further embellishment in the early medieval period. We have also have also included what survives of material by his Cornish contemporaries.

In 1191 the monks of Glastonbury announced the discovery of the grave of Arthur and Guinevere at the Abbey. Alongside the two bodies was a small cross identifying this site as the Island of Avalon. Whether or not this was a forgery, it was a propaganda coup and ensured that visitors and money flowed to the Abbey. The subsequent impact of the discovery was great. Since that time, this location has been embedded into the consciousness of Arthurian writers, and welded onto the existing narratives. Already one can see how ideologically Arthur was shifting, from being a champion of the Britons, towards becoming 'a great King of England', even though at first under the auspices of a French-speaking monarchy. In the aftermath of this find and in the centuries that followed numerous Cornish writers wove events here onto native ones.

Elsewhere a very new application of Arthurian legend was emerging in the French romances and courtly love poetry. Cornwall was not absent from these developing traditions. Cornwall has suffered the indignity of being considered very marginal in numerous histories of literature. Despite over thirty playing-place sites and a healthy mystery play culture,[9] only very recently has Cornwall's significance in the overall development of continental literature been considered.[10] It is very probable that forms and themes of drama crossed the Channel in both directions, principally via Brittany, and then onwards into the European hinterland. Arthurian legends may have become a staple of the French romances in the same way; the Tristan story was popular as far away as Sicily.

In the middle of the twelfth century, Robert Wace composed his version of the Arthurian legends, *Roman de Brut*,[11] dedicated to Eleanor of Aquitaine, recently married to Henry Plantaganet, a patron of both Geoffrey of Monmouth as well as Wace himself. It was in Wace's version that Arthur was portrayed as a heroic Christian king in the mould of Charlemagne. His version was all that was needed to set the trend. Chrétien de Troyes (1135–83) in writing his romances on Arthur introduced the element of courtly love.[12] It is likely that some of these romances passed back to Cornwall, though Cornish material was being supplanted in favour of gallantry, love from afar and imaginings of the 'faery' world of Arthur, far removed from the actuality of Arthur's life.[13]

In the aftermath of the crusades there had been growing Christian fervour and veneration of cult objects. The quest for the Holy Grail brought a spiritual dimension into Arthurian romances. In Cornwall, this particular symbol had even more resonance, since for centuries the Cornish had told narratives of the visit of the child Christ to Cornwall with Joseph of Arimathea, who travelled there to trade for tin. The legend of Christ in Cornwall has numerous local associations, not least with the Jesus Well of North Cornwall, and Creegbrawse Mine, between Chasewater and St Day, where the child Christ supposedly preached.[14] Joseph of Arimathea was also said to have visited Glastonbury itself, planting his staff at the foot of Glastonbury Tor.[15] It seems likely that these stories (and a connection between the St Michael sites, running from west Cornwall to Glastonbury)[16] were emergent during this phase.

Thomas Malory's *Le Morte D'Arthur* (c.1450) is based largely on the French romances yet interweaves into this more of the Celtic material concerning Cornwall. In Malory's re-telling, Arthur's legitimacy is questioned and this opens up the issue of civil war. It also foreshadows the later Renaissance concern, reflected in many of Shakespeare's dramas, with the questioning of kingship and government.[17] To understand this literary phase we need look no further than the so-called Round Table at Winchester, where the centrepiece is a large Tudor rose combined with a picture of King Arthur resembling Henry VIII. Despite his historical origin as a 'Celtic Briton', Arthur was here recast as the 'unifying' figure over England. As the seventeenth century opened up, Arthur, a King of Cornish origin, began to be rejected as a 'model' for all that was good. Even Cornishmen, such as Richard Carew, were happy to satirise Arthurian romance and see in it everything that was outmoded and worthless about old Cornwall. Paralleling the literary rejection, we also see the first signs of Tintagel Castle itself falling into ruin and decay. For the rest of the seventeenth century and during most of the eighteenth century, very few texts on Arthur were produced either in Cornwall or elsewhere. It seemed as if the 'great Celtic hero' had slipped from popular consciousness.

The republication of Malory's *Le Morte D'Arthur* in the early nine-teenth century was to change all that, however, as did the realisation that Britain had emerged as Victorian world superpower, with an Empire, a confident modern outlook and a kind of ideological realisa-tion that anything was possible and achievable. King Arthur was sud-denly hauled out of the mists of time, and began to look like the right kind of heroic image for this Victorian society.[18] Major writers such as William Morris and Alfred Tennyson constructed new verse epics to mirror this new society; Tennyson visited Cornwall. Cornish writers also reclaimed Arthur and investigated his origins. Robert Stephen Hawker delivered his vision of the Grail quest in his *The Quest of the Sangraal,* while folklorists began to collect 'authentic' versions of what Arthuriana had survived among the general populace. This was matched by a proliferation of new Anglo-Cornish poetry which saw Arthur as symbolic of a 'great' industrial Cornwall. In the wider cul-tural context, Pre-Raphaelite painters had begun to see the potential in depicting this Arthurian world, incorporating both Celtic and 'faery' elements into their paintings.[19]

In the wider British context Arthur had taken on a massive sym-bolic role – the projection of him as 'King of England' complete. However, in Wales and Cornwall, this wider role for Arthur was prob-lematical. In essence, much of this re-evaluation of Arthur there had come out of the folkloric activity of the mid-century. Initially, this had simply sought to record the narratives and stories for posterity, but increasingly such narratives and folklore were being used politically to reassert the regional territorial identities of the islands of Britain. In Cornwall, after the collapse of the industrial infrastructure at the end of the nineteenth century, there was a move to reconstruct Cornish identity. The reconstructionists looked back to a period of Cornish his-tory (which in their view at least) was more Cornish. Its tokens were Celtic saints, holy wells, Cornish language and literature, other pre-industrial folkloric survivals, and of course King Arthur. Thus, while Arthur, in the opening years of the twentieth century, continued to be celebrated in literature, art, decoration and symbol as everything great about Britain, paradoxically Cornish Revivalists took a different view. To them Arthur, no less than the Cornish chough, was symbol supreme of Celtic resistance, of nationhood, of language. In the liter-ature of the period, we see a rise in the use of this image, and in the development of the Cornish Gorseth a growing incorporation of Arthurian material which differentiated it from sister institutions in Wales and Brittany. Activists in Cornwall's twentieth-century Revival reappraised Arthurian sites, literature and place-names.

Not everything would go the way the Revivalists might have wished however. As Victorian fascination with Arthuriana rose to new heights, Tintagel became a kind of pilgrimage site and a wealth of Arthurian trappings was devised to support this tourist culture. Railway companies did much to play on Arthurian themes and all kinds of new expressions of Arthuriana started to emerge.[20] The depression of the 1930s and World War Two put paid to Arthur as symbol of Britain's greatness. Arthuriana was to emerge in the post-war period in new forms, in film and television (possibly best realised in John Boorman's *Excalibur* and ABC's *Merlin*, but also in Monty Python's comedy treatment *Monty Python and the Holy Grail*), in new spirituality as well as just about every cultural product possible, ranging from action figures and cartoons, to the popular paperback fiction of Marion Zimmer Bradley and Bernard Cornwell.

Linked to the specifically Arthurian legends were those of Tristan and Lyonesse, each with a separate origin, but by reason of cultural geography and cultural assimilation incorporated into the totality of the Arthurian corpus. The original teller of the story of Tristan must have been either a Cornishman or someone with intimate knowledge of the south Cornish coast and its landscape. A.S.D. Smith's *Trystan hag Isolt*, one of the finest poetic works in 'revived' Cornish effectively completed the circle between present imaginings of the love triangle and its first fashioning (certainly told or written in Cornish or proto-Cornish).

Lyonesse is a more recent incorporation. One of the more popular modern Arthurian re-tellings for children is Michael Morpurgo and Michael Foreman's *Arthur: High King of Britain* (1994), a story which begins on the Islands of Scilly and has the hero (a boy) taken down into Arthur's underworld, where he has resided since the ending of Camelot.[21] Various indigenous Cornish legends surround the flooding of Lyonesse. They are associated with the area surrounding St Michael's Mount (formerly known as 'the Hoar Rock in the Wood'), the escape of Trevilian onto the mainland Cornish coast, before the waves engulfed him (demonstrated by the family arms which bears a horse emerging from the sea) and the various literary references which record how Tristan was born on a ship returning from the land of Lyonesse. Like Tennyson, Thomas Hardy's fascination with the Tintagel area and his poem 'When I set out for Lyonesse' (1870) has also helped to fix the association between Arthur and Lyonesse in the collective consciousness.

Cornwall has generated and has helped to inspire a tremendous quantity of Arthurian literature, of great quality. When we think of Cornwall, we should never feel too much regret about what has been lost, but concentrate more on what has survived. To those who dismiss Cornwall's function in the Arthurian cycles I say re-examine the work here. Arthur, like Luke Skywalker, is with us for a long time yet.

Alan M. Kent

King Arthur and modern Cornwall

One of the most captivating characteristics of Arthur himself (and the legends surrounding him) is his mercurial ability to be all things to all people. That his origins lie in the dim and distant past, and his historical reality is tantalising difficult to secure, are perhaps two of the reasons why his popularity has been so enduring. Whether or not Arthur's origins lie in Cornwall is almost (but certainly not entirely) a moot point. What we do know is that the association of Arthur with Cornwall has profoundly affected both the Cornish and non-Cornish inhabitants of this peninsula. It is probable that Arthur has been a more powerful figure in Cornwall in the past one hundred and fifty years than ever before. The contemporary position of Arthur is in many ways as interesting as his origins. As we shall discover, myths and legends continue to grow and change, there is no single 'authentic' telling. Importantly, legendary material, aside from being entertaining and symbolic, impacts on and reflects cultural, political and economic developments. *Inside Merlin's Cave*, then is about the process of myth and legend making within one particular territory. By presenting these texts we hope to provide a detailed case study about why a story has continued to be relevant to a particular people over possibly a fifteen hundred year period. We can see how it changes and adapts, which features become locally the most salient and repeated, and which characters are the most popular. Stories are told for a reason, and it appears that the Cornish have always had a reason to tell stories about Arthur.

Arthur's most recent ascendancy to power began in the second half of the nineteenth century and has continued almost unabated ever since. There were a number of influences which led to the renewed interest in Arthur at that time. One of the most significant factors adding to his popularity was the overall rise in interest in mythology and folktale during this period, inspiring scholarly research into the nature and history of Arthur, as well as the collecting of localised variants of Arthurian and related legends and their relationship to particular landscapes.[22] Often, Arthurian research was motivated by theories suggesting that folklore was the repository of 'national' character.[23] It was theorised that if Arthur was a 'national' hero, his tales must therefore reflect aspects of 'essential Britishness'.

These theories concerning national identity reinforced other developments of the time. Particularly in England, Arthur became emblematic of the ideal imperial monarch and inspiring leader, unifying all lands under his crown while warding off all enemies, and demanding great moral and physical achievement from his knights.[24] During the Victorian period, Arthurian legend, particularly Tennyson's re-telling of it, became the touchstone for a number of typically Victorian moral projections about wider British society. Arthurian art and literature during this phase stressed conservatism, chivalry, romantic love, and importantly, reinforced arguments about the traditional position of women in society as both objects to be adored and as defenders of morality. Arthurian legend promoted a vision of an unsullied pre-industrial, pre-modern Britain, but also one which was unified, confident and imperially successful.

However, the way Arthur was interpreted in the Celtic regions was somewhat different. Even in England, much of the folklore research into Arthur attempted to trace his roots to the pre-Christian, pre-Roman mythology of the 'ancient Britons' and link them with mythological counterparts in Ireland which paradoxically never developed an Arthur tradition.[25] Although Malory's version of *Le Morte D'Arthur,* which established Arthur as an *English* monarch, was the version of the tale with which most people of the period were familiar, his Celtic roots were often acknowledged. This was certainly apparent in Arthurian inspired art which often adopted typically 'Celtic' ornamental motifs.[26] The concept that Arthur could belong to a 'purer' (i.e. pre-Roman) British Celtic culture was compelling, and reinforced notions of an imagined unified, uniform island. For some scholars these comparative theories provided an argument for the underlying similarities between Britain and Ireland during a period when Irish nationalist politics were being highlighted.[27] Arguing for a single parent culture was in fact a not-so-well concealed argument for political union between England and Ireland, and also helped justify the rest of the United Kingdom as well.

Cornwall's positioning within the growing Arthurmania was unique. Cornwall was at once different, separate and Celtic, yet simultaneously administered as an English county. In many ways Cornwall was the perfect place for the birth of Arthur, and ideal as a physical centre of Arthurian pilgrimage. However, the effects of the association of Arthur with Cornwall actually enhanced the recognition of Cornish difference (albeit in a variety of ways) both inside and outside the territory, and ultimately Arthur became a symbol of Cornish resistance.

Perhaps the earliest manifestation of Arthur in Cornwall in the modern era was in response to the newly-born tourist industry. Although it is likely that Arthurian material had been in popular circulation in Cornwall for centuries, like all folklore it too was subject to trends with both peaks and troughs. In the mid-nineteenth century, Arthurian lore among the Cornish in Cornwall appeared to be waning. According to folklorist Robert Hunt, who was collecting Cornish narrative material during this period, although there were many places in

Cornwall with Arthurian associations, the tales themselves did not appear to be among the corpus of narratives being told by the general population. Obviously this was not always the case, as this collection attests. However, this was to soon change. Two linked events occurred which reignited interest in Arthur in Cornwall; the publishing of Tennyson's *Idylls of the King* and widening access of travel into Cornwall.

The role of Tennyson in popularising Arthuriana cannot be underestimated. Tennyson's first visit to Cornwall in 1848 inspired his interest in the legends. The popularity of the *Idylls* throughout Britain was astounding.[28] A wide section of the population during this period was familiar with the *Idylls* and the series also inspired new interest in the French and German romances as well, particularly in Malory's *Morte D'Arthur*. This fascination was reflected in the visual arts and literature of the period, perhaps best exemplified by the Pre-Raphaelite school, the Arts and Crafts movement, and the William Morris studio, all of which drew heavily on Tennyson.[29]

Tennyson's journey was emblematic of the influx of visitors to Cornwall inspired by new-found depictions of Cornwall as a romantic periphery. Although at the time of Tennyson's visit Cornwall was still primarily conceived of as a heavily industrialised mining territory, within forty years the mining industry had collapsed and it began to be seen in new ways by visitors. The introduction of the railway to Cornwall in 1859 had a significant impact, as one might expect. The Great Western Railway company in particular promoted Cornwall as an ideal tourist destination within Britain, emphasising not only its climate and unique vegetation, but also its cultural difference.[30] Great Western Railway guide books depicted Cornwall as a remote land of myth and legend; somewhat different to the industrial centre it only just previously had been. This construction of Cornwall as an exotic yet domestic tourist destination was supplemented by romantic artists and writers coming to Cornwall to experience sweeping elemental landscapes and a 'timeless' culture.[31] Two in particular who had an impact on North Cornwall, Arthur's primary Cornish landscape, were the writer Thomas Hardy and the painter J.M.W. Turner, whose somewhat exaggerated portrayal of Tintagel island secured it firmly within popular imagination as a remote and rugged landscape.

This atmosphere formed just the right backdrop for a boom in Arthurian tourism in Cornwall. In some ways, Tintagel itself is a product of the tourist industry. Until the 1880s Tintagel was known as Trevena, only the headland itself was known as Tintagel.[32] For centuries the economy of the village was based on agriculture and slate-quarrying, but in the 1880s boarding houses and hotels bearing King Arthur's name were built to serve the newly developing tourist trade. One significant development in promoting Tintagel's Arthurian heritage was the building of King Arthur's Halls of Chivalry by custard magnate Fredrick Glasscock. In 1928, Glasscock, who had become entranced by the area, purchased what was then known as Trevena

Tintagel Haven. Engraving by George Cooke after the painting by J.M.W. Turner (1818).

House and in 1929 began rebuilding the house into the Halls of Chivalry.[33] The building was to become home to a neo-chivalric order based on loyalty, devotion and respect. The Hall itself was a tremendous centrepiece for Arthurian enthusiasms in Tintagel. It took four years to complete and includes original Pre-Raphaelite style paintings by William Hatherall and seventy-two outstanding stained glass windows by Veronica Whall, considered to be some of the best ever produced. Glasscock also amassed an impressive collection of manuscripts concerning Arthuriana and Celtic mythology. There is no doubt that the Halls were an important contributing feature to the Arthurian craze of the 1920s and 1930s, and also helped to highlight the other areas associated with Arthurian legend already present in the Cornish landscape.

In the late twentieth century there is a debate over the role of Arthurian tourism in Cornwall, particularly its impact on Tintagel itself. Some feel that the Arthurian overkill in Tintagel, particularly reflected in seemingly incongruous developments such as 'King Arthur's Car Park', cheapen the value and mystery of the original 'authentic' legendary material. Others perceive Arthurian tourism as a viable and crucial aspect of the economy. What is important to remember is that the industry, sites and artefacts which have developed around King Arthur in this century are themselves an important part of history, and reveal in microcosm the different ways in which Cornwall has been perceived over time.

Another aspect of the interest in Arthur in the 1920s directly linked to the growing conceptualisation of Cornwall as a romantic

Celtic territory was the development of Celtic spirituality. Since the 1920s, and possibly before, the area surrounding Tintagel has been a site of spiritual pilgrimage and also a place of settlement for alternative spiritual communities. Arthuriana is a central feature in this development, dating partially from trends in mythological scholarship of the nineteenth century. The predominant theory of mythology of the mid to late nineteenth century was solar mythology, popularised by Max Müller.[34] He theorised that because the movements of heavenly bodies must have been the main preoccupation of early societies, all mythological systems were invented to explain these phenomena. Mythologists seeking the Celtic and symbolic origins of Arthurian lore interpreted Arthur as an aspect of a Celtic solar deity. By the end of the nineteenth century this interpretation of mythology was actually quite prevalent and influential at a popular level.

By the 1920s both Tintagel and Glastonbury, with their Arthurian associations, were being interpreted as sites of early Celtic priesthoods of some significance. An important populariser of this theory was the Austrian educational philosopher Rudolph Steiner whose visit to Tintagel in 1924 had lasting effects. Steiner's lectures and essays form an important basis for many of the popular beliefs surrounding Tintagel and the relationship of Arthur to a Celtic spiritual inheritance. Steiner argued that 'Arthur' was not a personal name, but instead was a title of a priestly class, and that Tintagel was an ancient centre of learning dedicated to studying planetary phenomena and perpetuating the knowledge of the megalithic monument builders. Later esoteric writers such as Wellesley Tudor Pole, who developed the Chalice Well at Glastonbury, championed both Tintagel and Glastonbury as sites of St Michael, Archangel of Light, who also has solar significance. Writing in the 1950s, Tudor Pole argued for a new era of spiritual pilgrimage to sacred sites such as Tintagel which would lead to overall British spiritual regeneration.[35] Writers such as Paul Broadhurst still argue that Arthur was a solar hero and that Tintagel itself is situated on a ley line.

Although there were certainly many reasons why sites like Tintagel and Glastonbury might become the foci for alternative spirituality, there is no doubt that the mystique of Arthurian legend (especially the wider notion of a Grail quest), was a primary factor. Tintagel today remains an important centre for both Pagan and Christian religious activity. Aside from the village itself, which boasts a number of esoteric shops, the associated sites of St Nectan's Kieve, the Rocky Valley maze carving and the Museum of Witchcraft in neighbouring Boscastle have added to the esoteric attraction and draw thousands of visitors each year in addition to the residents for whom the sites are sacred. In fact, the Arthurian associations with the landscape of North Cornwall is part of a wider, mainly twentieth-century, construction of Cornwall in general as a site of particularly Celtic spiritual significance.[36]

As Cornwall was being sold as a mystical Celtic Otherworld by the

The Royal Institution of Cornwall

The Cornish Gorseth in 1933 at Roche Rock. Painting by Herbert Truman.

tourist industry and spiritual pilgrimages to the territory were becoming more common, another, slightly different version of Celtic Cornwall was also being promoted which since the 1920s has used King Arthur as one of its key symbols. Cornish ethnonationalism first started gaining ground in the first years of the of the twentieth century (1901–1904) when a very small number of Cornish activists, under the aegis of the *Cowethas Kelto-Kernuak* (Celtic Cornish Society) petitioned for Cornwall to be admitted into the Celtic Association, the organisation which was the vehicle for the nascent pan-Celtic movement.[37] The earliest aims of Cornish activism were not much different than they have always been: to promote Cornish culture and to revive the Cornish language. In addition, Cornish activists such as L.C. Duncombe-Jewell and Henry Jenner called for the establishment of a Cornish Gorseth similar to the ones in Wales and Brittany. After the initial stirrings, it took about twenty years for the Cornish movement to start gaining a popular base beyond scholars and antiquarians. King Arthur's association with the Cornish movement really begins in 1920 with the start of the Old Cornwall Societies by Robert Morton Nance in St Ives. Nance adopted the chough – the red beaked bird long associated with Cornwall believed to hold the soul of King Arthur – as the emblem for the Old Cornwall Societies. It remains a potent and visible symbol of the Societies to this day.

The chough and King Arthur were also adopted by the Cornish Gorseth. After the first calls for its formation in 1901, it took over a quarter of a century for a Cornish Gorseth to be established. The first Gorseth in 1928 was structurally almost identical to its Welsh counterpart, but within a couple of years the ceremony became more distinctive. Interestingly, its primary distinguishing features are Arthurian. The first Arthurian features were added in 1930 and the remainder in the following year. It is probably no coincidence that the Arthurian elements were added in the year that the International Arthurian Congress was held in Truro, attracting such renowned scholars as R.S. Loomis, and including lectures by Henry Jenner. Several speeches at the Congress argued that Cornwall had a special claim to Arthur, and a Gorseth ceremony was held in honour of the Congress participants. What better way to demonstrate that special relationship than by incorporating Arthur into the Cornish Gorseth ceremony?

Arthur was in many ways the perfect figure for Cornish ethnonationalists of the period to claim. First, he was the ideal British/Celtic hero redeemer figure, waiting to restore prosperity to his kingdom in times of their greatest need. However, Arthurian imagery also suited the aims of individual revivalists. Jenner was a committed royalist. He was also an Anglo-Catholic, and Arthurian legend, particularly the Grail quest, was heavily associated with that movement during the early part of the twentieth century. Nevertheless, Arthur has remained an important symbol for Cornish bards who call for his return every year at the Gorseth, and even for those who wear the chough necktie of the Old Cornwall Societies.

What these three strands of Arthurian interest in contemporary Cornwall have in common is that they all emphasise, in different ways, a distinctively Celtic Cornwall. Arthur's Cornwall is most certainly idealised, and romanticised, but it is also one which is ultimately saved – both spiritually and politically. Arthur's status as redeemer, liberator and figure of resistance has formed the basis for many of the works we have presented in this collection.

Amy Hale

King Arthur and ideology

The matter of Arthur has seeded nearly every literature in Europe. We see in his story every permutation of virtue and horror, of solidarity and cowardice, of delicacy and vice that we can imagine. Above all, there is loyalty to a just cause, whatever the cost, because if justice triumphed once, it can triumph again. In addition to any political, ethnic or social significance, a primary reason for Arthur's continuing popularity is that there are certain constant themes relevant to people from all ages and places. Some of these themes are not necessarily consistent with one another. There is Arthur the rejected child, the orphan in whom nobody believes, and there is Arthur the invincible inheritor of the sacral kingship. There is the wise, all-powerful leader, and there is the mere figurehead who lets his family and his entourage slide out of control. He belongs intimately to us yet ultimately he is everywhere.

Nevertheless, extant sources are tantalisingly scarce in the two linguistic domains closest to whatever historical events lie at the root of the Arthurian legends. How much of the native Brythonic was put into writing during the Roman period we do not know. The climate of north-western Europe has left us no Irish Sea Scrolls, and there is no equivalent to the Rosetta Stone in Wales. The document closest to Arthur's likely period, Gildas' *De Excidio Britanniae*, does not mention him.[38] References to him in the Latin that provided most documentation for centuries are sparse and obscure until at least the turn of the millennium. It is therefore quite fair to ask what proportion of the Arthurian Matter derived from Late Roman Britain and Armorica (Brittany), and how much from the needs of a continental audience several hundred years afterwards. Obviously, different times and places will have different needs from a hero like Arthur. He is a remarkably flexible character.

Arthur is first an icon for that time of troubles during which Roman power dissolved in these islands, and the four modern territories of Britain began to emerge. The present outcome of Scotland, Wales, England and Cornwall was certainly not inevitable. The new Germanic-speaking peoples might not have taken over all the land now known as England. The Cumbrian language, a Brythonic language, related to Cornish, might have survived.[39] The Vikings might have established a distinct nationality in what is now north-east England. But catastrophic change could not be avoided. In times of social and political breakdown, those who strive hardest to defend the existing social structures often precipitate the most far-reaching changes. Arthur may have been one such figure.

The picture of Arthur in the British texts where he is first mentioned perhaps reveals something of Arthur's original societal position. Texts such as *Culhwch and Olwen* or *Arthur and Eliud* portray a military strongman whose retinue provides the context for the adventures of the great, the good and the ghostly. He himself delights in both endless board-games and long border-crossing hunts. He is described in Latin as *tyrannus* (tyrant) and in Welsh as *ymerawdwr* (modern Welsh, emperor). Yet these terms have a historical context as well, and their modern connotations can obscure their original sense. The first term does not necessarily denote a tyrant in the modern sense: while his conduct may in fact generally be exemplary, the *tyrannus* rules without state sanction. Again *ymerawdwr* in the early texts does not denote emperor as in modern Welsh. Derived from the Latin *imperator*, it refers to a military commander. The sixth-century British poet Aneurin says of a dead cavalryman that, although he was not Arthur, he fought well. This may indicate that Arthur the warlord was a touchstone for martial virtue.

There were early writings from Cornwall as well which can help illuminate the early social and cultural context for the Cornish development of an Arthurian tradition. Much of the evidence from the immediate post-Roman period (itself a not wholly relevant concept in Cornwall where there was little or no direct Roman occupation[40]), is physical rather than strictly historical or literary, and perhaps more appropriately, the province of archaeology. However, *The Old Cornish Vocabulary*,[41] dating from about AD1000 is the closest we shall come to the speech of the Cornish in the Arthurian period, and may give us some clues about his position, if not his role. For instance, the Cornish word for a king, *maghtern*, originating in indigenous Cornish legal terminology, originally denoted a minor chieftain operating largely by consent. The word for knight, *marghogyon*, is a compound of *margh* (horse), which also echoed indigenous notions of kingship, most obviously observed in King Mark of the *Tristan and Isolde* material. This link between horses and sovereignty has parallels in both Irish and Welsh legendary material.[42] Words like *caid* (bondsman), *guidthiat* (guard), *kelegel* (chalice), *ruy* (king), *ruifanes* (queen) and *teleinor* (harper) denote social and cultural functions in Cornish, and wider British culture at the time when Arthur would have lived.

What seems clear is that there was a distinctly British need for a hero like Arthur, a strong leader and warrior who battled against an invading and culturally alien force. It arose in what is broadly known as the post-Roman period of the sixth to the tenth century. However, what is truly interesting is the spread and persistence of Arthurian material across the European continent during the medieval period. How is this to be accounted for and under what historical circumstances did it occur? The Arthurian Matter (including the important sub-theme of Tristan and Isolde) was the only Celtic theme to catch on within the rest of Europe until the Ossianic craze of the eighteenth century.[43] The popularity of the work of Geoffrey of Monmouth on the continent may provide a key. Geoffrey of Monmouth was able to create a figure who would be significant to the insular British population and the Breton-speaking population of Brittany and France, many of whom would have been involved in the Norman conquest of Britain. The Normans themselves were a fusion of Viking settlers and northern French farmers and artisans expanded into medieval forerunners of today's multinational corporations.[44] They recruited brave and able people wherever they went, and their leaders made a point of marrying everywhere into the local elite. So it was that many of William the Conqueror's men were by origin Bretons, who were given lands in Cornwall and in the Welsh Marches. These Bretons would have provided a perfect audience for Geoffrey's *History of the Kings of Britain* and may have also been a link to the potential readership and further literary innovations generated on the European Continent.

Thus, Arthur became an expression of national legitimacy in a number of contexts, and also symbolised the refusal to surrender and the determination to endure and prevail. He became a figure of authority and order, his Saxon enemies mutating into every imaginable kind of adversary, natural and supernatural. To this day, 'Arthur' is a name of power amongst the families providing heads of state for the British polity. It was Henry Tudor who brought a new dynamism into the 'British Project', ironically in the process giving Cornwall a Duke called Arthur. The Britons of Cornwall and Wales had played an important part in the revolutionary religious changes of the Tudor period.[45] Those changes in turn transformed the lives of the Cornish and Welsh. One consequence was a decline in the importance of the Arthurian Matter, both amongst the Insular Britons and elsewhere. In England, Arthur subsided into fancy. Throughout the West, a more rigorous historiography was dissolving the substance of the kind of world-view that Geoffrey of Monmouth had successfully created.

Yet as the present volume demonstrates, despite Arthur's ongoing vestigial relevance in Cornish ideology, Arthurian literature in Cornwall declined further during the seventeenth and early eighteenth centuries. During the seventeenth century, historical speculations on Cornish origins began to look to the eastern Mediterranean, to Phoenicia and Judea, rather than to Troy as Geoffrey of Monmouth had claimed. Arthur would have to take his place in an expanded pantheon of prominent 'early Cornishmen', alongside Phoenician traders and stray members of the Lost Tribes of Israel.[46] In any event, the issue of origins was hardly a central one for Cornwall of the six or seven generations following Edward Lhuyd's visit to study the declining language.[47] Confident in its industrial and technological prowess, and in the efficiency of its laws and institutions, Cornwall had no pressing need for defining images of its origins and continuity. But when that need did emerge, towards the end of the nineteenth cen-

Tintagel Castle. Engraving by F.R. Hay after a drawing by J. Farington (1813).

tury, such images would be ready and an Arthurian revival began in earnest among the Cornish.

There were a number of cultural responses in the second half of the nineteenth century which arose from the dramatic social and political changes which occurred in the first half of that century and led to renewed interest in Arthur. Again, this hero would provide a solution to a number of social ills. A rise in cultural nationalism throughout Europe resulted in the promotion of national and native heroes as role models.[48] In Cornwall this was perhaps best exemplified by Arthur's stoutest champion Henry Jenner, who completed the Cornish repatriation of the Arthurian Matter. Jenner's theory of Cornish nationality rested on a trinitarian dialectic of race, faith and language, very much in keeping with the European Romantic nationalism derived from German eighteenth-century thought.[49] There was simultaneously a reaction to the very grim realities of the Industrial Revolution and the horrible conditions that many people faced. In this temporal context, Arthur and his knights become defenders of a nobler, more humane order against the encroaching darkness of industrialism and the ruthlessness of the cash nexus. Arthur and his knights suggested a simpler, less chaotic and unjust era.

In the new millennium the Arthurian ideology leads us in two directions, both backward and forward. It can take us towards the past, drawing us close to the remaining evidence for life in Cornwall during the post-Roman period. What does *this* document tell us about the people who wrote and read it? What does *that* hewn stone tell us about the people who set it up and who saw it? On the way into the past we encounter other people asking their own questions – about sovereignty, identity or spirituality. People will interpret the past in a variety of ways, and create different meanings out of historical documents. Arthur is a central component of the heritage industry in Cornwall[50] (as elsewhere[51]), and the contestations in that arena over ownership and site management, not to mention the conflict between English Heritage and the Cornish Stannary Parliament, have focused many of these issues surrounding Arthur.[52] An understanding of the heritage industry, itself a very modern manifestation, helps us to understand how Arthur is marketed and sold, and how he fits into a general image of Celtic Cornwall. As John Lowerson has shown, the 'modern Celtic spirituality movement' (however contentious that may be), of which Arthuriana has been a key feature, has been a central component in promoting Cornwall as a tourist destination.[53]

People will read and understand history in differing ways according to their own needs for legitimacy. Certainly legend, with its multifarious interpretations, and necessary ambiguities will be used for a variety of purposes. Like Cornish nationalists, practitioners of this 'modern Celtic spirituality movement' will have their own readings of history, and may find their authority and legitimacy comes from a variety of sources.[54] In all likelihood, this volume itself will contribute its own message to the continuum. At the same time, typing in *King Arthur* or *Merlin* into any search engine on the world-wide web will provide the scholar with a hundred sites to consider. In this we see the Celtic texts of the past fast becoming the hypertext of the future. The changes that this will bring are only just beginning to be imagined. This vision leads us towards Arthur's role in representing the future. In modern times, many people in Cornwall have seen in the legend of Arthur's return an assurance that Cornwall could once more attain lost glories. For some people, this meant re-establishing an imagined state of goodness and beauty from the past. For others, it meant establishing a new one. In any event, the net result will be to precipitate change. Even those striving to recapture the past find themselves changing the future. Ever present, ever changing, this is the Arthur of the Cornish.

Tim Saunders

Notes

1. Mary Henderson (1997) *Star Wars: The Magic of the Myth*, New York and London: Bantam Books, pp.1–47.
2. Joseph Campbell (1993 [1949]) *The Hero with a Thousand Faces*, London: Fontana Press.
3. See Alan Lupack (ed.) (1992) *Modern Arthurian Literature: An Anthology of English and American Arthuriana from the Renaissance to the Present*, New York and London: Garland; James J. Wilhelm (ed.) (1994) *The Romance of Arthur: An Anthology of Medieval Texts in Translation*, New York and London: Garland; Richard White (ed.) (1997) King Arthur in History and Legend, London: Dent, pp.xv–xxv.
4. Paul Russell (1995) *An Introduction to Celtic Languages*, Harlow: Longman, pp.1–24.
5. Philip Payton (1992) *The Making of Modern Cornwall: Historical Experience and the Persistence of "Difference"*, Redruth: Dyllansow Truran; M. Wynn Thomas (1992) *Internal Difference: Literature in 20th-Century Wales*, Cardiff: University of Wales Press.
6. Peter Berresford Ellis (1974) *The Cornish Language and its Literature*, London and Boston: Routledge & Kegan Paul, pp. 21–22.
7. Lewis Thorpe (ed. and tr.) (1966) *Geoffrey of Monmouth: The History of the Kings of Britain*, Harmondsworth: Penguin.
8. Peter Goodrich (ed.) (1990) *The Romance of Merlin*, New York and London: Garland, pp.3–70.
9. Jane Bakere (1980) *The Cornish Ordinalia: A Critical Study*, Cardiff: University of Wales Press, pp.14–49.
10. Brian Murdoch (1993) *Cornish Literature*, Cambridge: D.S. Brewer; Alan M. Kent (2000) *The Literature of Cornwall: Continuity, Identity, Difference*, Bristol: Redcliffe.
11. See White (ed.) op.cit., pp.45–60.
12. William W. Kibler and Carleton W. Carroll (eds. and trs.) (1991) *Chrétien de Troyes: Arthurian Romances*, Harmondsworth: Penguin.
13. Ultimately embodied in the work of Edmund Spenser.
14. Tony Deane and Tony Shaw (1975) *The Folklore of Cornwall*, Totowa, New Jersey: Rowman & Littlefield, pp.62–3.
15. John Michell (1983) *The New View over Atlantis*, London: Thames & Hudson, pp.167–9.
16. Hamish Miller and Paul Broadhurst (1989) *The Sun and the Serpent*, Launceston: Pendragon Press, pp.19–36.
17. See obviously Henry V, Macbeth and King Lear. Also a comedy attributed to Shakespeare and William Rowley: R.J. Stewart, Denise Coffey and Roy Hudd (eds.) (1989) *The Birth of Merlin*, Shaftesbury: Element Books.
18. See Lupack (ed.) op.cit., pp.134–429.
19. See Christine Poulson (1999) *The Quest for the Grail: Arthurian Legend in British Art 1840–1920*, Manchester: Manchester University Press.
20. Charles Thomas, 'Hardy and Lyonnesse: Parallel Mythologies' in Melissa Hardie (ed.) (1992) *A Mere Interlude: Some Literary Visitors in Lyonnesse*, Penzance: Patten Press, pp.13–26.
21. Michael Morpurgo and Michael Foreman (1994) *Arthur: High King of Britain*, London: Pavilion Books.
22. For these collections in Cornwall, see Robert Hunt (ed.) (1865) *The Drolls, Traditions, and Superstitions of Old Cornwall: Popular Romances of the West of England (First and Second Series)*, London: John Camden Hotten; William Bottrell (ed.), *Traditions & Hearthside Stories of West Cornwall: First, Second and Third Series*, Penzance: W.

Cornish, Beare and Son, and F. Rodda, 1870, 1873 and 1880.

23. See Amy Hale, 'Re-thinking Celtic Cornwall: An Ethnographic Approach' in Philip Payton (ed.) (1997) *Cornish Studies: Five*. Exeter: University of Exeter Press, pp 87–8

24. Poulson, op.cit.

25. R.S. Loomis (1927) *Celtic Myth and Arthurian Romance*, New York: Columbia University Press.

26. Poulson, op.cit. For later examples, see Courtney Davis (1994), *The Art of Celtia*, London: Blandford.

27. Loomis, op.cit.; Alfred Nutt (1904) *The Influence of Celtic upon Medieval Romance*, London: David Nutt.

28. See J.M Gray (ed.) (1983) *Alfred Lord Tennyson: Idylls of the King*, Harmondsworth: Penguin, p.11.

29. Poulson, op.cit.

30. See Chris Thomas, 'See Your Own Country First: The Geography of a Railway Landscape' in Ella Westland (ed.) (1997) *Cornwall: The Cultural Construction of Place*, Penzance: Patten Press, pp.107–28.

31. For evidence of this, see Denys Val Baker (1973) *The Timeless Land: The Creative Spirit in Cornwall*, Bath: Adams and Dart.

32. See A.C. Canner (1982) *The Parish of Tintagel: Some Historical Notes*, Middlesex: Friary Clark Limited.

33 See Charles Thomas (1993) *Tintagel: Arthur and Archaeology*, London: Batsford.

34. See Richard Dorson (ed.) (1968) *Peasant Customs and Savage Myths: Selections from the British Folklorists, Volume One*, Chicago: University of Chicago Press, pp.66–119.

35. For more comprehensive historical information on esoteric interpretations of Tintagel, see Paul Broadhurst (1992) *Tintagel and the Arthurian Mythos*, Launceston: Pendragon Press; Richard Seddon (1990) *The Mystery of Arthur at Tintagel*, London: Rudolph Steiner Press.

36. See Amy Hale (1998) *Gathering the Fragments: Performing Contemporary Celtic Identities in Cornwall*, Ph.D. thesis, University of California, Los Angeles, pp. 176–213.

37. Amy Hale (1997) 'Genesis of the Celto-Cornish Revival? L.C. Duncombe-Jewell and the Cowethas Kelto-Kernuak' in Philip Payton (ed.) (1997), op.cit., pp.100–11.

38. White, op.cit., pp.3–4.

39. Russell, op.cit., p.16.

40. See Martyn Wakelin (1975) *Language and History in Cornwall*, Leicester: Leicester University Press, pp.48–9.

41. Murdoch, op.cit., pp.10–11.

42. See commentary in Patrick K. Ford (ed. and tr.) (1977) *The Mabinogi and Other Medieval Welsh Tales*, Berkeley and Los Angeles: University of California Press, pp.8–13.

43. Fiona Stafford 'Primitivism and the "Primitive" Poet: A Cultural Context for Macpherson's Ossian' in Terence Brown (ed.) (1996) *Celticism*, Amsterdam: Rodopi, pp.79–96.

44. See Thorpe, op.cit., p.10.

45. Brendan Bradshaw and John Morrill (eds.) (1996) *The British Problem c 1534–1707: State Formation in the Atlantic Archipelago*, Basingstoke, Macmillan; Ian Arthurson (1994) *The Perkin Warbeck Conspiracy 1491–1499*, Stroud: Sutton, pp.168–9.

46. Myths deconstructed by contributors to Keith Pearce and Helen Fry (eds.) (2000) *The Lost Jews of Cornwall*, Bristol: Redcliffe.

47. See Derek R. Williams (1993) *Prying into Every Hole and Corner: Edward Lhuyd in Cornwall*, Redruth: Dyllansow Truran.

48. See Eric Hobsbawm (1993) *Nations and Nationalism Since 1780*, Cambridge: Cambridge University Press.

49. Ibid., pp.58–9.

50. See for example Brian K. Davison (1999) *Tintagel Castle*, London: English Heritage; The Land of Lyonesse at Land's End; The Halls of Chivalry, Tintagel.

51. For Wales, see King Arthur's Labyrinth at Corris, Powys; for Glastonbury, see the Chalice Well; for Brittany, see Antone Minard 'Pre-Packaged Breton Folk Narratives' in Amy Hale and Philip Payton (2000), *New Directions in Celtic Studies*, Exeter: University of Exeter Press, pp. 52–68.

52. John Angarrack (1999) *Breaking the Chains: Censorship, Deception and the*

Manipulation of Public Opinion in Cornwall, Camborne: Stannary Publications, pp. 445–6.

53. John Lowerson 'Celtic Tourism - Some Recent Magnets' in Philip Payton (ed.) (1994) *Cornish Studies: Two*, Exeter: University of Exeter Press, pp.128–37.

54. Marion Bowman 'Contemporary Celtic Spirituality' in Hale and Payton, op.cit., pp. 69–91.

1 Stone Inscriptions of Cornwall (500–800AD)

The Arthur Stone, inscribed stone, Tintagel (6th Century)
PATER COLIAVI–FICIT ARTOGNOV
[*Artognou,*[1] *father of a descendent of Coll, has had this constructed*]

Slaughter Bridge, inscribed stone, Camelford (6th–7th Century):
LATINI IC IACIT FILIVS MAGARI
[*Latinus lies here, son of Magarus*]

Selus Stone, inscribed stone, St Just (5th–6th Century):
SELVS IC IACIT
[*Selus lies here*]

The Tristan Stone, inscribed stone, Fowey (6th Century):
DRVSTANVS HAC IACIT CVNOMORI FILIVS
[*Drustanus*[2] *lies here, son of Cunomorus*[3]]

2 The Dialogue of Arthur and Eliud by Taliesin (c.550)

Arthur
I marvel at it, since I am a poet,
before an oak tree with a beautiful top,
Why does the eagle stare? Why does it laugh?

Eliud[1]**/Eagle**
O Arthur, who won long-lasting praise,
bear[2] of the hosts, refuge of happiness,
the eagle has seen you before.

Arthur
I marvel at it, close to the seas,
and I ask it cautiously:
Why does it laugh? Why does the eagle stare?

Eliud/Eagle
O Arthur, whose career found long-lasting praise,
bear of the hosts, with a look of joy:
the eagle has seen you before.

Arthur
The eagle stands on the top of an oak:
if you sprang from bird-kind,
you would not be tame or gentle.

Eliud/Eagle
O Arthur, charging with sword in hand,
your enemies will not stand before your assault:
I am the son of Madog, son of Uthyr.[3]

Arthur
O eagle, I do not know your kind
that travels the wooded valley of Cornwall:
Madog the son of Uthyr is not alive.

Eliud/Eagle
O Arthur, of language and fierceness,
bear of men, anger will not preserve you:
I was was once called Eliud.

3 *From* **How Culhwch Won Olwen**[1] **(c.1000)**

Twrch Trwyth went between Tawy[2] and Ewyas.[3] Arthur summoned Cornwall and Devon to meet him at the mouth of the Severn. And Arthur said to the soldiers of this island, "The Twrch Trwyth has killed many of my men. By the courage of men, while I am alive he will not go to Cornwall. I shall not pursue him further but strive with him soul for soul. You do as you may." What they did on his advice was to send out a troop of horsemen, with the dogs of the Island as far as Ewyas and he returned from there to the Severn and there, all the experienced soldiers of this Island ambushed him, and drove him by main force into the Severn, and Mabon son of Modron on Gwyn of the Dark Mane, the stallion of Gweddw, went with him into the Severn, and also Gorau, son of Cystenin, and Menw, son of Teirgwaedd, between Lake Lliwan and the Mouth of the Wye and there, Arthur and the champions of Britain fell on him. Osla of the big knife approached and also Manawydan, son of Llyr, and Cacmwri, the servant of Arthur, and Gwyngelli assailed him and grabbed hold first of his feet and ducked him in the Severn until he was covered by the billows. Mabon, son of Modron, spurred fiercely from one side and got the razor from him, and from the other side, Cyledr the Wild approached on his horse and took the shears from him. Before they got the comb he got his feet on dry land, and as soon as he reached the land, no dog or man or horse could keep up with him until he reached Cornwall. For all the evil they suffered trying to get those treasures from him, they got worse trying to save the two men from drowning. As Cacmwri was being pulled up two millstones dragged him into the deep. As Osla of the big knife was running after the boar, the knife fell from his sheath and he lost it. After that, his sheath was full of water: as he was pulled up, it pulled him into the deep. From there Arthur and the hosts went on until they overtook him in Cornwall. The evil that they had got from him up till then was like play compared with what they got from him in trying to get the comb. For all the evils the comb was got from him. From there, he was hunted out of Cornwall, and he was driven towards the sea. It was not known from then on where he went, or Aned and Alhlern either. And from there, Arthur went to bathe and to rest from his tiredness in Kelli Weg in Cornwall.

4   *From* **The History of the Kings of Britain by Geoffrey of Monmouth (1136)**

While I was thinking about these things and many related matters, Walter the Archdeacon of Oxford, a man very learned in the art of public speaking and the history of distant lands, brought me a certain very old book in the British tongue which set out the acts of all the Kings of the Britons from the first one, Brutus, right down to Cadwaladr,[1] son of Cadwallon in a continuous and very elegant narrative. Prompted therefore by his request, even if I would not gather ornate words in the gardens of other men, but satisfied with the rustic style of my own pens I took great care to translate that book into the Latin tongue.

While these things were being done at Winchester, a star of wonderful appearance and brightness appeared, with one beam coming from it. On this beam was a fiery globe, stretched out in the likeness of a dragon, and from its mouth emerged two beams, of which one appeared to stretch out its length over the sky of Gaul, and the other bent towards the Irish sea, and ended in seven smaller beams. When this star had made its appearance, all of those who were looking at it were struck by fear and wonder. Now Uther, the King's brother, driving the enemy army into Wales, was struck by no less a fear, and consulted all the wise men, so that they might inform him what the star might bring. Amongst the others he ordered Merlin to be called, for he had come into the army, so that military matters might be dealt with by his advice. He, having been led into the presence of the King, took up his position, and was ordered to explain the meaning of the star. He, quickly bursting into tears and having called up a spirit, cried out and said, "Oh, irrecoverable hurt! Oh, orphaned people of Britain! Oh, passing of the most noble King! Dead is the famous King of the Britons, Aurelius Ambrosius by whose death we shall all die, unless God brings help. Hasten therefore, most noble duke Uther, hasten, and to make combat with the enemy do not delay. Victory will be in your hands, and you will be King of all Britain. For it is you that yonder star means, and the fiery dragon beneath the star. The beam, which towards the shore of Gaul is stretched out, foretells the most powerful son that will be yours, whose power will possess all the kingdoms that it covers. The other beam means a daughter, whose sons and grandsons, one after another, will possess the kingdom of Britain."

For that mountain was steep, having a hazel grove on its summit, and half-way up broken rocks suitable as lairs for wild beasts. The Britons occupied it and all the night they remained between the rocks and the hazel groves. As the Bear[2] began to revolve round its pole, Uther ordered his consuls and principles to be called to him, so that with their advice he might discuss how they should make an attack on the enemy. They quickly came together in the presence of the King, and he ordered them to say what they advised. They urged Gorlois, Duke of Cornwall, to offer his opinion first. He was a man of great wisdom and mature age. "It is not a matter," he said, "of long-winded chatter and talk, while the night still remains. You should apply boldness and courage, if you wish to enjoy life and freedom any longer. Great is the host of the pagans who are eager for the fray, but we are far fewer. If we wait for the day to break, I do not consider it worthwhile for us to engage them. Therefore, while the darkness persists, let us go down in serried ranks and fall upon them in their camp with a sudden assault. They will not have expected anything, or have foreseen that we might approach in this way. If we boldly rush upon them all of one mind, we shall without doubt be capable of victory." His advice pleased the King and all the others, and they obeyed his warnings. When they were drawn up into units and armed, they sought the camp of the enemy, and decided to charge them with single-minded zeal. But as they drew near, the guards observed their approach, and woke their sleepy comrades with the sound of trumpets. The enemy therefore were stirred up and confused. Some of them hastened to arm themselves, some were overwhelmed with fear, and ran away wherever the impulse led them. But the Britons, moving forward in close formations, quickly came to the camp and rushed in. The entrance having been found, they closed upon the enemy with swords drawn. As the Saxons had been engaged unexpectedly, they did not give battle in a manly way, while the Britons took boldness from their forethought. Then the Britons set about charging fiercely, and they killed the pagans in their thousands. In the end, Octa and Eosa[3] were taken, and the Saxons were completely scattered.

Very many prominent men had come, together with their wives and daughters, worthy of a joyful feast. There was present among the others Gorlois, Duke of Cornwall, with Igerna his wife, whose beauty was greater than that of all the women of Britain. When the King beheld her amongst the other women, he suddenly warmed with love for her, so that, ignoring the others, he turned all his attention to her. She was the only one to whom he constantly sent dishes and to whom he sent gold cups by trusted messengers. He smiled at her constantly and he interjected light-hearted words. When her husband noticed this, he became so angry that he left the court at once without permission. There was nobody there who managed to call him back, because he feared to lose that one thing that he loved above all others. Therefore Uther became angry and ordered him to return to his court so that he might claim from him recompense for the injury suffered. When Gorlois recoiled from obeying this, the King grew so angry that he swore by an oath that he would devastate his territory, unless he hastened to grant satisfaction. Without delay, while the aforesaid anger remained between them, the King gathered a great army, set out for the province of Cornwall, and set fire to cities and castles. Now Gorlois did not dare to engage him, for his force of armed men was smaller. At this he decided to fortify his castles, until he might receive his help from Ireland, and as he was more concerned for Igerna than he was for himself, he placed her in the castle of Tintagel on the shore of the sea, which he had as a safe retreat. But he himself went to his castle of Demeliock,[4] so that if ill-fortune should overtake them, both should not be endangered. When the King has been informed of this, he went to the castle where Gorlois was, and besieged it, and shut off its approaches. When at last a week had gone by, remembering his love for Igerna he said to a certain retainer of his, called Ulfin of Ricaradoch,[5] "I am burning with love of Igerna, and I believe that I shall have no joy, nor escape danger to my body, unless I possess her. You, therefore, advise me how I can fulfil my desire, or else I shall perish from my inner woes." To this Ulfin replied, "And whose while will it be worth advising you, when there is no route whereby we may reach her in the castle of Tintagel? It is set on the sea, and is on every side surrounded by it, nor is there another entrance, apart from that offered by a narrow rock. Three armed soldiers can bar it, even though you take your stand with the whole realm of Britain. But if the prophet Merlin were to concentrate on the matter, I consider that by his advice you could attain your desire." Convinced, the King therefore ordered Merlin to be called, for he too had come to the siege. Merlin was immediately called and when he presented himself to the King, he was ordered to give advice on how the King might fulfil his desire on Igerna. He, perceiving the agony that the King suffered was moved because of his love for her was so great and said, "In order for you to be able to have your way, you must use arts that are new and unheard of in your time. I know how, by my drugs, to give the form of Gorlois, so that in every way you seem like him. Therefore if you obey, I will give you his exact appearance, and Ulfin that of Jordan of Tintagel, his retainer. For my part, having adopted another appearance, I shall come along as a third man, and you will be able to enter the castle safely, to Igerna, and have admittance." The King therefore obeyed, and paid attention. Finally he entrusted the siege to his retainers, dosed himself with Merlin's drugs, and was changed into the appearance of Gorlois. Ulfin was changed into Jordan, and Merlin into Bricelm, so that to nobody would they resemble what they had been. They then set out on the way towards Tintagel and at twilight came to the castle. Immediately the gate-keeper had been informed that the leader was approaching, the gates were opened and the men were admitted.

Who else could be approaching, when it seemed that Gorlois himself was approaching? Therefore the King stayed that night with Igerna, and satisfied his desires by love. He had deceived her by the false appearance he had taken on. He had deceived her also by made-up sayings, which he cunningly put together. He said that he had come out of his besieged castle, so that he might see to the one he loved, and to his castle. She, believing him, refused him nothing that he demanded. Therefore that night she conceived the most renowned Arthur, who afterwards was renowned for his wonderful uprightness. Meanwhile, when it was discovered at the siege that the King was not present, his army, acting without consultation, attempted to overthrow the walls and so called the besieged count[6] out to battle. He, also acting ill-advisedly, went out with his fellow soldiers, believing that with a small force he would be able to resist so many armed men. As they fought hither and thither one of the first to be killed was Gorlois, and his comrades were scattered. Also the castle that they had besieged was captured, and the treasure placed there was shared out in a far from fair way. Each one savagely grabbed whatever luck and strength allowed him. When the action of this had died down, messengers came to Igerna, to inform her of the death of the Duke and the outcome of the siege. But when they looked at the King sitting by her in the guise of their leader, they, blushing, marvelled at him. He, whom they had left dead in the siege, had arrived unharmed. They did not know what drugs Merlin had concocted. The King laughed at such tales, and with these words he embraced the Countess, "I have not, of course, been killed, but as you see, I live, although I grieve at the destruction of my fortress, and the slaying of my companions. We should fear that the King may prevail because of this, and seize us in this castle. Therefore I shall go out first to meet him, and I shall make peace with him, less worse befall us." Having gone out thus, he sought out his own army, put off the likeness of Gorlois and returned to being Uther Pendragon. When he heard all that had happened, he grieved the death of Gorlois, but he rejoiced at Igerna's being released from her marriage bonds. Going back to the castle of Tintagel, he took it. He also took Igerna, and his desire was attained. They remained together from then on as equals, bound by a great love. They had a son called Arthur and a daughter called Anna.

And Arthur, had become more bitterly angry because he had lost so many hundreds of his fellow-soldiers. When the slain had first been placed in the tomb on the third day, he approached the city. He besieged his nephew[7] who had been admitted to it. He, nevertheless, being unwilling to abandon his enterprise, but encouraging those who followed him in very many ways, ventured out with his columns and prepared to do battle with his uncle. When the engagement had begun, great slaughter was done on both sides, which bore more heavily on his side, so he abandoned the field in ignominy. Thereupon, he, not taking much care for the burial of his slain, quickly carried away in flight by boat, setting a course towards Cornwall. Now Arthur was tormented by inner anguish, because he had escaped so many times, and immediately followed him into the aforesaid country, right to the river Camel, where Mordred was awaiting his arrival. Then Mordred, as he was the boldest of all, and always the swiftest to give battle, immediately drew up his men in their units, endeavouring rather to live or die than continue to flee. There still remained sixty thousand of his comrades from the aforesaid host, from whom he formed three divisions. In every one of them he placed six thousand, six hundred and sixty-six armed men. After that he made one division from the remainder who were left over, and when a leader had been given to each of the others, he placed that one under his own command. When they had been drawn up, he encouraged each one, promising them the possessions of others, if they held fast unto victory. On the opposite side Arthur also set out his army, which he divided into nine columns of infantry drawn up in a square with a left and a right wing. Having assigned a commander to each one, he urged them to wipe out the oath-breakers and robbers who had been shipped into the island[8] from foreign parts at the instigation of his betrayer, and to strive to deserve their honour. He also said that the jumbled collection of Barbarians from various countries were unfit for war and unfamiliar with battle, and those people could in no way be as courageous as they themselves had been in many battles, if the Britons were eager to attack them boldly or to fight manfully. While they went hither and thither urging on their respective soldiers, the front ranks suddenly clashed, and strove with repeated blows to join in close combat. In this way such great slaughter was made on both sides, so many cries of the dying and so much fury of the attackers, that it is too great and painful to describe it all. Everywhere men were wounding and being wounded. They were killing and being killed. When they had spent much of the day in this manner, Arthur charged with his column, in which he had placed six thousand, six hundred and sixty-six men, onto that division where he knew Mordred to be, and, opening a way with a sword, he broke into it, and perpetrated a most grievous slaughter. There his execrable betrayer fell, and many thousands with him. Nevertheless, the host did not flee because of his fall, but streamed together from the entire field and gave all of their boldness to try and stand their ground. A most fierce combat was therefore joined between them, for nearly all the leaders who were present on both sides fell, together with their units. There fell on Mordred's side: Cheldric, Elaf, Egbrict, Bunign, Saxons: Gillapatric, Gillamor, Gislafel, Gillar, Irish, and the Scots and Picts, with almost all who commanded them. On Arthur's side Olbrict, King of Norway, Aschill, King of Dacia, Cador Limenic, Casibelan, together with many thousands of his men, both Britons and of other nations, whom he had brought with him. But that famous King Arthur was fatally wounded, and was taken from there to heal his wounds on the island of Avalon, and gave the crown of Britain to his kinsman Constantine, son of Cador, Duke of Cornwall in the five hundred and forty second year from the Incarnation of the Lord.

5   Concerning the Miracles of St Mary of Laudun by Hermann of Tournai (1146)

Then we came from Exeter into the area which is called Dumnonium,[1] where people showed us the chair and oven of King Arthur, famous in the stories of the Britons, and they said that this had been Arthur's land ... In the town which is called Bodmin ... there was a certain man with a withered hand, who was keeping watch beside the shrine, hoping to recover his health. However, just as the Bretons[2] are accustomed to quarrel with the French about King Arthur, so this man began to dispute with one of our household, called Little Hagan, who was from the household of Guy, archdeacon of Laon, saying that Arthur was still alive. From this argument arose a great uproar; many people rushed into the church with weapons and, if Algard the cleric had not intervened, it would probably have resulted in bloodshed. We believe that God was displeased with the riot beside his shrine, for the man with the withered hand, who caused the disturbance over Arthur, did not recover his health.

6   The Prophecy of Merlin by John of Cornwall (c.1150)

> O East wind, your seed uproots the South Wind
> from our gardens, and the tithed follows the example of
>   the tither;
> there shall be born across in timber, keen and encased in
>   iron,
> fighting in the fields in threefold armour,
> a people fierce in wars, burning for the slaughter of the
>   Saxon.
> Afterwards those who gave their effort to rakes and
>   ploughs
> will not spare their mother and will reach into her entrails.
> Every wrong that makes a yoke of slavery for a people
> they owe to Treachery; let me not be troubled to remember
>   it.
> > How many years will the Prince have lived to restore our
> > people? Twice over seven you will reckon the same
> > number,
> Cruel Northern France, parent of a fertile soil, rejoicing
> that twin heirs of an avenger are growing up as dragons.
> First, a bow is bent for the destruction of one;
> the other laughs under the melancholy shadow of a name,
> he will be feared four times twice and five years.
> > But the lion of justice, to whom all things indeed are

fulfilled, that lion lasts twice seven over eight;
clipping the claws of hawks and the teeth of wolves,
he gives all forests and all harbours everywhere.
Every nine this one rears, the town eroded by the Seine
trembles, and in the Atlantic each island of Dragons.
Then the curly-headed one will put on a many-coloured
    cloak
and his clothes will not protect him from the misdeeds of
    an unsound mind; then there will be squeezed from
    the narcissus and the thorn
and gold will flow from the horns of the grazing cattle.
Therefore, willing or not, with a foot cut off, the barking
    one
will make a treaty with the stag. The appearance of money
    is split
to this; also the form of half a circle is added.
   Henceforth the Aarau, the most famous flying creature,
will seize its nest and Scotland will weep for its snatched
    cubs.
Alas! what crime of the sea will the third bring forth!
The one unmoved by that was ransomed for his threefold
    fierceness.
On seven French-born of the blood on one mother
a sad, ruddy-throne, having suffered so many deaths, so
    many ends,
cries out and declares: 'Normandy, do you know what is
    going on?'
Recently I too suffered, recently I poured out my entrails;
only through these destructions can destruction be
    relieved.
O wide island, you are swimming with tears! There is
    scarcely me,
and all are kings today, because the sword is used too
    sparingly.
From now on, this one is the possessor surrounded by
    unfilial terror;
With his face covered in shadows of night, the lion's
progeny, hostile once more, will shine against the stars.
A broken law will call an eagle to anger with a cub
and those who skulk in the woods hunting to the very
    walls,
that the bulls will sometime hate those whom they fear.
No love of brothers or true faith of allies,
or very little calm, over willows climb brambles.
Alas, too great a licence is given to wolves and kites.
Three times six revolutions shall this age last.
   You, House of Arthur, a subjected faith-breaking people,

then you will see the seizure of cattle of the plains of
    Reont.
But what are you doing in defiance? O Victorious one, wait
    a while;
why, effeminately painted with make-up and with curled
    hair,
lost people, why do you dress with rings, why do you love
    to make yourself vulgarly familiar with the trivia of
    Venus?
You are punished: one plague, one pain condemns us all;
Abandoned you will lie, unless you can bring comfort.
Flame, hunger, diseases or whatever new upheavals, your
    fates
conspire against you, these things also whip others.
Behold, in the pillaging of his father, with lightning, round
    the hard
head, girdled about and bringing low the crest of the
    helmeted one,
the pale adopted one shall walk round the springs of
    Periron.
What is his standing? What hope in our seed?
Let him serve or let him perish, or let him lose wealth and
    name,
the translateral hills of Scotland will approach,
in the land of Arfon the brass plague is being forged;
a bird of prey reins in a boar and reveals the ancestral
    time.
This third nest will fall apart again;
a year will come, London will yield up the remains of the
    sceptre.
I was amazed at first, I am amazed that he stood forth
    second,
or fourth, or fifth. Soon there will arise from the citadel of
    the Britons
so that he may grow, so that the javelin may be made into
    a lance,
make a tomb for all will be raised up as a sad machine;
death will be envied, nor will the shape of money be
    simple.
    Learn the way at last, Cornwall, learn the work.
And our cradles shall bring back the Saxon mourning.
Why is our hand so generous? Who thereafter will be
    thought free?
    Where the Great Bear[1] looks, where the Tamar flows
    South,
by the yoke of Brentigia the French lord it everywhere,
if you would continue to live, O Queen, you will so
    unplough,

out of which rat-catchers and buck goats are multiplied in
    value,

The fury of the winds and every revolt against the citizens
will rage until the sad anger of the thunder ceases.

Therefore, let the unfortunate common people share the
    favour,

and in the meantime for itself, it will make unimportant
    prayers.

Religion weeps, the frocked ones prays vainly,
he who turns the heaven, who forges the lightning listens.
In the past, Ireland lies down for the sixth;
Also the offspring of the West reach out for the North.
And why so late paying the menacing castle?
When the shield was permitted it was useful to pay the
    fare.

Is he more praiseworthy for his piety or his prowess in
    arms?

Demolishing fortifications, reducing groves to level
    ground,

he will make the hills naked, he will renew the statutes
    and laws.

He who will put onto his side, wings previously cut off
and also with a lion's mane placed in his locks
more sure in affection, he will reach into high places by
    flight,

for indeed he will separate the temples of holy men,
and the dragon will not send alert kings into the pastures.
He will bedeck cloaks with cities and attractive jewels
and joyously bestow his own favours on virgins;
then seeking one, he will gladly marry her.
His years will be few, and swift for the little ones.
Go, days of the Lynx! May you be ashamed, German
    worm,

that you and your gods crossed our frontiers.
It will anger and act for itself, why did Northern France
    burn more slowly? And like an old keystone England
    will place its old name.

Thus may she go to hers, may my race eradicate her.
  May the weather be fine. Conan[2] will sail the waves
and may he who commands the East support Cadwaladr.
A horseman whiter than snow loosening the reigns of his
    mount,

all for duty having passed the whirlpool of Periron,
with a whitening rod snatches the streams in the middle of
    a circle,

and measures a mill over it.
After so many disasters and often stormy labours,
the Severn will hear so many trumpets, so many of its

battles to be mixed, your rivers laugh, O Tevi![3]
And the thorns tremble, the twins pitch their tents.
Now there, now in another place, the first things are owed
    to Reont.
The enemy will receive lances, stakes, swords and darts in
    their warm flanks; gore flows and stains everybody;
I bear witness that the waves are happy, the sands are
    happy.
The German tyrants would have been happy if they had
    ceased before.
Whoever are worthy of their horses and close in handling
    spears,
they will learn to conquer, few will desert the standards.
For shame! Eight and ten thousand there just now.
Four turn back in ignoble disgrace.
Behold what Gwynedd[4] wanted, and it rises again
to its golden head and leads the people back together,
a woman will change fleeces for purple cloths,
a man brings silver until the City of the Legions[5] has
    squeezed;
the valleys burst out and the oaks are green,
the mountains of Arfon[6] reach the clouds with their peaks.
Posterity will lift up the crown of the Great Briton;
The good appearance of the leaders extends to deserved
    honours,
the appearance of the two extends to ordinary customs.
Three times twenty, three times a hundred finish the years,
golden freedom and age the same colour in heaven

Here endeth the Prophecy of Ambrosius Merlin
    about the seven kings.

7   *From* **The Cornish Glosses of the Prophecy of Merlin by John of Cornwall (c.1150)**[1]

(46)   [*He lasts*] He lasts in an aforesaid rhythm that is eight and
they all make thirty-five; which is again divided in this manner; that
is twenty-five years and a half; by that is not to be understood a half
of a half, but rather a half of twenty, namely ten.[2]
(61)   [*Three-fold fierceness*] For he was partly Norman, partly
Scots, and partly descended from the direct nobility of the Cornish.
(63)   [*Solium*] The Kingdom that is Cornwall which in history is
called the House of Coronius because that man Coronius got it by lot
from Brutus in ancient times; the House is also called the Kingdom of
Arcturus[3] because he arose as the greatest of Kings amongst them.
(66)   [*He now*] He now, then etc. All this was brought about when
the Viscount Frewin and other Cornishmen conspired in his punish-

ment and they killed them at a town which is called Treruf and even more things are said here that I shall pass by lest my speech be seen.

(87) [*Flame and Hunger*] Flame, that is copious burning. Hunger. That hunger sometimes rises from the menacing greed of the despoilers and sometimes from barbarity. For in that time the wind raves like one possessed, so that it leaves the prayers of the husbandmen unfulfilled. This evil he calls in the British tongue the wind of the leaves, which means the shaking out of the wind.

(91) [*Canus adoptatus*] This is what is said in the British tongue; a King grey like his mare. Of Periron. He says this about his arrival in Cornwall and because he then besieged the castle at Periron which is called Tintagel.

(107) [*Tamar*] Tamar is the river which divides Cornwall and Devon.

(108) [*Brentigia*] Brentigia is a certain wilderness in Cornwall and in our language it is called the Down of the Tree, in the language of the Saxons Fowey Moor.

(111) [*Ventorum*] The which evil Merlin calls rough wind, that is rough wind and it is widely accepted as whatever cruelty it is possible to name.

(119) [*Fatal castle*] The fatal castle is a town in our area which in English is called Ashbury,[4] in the British tongue the Fortress of Beli, or as it pleases some, the castle of the High Wood.

(133) [*German reptiles*] German reptiles, that is the white dragon stands for the Saxons as the red one stands for the Britons.

8   *From* **The Romance of Tristan by Béroul (c.1150)**

They were in the forest of Moresk;[1]
that night they lay on a hill.
Now Tristan is as safe
as if he were in a castle with a wall.
  Tristan was a good archer,[2]
He knew how to use a bow very well.
Governal[3] had taken one
from a forester who owned it;
and two arrows feathered
and tipped that he had taken.
Tristan took the bow, and went into the wood;
he saw a deer, fitted an arrow and shot,
and fiercely struck the right flank:
it cried out, leapt high and sank down.
Tristan took it and came back with it.
He made a shelter: with the sword that he held
he cut the branches, made a bower;
and strew flowers on the ground inside.
Tristan sat down with the Queen.

Governal knew how to cook:
with dry wood, he made a good fire.
Cooks have much to do!
They had neither milk nor salt
at that time in their lodging.
The Queen was very tired
because of the ordeal that she had gone through;
slumber took her, she wished to sleep,
she wanted to sleep resting on her lover.
My Lords, they remained for a long time
deep in the forest;
they were a long time in that wilderness.

—————————

Yseut had not delayed:
through Perinis[4] she reminded Tristan
of all the pain and all the anguish
that she had borne for him that year.
Now the value of it would be returned to her!
If he willed it, she would be able to live in peace:
"Tell him that he knows the marsh well,
at the end of the plank-bridge at Malpas:[5]
There, I soiled my clothes a little.
On the mound, at the end of the plank-bridge,
and a little this side of the Lande Blanche,[6]
let him be dressed in the clothes of a leper;
let him carry a wooden cup,
let him have a bottle beneath
tied on with a strap;
in the other hand, let him carry a stick.
This is the stratagem he must keep in mind.
At the appointed time let him be seated on the ground:
let his face be very pock-marked.
Let him carry the cup in front of his face:
to those who pass by him
let him simply ask for alms:
they will give him gold and silver;
let him keep the silver for me, until I see him
privately, in a quiet room."
Perinis[7] said: "Lady, in faith,
I shall certainly tell him all this."

9   The Sicilian Coverlet (c.1400)

1. COMU: LU AMOROLDU FA BANDIRI: LU OSTI: In CORNUUALGIA
[*How the Morold[1] made the host go to Cornwall*]

2. COMU:LU RRE: LANGUIS: CUMANDA: CHI UAIA : LO OSTI: CORNUAGLIA
[*How King Languis[2] ordered that the host should go to Cornwall*]

3. COMU: LU RRE: LANGUIs: MANDA: per LU TRABUTU In CORNUALIA
[*How King Languis sent to Cornwall for the tribute*]

4. (imperfect) COMU: (li m) ISSAGIEIRI: SO UINNITI AL (lu) RRE: MARCU: Per LU TRIBUTU DI SECTI ANNI
[*How the ambassadors come to King Mark for the tribute of seven years*]

5. COMU: LU AMOROLDU: UAI: IN CORNUUALGIA
[*How the Morold comes to Cornwall*]

6. COMU: LU AMOROLDU: FA SULDARI: LA GENTI.
[*How the Morold made the people pay*]

7.COMU: TRISTAINU DAI: LU GUAnTU ALLU AMOROLDU DELA BACTAGLIA
[*How Tristan gives the glove of battle to Morold*]

8. COMU: LU AMOROLDU: UUINUTU: IN CORNUUALGIA: Cum XXXX GALEI
[*How the Morold is come to Cornwall with forty galleys*]

9. COMU TRISTAINU BUOTA: LA UARCA: ARRETU: INTU: ALLU MARU
[*How Tristan thrust his boat into the sea*]

10. COMU: TRISTAINU: ASPECTA: LU AMOROLDU: ALLA ISOLA DI LU MARU: SANSA UINTURA
[*How Tristan awaits the Morold on the Isle of Sansa Ventura in the sea*]

11. COMU: TRISTAINU FERIU LU AMOROLLDU In TESTA
[*How Tristan wounded the Morold in the Head*]

12. COMU: LU InNA (?) DELLU AMOROLDU: ASPECTAVA LU PATRUNU
[*How the Morold's page(?) awaited his master*]

13. COMU LU AMOROLDU FERIU: TRISTAINU A TRADIMENTU
[*How the Morold wounded Tristan to the point of death*]
14. (imperfect)..SITA IN AIRLANDIA....
[*In Ireland*]

10 *From* **Arthur, a short sketch of his life and history in English verse by the Marquis of Bath (c.1428)**

Armorica[1] on latyn me clepeyd that lond
Tyl Maxymyan[2] conqueryd hyt wyth honde,
And called hyt lyte Bretayne that,
So hyght this lond that he coom fram;
For perpetuell Mynde of grete Bretayne[3]
He called hyt lyte Bretayne
That men schulde kepe in Mynde and wytt
How this lond conquered hytt;
For Walsch Men[4] beth Bretouns of kynde –
Know that well fast on Mynde
Englysh men beth Saxoynes,
That beth of of Engistes Soones;
There-fore the walsch man Breton
Seyth and clepeth vs 'Sayson'[5]
(That to seye vpon a reess,
'Stynkyng Saxone, be on pees')
And seyth (.) 'taw or (.) Peyd Sayson brount'[6]
Whan he ys wroth (:) or ellys drounke;
Hauyng Mynde of Engystis[7] Men
That wyth gye sclow there kyn:[8]
At the place of the Stonehenge
Ghut they thenketh for to venge:
  And that hyt neuere be so,
  Seyth a Pater noster[9] more to ...

  Wyth gret Myght & strong hond,
  and Mordred[10] saingh fayl
Gaf hym tho a strong batayl;
Many a man, as y rede
That day was there dede;
Arthoures nevew Waweyn[11]
That day was thre y-sclayn,
And other knyghtes Many moo:

Than Arthour was heuy &woo.
Mordred fly toward Londoun,
He most nat come in the toun;
Than fled he to Wynchester
And wyth hys Mayn kep hym ther;
And Arthour on gret haste
Pursywed after him faste.
Mordred wythoute fayle
Fled in-to Cornewayle.
The quene wythoute lesyng
Hurde of this tyding,
And how Mordred was flow,
And how to Cornewale he hym drow
Heo of Mercy hadde noon hoope,
Ther-for he dude on a Russet cote
And to Carlyon[12] ys preuyly Roñne
And made heore self tho a Noñne;
Fro that place neur heo wende,
But of heore lyf there made an ende.
Waweynes body, as y reede,
And other lordes that weere deede,
Arthour sente into Skotlonde,
And buryed ham there, y vnderstonde,
Muche folke therhenne he toke tho,
Of Northumber-lond also
Fram dyverse places to Arthour come
His wyll to werk and done:
Thus he sembled a full great Ost;
To Cornewyle he draweth hym fast
After that Mordred the traytour
That hadde do hym Much dyshonour.
That treytour hadde gret Strength
And fulled that lond on brede and length,
Such a battell as there was redy tho
Hadde neuer Arthour byfore y-doo:
They fowght tyl ther come down bloode
As a (.) Ryver or (.)a(.) flood;
They fowght euer soore and sadde;
Men nyst ho the betere hadde;
But at the last Certyn
Was Mordred and alle hys y-sclayn;
And Arthour y-bete wyth wounde,
He Myght not stonde on grounde;
But on lyter ryght anon
Was brwght to Aueloñ[13]
That was a place fayr and Mury;
Now hyt hooteth Glastyngbury.
Ther Arthour that worthy kyng

Maked hys lyues endyng;
But for he skaped that battell y-wys,
Bretoñs and Cornysch seyeth thus,
"That he leuyth ghut parde,
and shall come and be a kyng aghe."
At Glastyngbury on the qweer
They made Artouregh toumbe there
And wrote wyth latyn thus
Hic iacet Arthurus, rex quondam, rex que futurus.[14]
Thys was thus forsothe ydone
The yheer after the incarnacione,
Vyf hundred (.) fourty and two.[15]
Now saue vs alle fra woo
Ihesu cryst, heuenly kyng,
And graunt vu alle hys blessyng;
And that hyt Moote so be
Seyeth alle Pater and Aue.[16]

11   *From* **Le Morte D'Arthur by Thomas Malory (1485)**

1:1

How Uther Pendragon sent for the duke of Cornwall and Igraine his wife, and of their departing suddenly again.

It befell in the days of Uther Pendragon, when he was king of all England,[1] and so reigned, that there was a mighty duke in Cornwall that held war against him long time. And the duke was called the Duke of Tintagil. And so by means King Uther sent for this duke, charging him to bring his wife with him, for she was called a fair lady, and a passing wise, and her name was called Igraine.

So when the duke and his wife were come unto the king, by the means of great lords they were accorded both. The king liked and loved this lady well, and he made them great cheer out of measure, and desired to have lain by her. But she was a passing good woman, and would not assent unto the king. And then she told the duke her husband, and said, I suppose that we were sent for that I should be dishonoured, wherefore, husband, I counsel you, that we depart from hence suddenly, that we may ride all night unto our own castle. And in like wise as she said so they departed, that neither the king nor none of his council were ware of their departing. All so soon as King Uther knew of their departing so suddenly, he was wonderly wroth. Then he called to him his privy council, and told them of the sudden departing of the duke and his wife.

Then they advised the king to send for the duke and his wife by a great charge; and if he will not come at your summons, then may ye do your best, then have ye cause to make mighty war upon him. So that was done, and the messengers had their answers; and that was this shortly, that neither he nor his wife would not come at him.

Then was the king wonderly wroth. And then the king sent him plain word again, and bade hlrn be ieady and stuff him and garnish him, for within forty days he would fetch him out of the biggest castle that he hath.

When the duke had this warning, anon he went and furnished and garnished two strong castles of his, of the which the one hight[2] Tintagil, and the other castle hight Terrabil. So his wife Dame Igraine he put in the castle of Tintagil, and himself he put in the castle of Terrabil, the which had many issues and posterns out. Then in all haste came Uther with a great host, and laid a siege about the castle of Terrabil. And there he pight[3] many pavilions, and there was great war made on both parties, and much people slain. Then for pure anger and for great love of fair Igraine the king Uther fell sick. So came to the king Uther Sir Ulfius,[4] a noble knight, and asked the king why he was sick. I shall tell thee, said the king, I am sick for anger and for love of fair Igraine, that I may not be whole. Well, my lord, said Sir Ulfius, I shall seek Merlin, and he shall do you remedy, that your heart shall be pleased. So Ulfius departed, and by adventure he met Merlin in a beggar's array, and there Merlin asked Ulfius whom he sought. And he said he had little ado to tell him. Well, said Merlin, I know whom thou seekest, for thou seekest Merlin, therefore seek no further, for I am he; and if King Uther will reward me, and be sworn unto me to fulfil my desire, that shall be his honour and profit more than mine; for I shall cause him to have all his desire. All this will I undertake, said Ulfius, that there will be nothing reasonable but thou shalt have thy desire. Well, said Merlin, he shall have his intent and desire. And therefore, said Merlin, ride on your way, for I will not be long behind.

1:2
How Uther Pendragon made war on the Duke of Cornwall, and how by the mean of Merlin he lay by the duchess and gat Arthur.

Then Ulfius was glad, and rode on more than a pace till that he came to King Uther Pendragon, and told him he had met with Merlin. Where is he? said the king. Sir, said Ulfius, he will not dwell long. Therwithal Ulfius was ware where Merlin stood at the porch of the pavilion's door. And then Merlin was bound to come to the king. When King Uther saw him, he said he was welcome. Sir, said Merlin, I know all your heart every deal; so ye will be sworn unto me as ye be a true king anointed, to fulfil my desire, ye shall have your desire. Then the king was sworn upon the Four Evangelists. Sir, said Merlin, this is my desire: the first night that ye shall lie by Igraine ye shall get a child on her, and when that is born, that it shall be delivered to me for to nourish there as I will have it; for it shall be your worship, and the child's avail, as mickle as the child is worth. I will well, said the king, as thou wilt have it. Now make you ready, said Merlin, this night ye shall lie with Igraine in the castle of Tintagil; and ye shall be like the duke her husband, Ulfius shall be like Sir Brastias, a knight of the duke's, and I will be like a knight that hight Sir Jordanus, a knight of the duke's. But wait ye make not many questions with her nor her men, but say ye are diseased, and so hie you to bed, and rise not on the morn till I come to you, for the castle of Tintagil is but ten miles hence; so this was done as they devised. But the duke of Tintagil espied how the king rode from the siege of Terrabil, and therefore that night he issued out of the castle at a postern for to have distressed the king's host. And so, through his own issue, the duke himself was slain or ever the king came at the castle of Tintagil.

So after the death of the duke, King Uther lay with Igraine more than three hours after his death, and begat on her that night Arthur, and on day came Merlin to the king, and bade him make him ready, and so he kissed the lady Igraine and departed in all haste. But when the lady heard tell of the duke her husband, and by all record he was dead or ever King Uther came to her, then she marvelled who that be might be that lay with her in likeness of her lord; so she mourned privily and held her peace. Then all the barons by one assent prayed the king of accord betwixt the lady Igraine and him; the king gave them leave, for fain would he have been accorded with her. So the king put all the trust in Ulfius to entreat between them, so by the entreaty at the last the king and she met together. Now will we do well, said Ulfius, our king is a lusty knight and wifeless, and my lady Igraine is a passing fair lady; it were great joy unto us all, an it might please the king to make her his queen. Unto that they all well accorded and moved it to the king. And anon, like a lusty knight, he assented thereto with good will, and so in all haste they were married in a morning with great mirth and joy.

And King Lot of Lothian and of Orkney then wedded Margawse that was Gawaine's mother, and King Nentres of the land of Garlot wedded Elaine. All this was done at the request of King Uther. And the third sister Morgan le Fay was put to school in a nunnery, and there she learned so much that she was a great clerk of necromancy. And after she was wedded to King Uriens of the land of Gore,[5] that was Sir Ewain's le Blanchemain's father.

1:3
Of the birth of King Arthur and of his nurture.

Then Queen Igraine waxed daily greater and greater, so it befell after within half a year, as King Uther lay by his queen, he asked her, by the faith she owed to him, whose was the child within her body, then she sore abashed to give answer. Dismay you not, said the king, but tell me the truth, and I shall love you the better, by the faith of my body. Sir, said she, I shall tell you the truth. The same night that my lord was dead, the hour of his death, as his knights record, there came into my castle of Tintagil a man like my lord in speech and in countenance, and two knights with him in likeness of his two knights

Brastias and Jordanus, and so I went unto bed with him as I ought to do with my lord, and the same night, as I shall answer unto God, the child was begotten upon me. That is truth, said the king, as ye say, for it was I myself that came in the likeness, and therefore dismay you not, for I am father of the child; and there he told her all the cause, how it was by Merlin's counsel. Then the queen made great joy when she knew who was the father of her child.

Soon came Merlin unto the king, and said, Sir, ye must purvey you for the nourishing of your child. As thou wilt, said the king, be it. Well, said Merlin, I know a lord of yours in this land, that is a passing true man and a faithful, and he shall have the nourishing of your child, and his name is Sir Ector, and he is a lord of fair livelihood in many parts in England and Wales; and this lord, Sir Ector, let him be sent for, for to come and speak with you, and desire him yourself, as he loveth you, that he will put his own child to nourishing to another woman, and that his wife nourish yours.[6] And when the child is born let it be delivered to me at yonder privy postern unchristened. So like as Merlin devised it was done. And when Sir Ector was come he made fiaunce to the king for to nourish the child like as the king desired; and there the king granted Sir Ector great rewards. Then when the lady was delivered, the king commanded two knights and two ladies to take the child, bound in a cloth of gold, and that ye deliver him to what poor man ye meet at the postern gate of the castle. So the child was delivered unto Merlin, and so he bare it forth unto Sir Ector, and made an holy man to christen him, and named him Arthur; and so Sir Ector's wife nourished him with her own pap.

1:6
How Arthur pulled out the sword divers times.

Now assay, said Sir Ector unto Sir Kay. And anon he pulled at the sword with all his might; but it would not be. Now shall ye assay, said Sir Ector to Arthur. I will well, said Arthur, and pulled it out easily. And therewithal Sir Ector knelt down to the earth, and Sir Kay. Alas, said Arthur, my own dear father and brother, why kneel ye to me? Nay, nay, my lord Arthur, it is not so; I was never your father nor of your blood, but I wot well ye are of an higher blood than I weened ye were. And then Sir Ector told him all, how he was betaken him for to nourish him, and by whose commandment, and by Merlin's deliverance.

Then Arthur made great dole when he understood that Sir Ector was not his father. Sir, said Ector unto Arthur, will ye be my good and gracious lord when ye are king? Else were I to blame, said Arthur, for ye are the man in the world that I am most beholden to, and my good lady and mother your wife, that as well as her own hath fostered me and kept. And if ever it be God's will that I be king as ye say, ye shall desire of me what I may do, and I shall not fail you; God forbid I should fail you. Sir, said Sir Ector, I will ask no more of you, but that ye will make my son, your foster brother, Sir Kay, seneschal of all your lands. That shall be done, said Arthur, and more, by the faith of my body, that never man shall have that office but he, while he and I live. Therewithal they went unto the Archbishop, and told him how the sword was achieved, and by whom; and on Twelfth-day all the barons came thither, and to assay to take the sword, who that would assay. But there afore them all, there might none take it out but Arthur; wherefore there were many lords wroth, and said it was great shame unto them all and the realm, to be overgoverned with a boy of no high blood born. And so they fell out at that time that it was put off till Candlemass, and then all the barons should meet there again; but always the ten knights were ordained to watch the sword day and night, and so they set a pavilion over the stone and the sword, and five always watched. So at Candlemass many more great lords came thither for to have won the sword, but there might none prevail. And right as Arthur did at Christmas, he did at Candlemass, and pulled out the sword easily, whereof the barons were sore aggrieved and put it off in delay till the high feast of Easter. And as Arthur sped before, so did he at Easter, yet there were some of the great lords had indignation that Arthur should be king, and put it off in a delay till the feast of Pentecost.

Then the Archbishop of Canterbury by Merlin's providence let purvey then of the best knights that they might get, and such knights at Uther Pendragon loved best and most trusted in his days. And such knights were put about Arthur as Baudwin of Britain, Sir Kay, Sir Ulfius, Sir Brastias. All these, with many other, were always about Arthur, day and night, till the feast of Pentecost.

1:7
How King Arthur was crowned and how he made officers.

And at the feast of Pentecost all manner of men assayed to pull at the sword[7] that would assay; but none might prevail but Arthur, and pulled it out afore all the lords and commons that were there, wherefore all the commons cried at once, We will have Arthur unto our king, we will put him no more in delay, for we all see that it is God's will that he shall be our king, and who that holdeth against it, we will slay him. And therewithal they kneeled at once, both rich and poor, and cried Arthur mercy because they had delayed him so long, and Arthur forgave them, and took the sword between both his hands, and offered it upon the altar where the Archbishop was, and so was he made knight of the best man that was there. And so anon was the coronation made. And there was he sworn unto his lords and the commons for to be a true king, to stand with true justice from thenceforth the days of this life. Also then he made all lords that held of the crown to come in, and to do service as they ought to do. And many complaints were made unto Sir Arthur of great wrongs that were done since the death of King Uther, of many lands that were bereaved lords, knights, ladies, and gentlemen. Wherefore King Arthur made the lands to be given again unto them that owned them.

When this was done, that the king had stablished all the countries about London, then he let make Sir Kay seneschal of England; and Sir Baudwin of Britain was made constable; and Sir Ulfius was made chamberlain; and Sir Brastias was made warden to wait upon the north from Trent forwards, for it was that time the most party the king's enemies. But within few years after Arthur won all the north, Scotland, and all that were under their obeissance. Also Wales; a part of it, held against Arthur, but he overcame them all, as he did the remnant, through the noble prowess of himself and his knights of the Round Table.

4:1

How Merlin was assotted and doted on one of the Ladies of the lake, and how he was shut in a rock under a stone and there died.

So after these quests of Sir Gawaine, Sir Tor, and King Pellinore, it fell so that Merlin fell in a dotage on the damosel that King Pellinore brought to court, and she was one of the damosels of the lake, that hight Nimue.[8] But Merlin would let her have no rest, but always he would be with her. And ever she made Merlin good cheer till she had learned of him all manner thing that she desired; and he was assotted upon her, that he might not be from her. So on a time he told King Arthur that he should not dure long, but for all his crafts he should be put in the earth quick. And so he told the king many things that should befall, but always he warned the king to keep well his sword and the scabbard, for he told him how the sword and the scabbard should be stolen by a woman from him that he most trusted. Also he told King Arthur that he should miss him, – Yet had ye liefer than all your lands to have me again. Ah, said the king, since ye know of your adventure, purvey for it, and put away by your crafts that misadventure. Nay, said Merlin, it will not be; so he departed from the king. And within a while the Damosel of the Lake departed, and Merlin went with her evermore wheresomever she went. And ofttimes Merlin would have her privily away by his subtle crafts; than she made him to swear that he should never do none enchantment upon her if he would have his will. And so he sware; so she and Merlin went over the sea unto the land of Benwick, whereas King Ban was king that had great war against King Claudas, and there Merlin spake with King Ban's wife, a fair lady and a good, and her name was Elaine, and there he saw young Lancelot. There the queen made great sorrow for the mortal war that King Claudas made on her lord and on her lands. Take none heaviness, said Merlin, for this same child within this twenty year shall revenge you on King Claudas, that all Christendom shall speak of it; and this same child shall be the most man of worship of the world, and his first name is Galahad, that know I well, said Merlin, and since ye have confirmed him Lancelot. That is truth, said the queen, his first name was Galahad. O Merlin, said the queen, shall I live to see my son such a man of prowess? Yea, lady, on my peril ye shall see it, and live many winters after.

And so, soon after, the lady and Merlin departed, and by the way Merlin showed her many wonders, and came into Cornwall. And always Merlin lay about the lady to have her maidenhood, and she was ever passing weary of him, and fain would have been delivered of him, for she was afeard of him because he was a devil's son, and she could not beskift him by no mean. And so on a time it happed that Merlin showed to her in a rock whereas was a great wonder, and wrought by enchantment, that went under a great stone. So by her subtle working she made Merlin to go under that stone to let her wit of the marvels there; but she wrought so there for him that he came never out for all the craft he could do. And so she departed and left Merlin.

5:5
How a man of the country told to him of a marvellous giant, and how he fought and conquered him.

Then came to [Arthur] an husbandman of the country, and told him how there was in the country of Constantine, beside Brittany, a great giant which had slain, murdered, and devoured much people of the country, and had been sustained seven year with the children of the commons that land, insomuch that all the children be all slain and destroyed; and now late he hath taken the Duchess of Brittany as she rode with her meiny, and hath led her to his lodging which is in a mountain, for to ravish and lie by her to her life's end, and many people followed her, more than five hundred, but all they might not rescue her, but they left her shrieking and crying lamentably, wherefore I suppose that he hath slain her in fulfilling his foul lust of lechery. She was wife unto thy cousin Sir Howell, whom we call full nigh of thy blood. Now, as thou art a rightful king, have pity on this lady, and revenge us all as thou art a noble conqueror. Alas, said King Arthur, this is a great mischief, I had liefer than the best realm that I have that I had been a furlong way to-fore him for to have rescued that lady. Now, fellow, said King Arthur, canst thou bring me thereas this giant haunteth? Yea, Sir, said the good man, look yonder whereas thou seest those two great fires, there shalt thou find him, and more treasure than I suppose is in all France. When the king had understood this piteous case, he returned into his tent.

Then he called to him Sir Kay and Sir Bedivere, and commanded them secretly to make ready horse and harness for himself and them twain; for after evensong he would ride on pilgrimage with them two only unto Saint Michael's mount.[9] And then anon he made him ready, and armed him at all points, and took his horse and his shield. And so they three departed thence and rode forth as fast as ever they might till that they came to the foreland of that mount. And there they alighted, and the king commanded them to tarry there, for he would himself go up into that mount. And so he ascended up into that hill till he came to a great fire, and there he found a careful widow wringing her hands and making great sorrow, sitting by a grave new made. And then King Arthur saluted her, and demanded of her wherefore she made such lamentation, to whom she answered and said, Sir knight, speak soft, for yonder is a devil, if he hear thee speak he will come and destroy thee; I hold thee unhappy; what dost thou here in this mountain? for if ye were such fifty as ye be, ye were not able to make resistance against this devil: here lieth a duchess dead, the which was the fairest of all the world, wife to Sir Howell, Duke of Brittany, he hath murdered her in forcing her, and hath slit her unto the navel.

Dame, said the king, I come from the noble conqueror King Arthur, for to treat with that tyrant for his liege people. Fie on such treaties, said she, he setteth not by the king nor by no man else; but an if thou have brought Arthur's wife, dame Guenever, he shall be gladder than thou hadst given to him half France. Beware, approach him not too nigh, for he hath vanquished fifteen kings, and hath made him a coast full of precious stones embroidered with their beards, which they sent him to have his love for salvation of their people at his last Christmas. And if thou wilt, speak with him at yonder great fire at supper. Well, said Arthur, I will accomplish my message for all your fearful words; and went forth by the crest of that hill, and saw where he sat at supper gnawing on a limb of a man, baking his broad limbs by the fire, and breechless, and three fair damosels turning three broaches whereon were broached twelve young children late born, like young birds.

When King Arthur beheld that piteous sight he had great compassion on them, so that his heart bled for sorrow, and hailed him, saying in this wise: He that all the world wieldeth give thee short life and shameful death and the devil have thy soul; why hast thou murdered these young innocent children, and murdered this duchess? Therefore, arise, and dress thee, thou glutton, for this day shalt thou die of my hand. Then the glutton anon started up, and took a great club in his hand, and smote at the king that his coronal fell to the earth. And the king hit him again that he carved his belly and cut off his genitours, that his guts and his entrails fell down to the ground. Then the giant threw away his club, and caught the king in his arms that he crushed his ribs. Then the three maidens kneeled down and called to Christ for help and comfort of Arthur. And then Arthur weltered and wrung, that he was other while under and another time above. And so weltering and wallowing they rolled down the hill till they came to the sea mark, and ever as they so weltered Arthur smote him with his dagger.

And it fortuned they came close to the place whereas the two knights were and kept Arthur's horse; then when they saw the king fast in the giant's arms they came and loosed him. And then the king commanded Sir Kay to smite off the giant's head and to set it upon a truncheon of a spear, and bear it to Sir Howell, and tell him that his enemy was slain; and after let this head be bound to a barbican that all the people may see and behold it; and go ye two up to the mountain, and fetch me my shield, my sword, and the club of iron; and as for the treasure, take ye it, for ye shall find there goods out of number, so I have the kirtle and the club I desire no more. This was the fiercest giant that ever I met with, save one in the mount of Araby, which I overcame, but this was greater and fiercer. Then the knights fetched the club and the kirtle, and some of the treasure they took to themselves, and returned again to the host. And anon this was known through all the country, wherefore the people came and thanked the king. And he said again, Give the thanks to God, and depart the goods among you.

And after that King Arthur said and commanded his cousin Howell, that he should ordain for a church to be builded on the same hill in the worship of Saint Michael. And on the morn, the king removed with his great battle, and came into Champayne and in a valley, and there they pight their tents; and the king being set at his dinner, there came in two messengers, of whom that one was Marshal of France, and said to the king that the emperor was entered into France, and destroyed a great part, and was in Burgoyne, and had destroyed and made great slaughter of people, and burnt towns and boroughs; wherefore, if thou come not hastily, they must yield up their bodies and goods.

8:3
How Sir Tristram was sent into France, and had one to govern him named Gouvernail, and how he learned to harp, hawk and hunt.

And then he let ordain a gentleman that was well learned and taught, his name was Gouvernail;[10] and then he sent young Tristram with Gouvernail into France to learn the language, and nurture, and deeds of arms.[11] And there was Tristram more than seven years. And then when he well could speak the language, and had learned all that he might learn in that country, then he came home to his father, King Meliodas, again. And so Tristram learned to be an harper passing all other, that there was none such called in no country, and so on harping and on instruments of music he applied him in his youth for to learn.

And after, as he grew in might and strength, he laboured ever in hunting and in hawking, so that never gentleman more, that ever we heard read of. And as the book saith, he began good measures of blowing of beasts of venery, and beasts of chase, and all manner of vermin, and all these terms we have yet of hawking and hunting. And therefore the book of venery, of hawking, and hunting, is called the book of Sir Tristram. Wherefore, as meseemeth, all gentlemen that bear old arms ought of right to honour Sir Tristram for the goodly terms that gentlemen have and use, and shall to the day of doom,

that thereby in a manner all men of worship may dissever a gentleman from a yooman, and from a yeoman a villein. For he that gentle
is will draw him unto gentle tatches, and to follow the customs of
noble gentlemen.

Thus Sir Tristram endured in Cornwall until he was big and strong,
of the age of eighteen years. And then the King Meliodas had great joy
of Sir Tristram, and so had the queen, his wife. For ever after in her
life, because Sir Tristram saved her from the fire, she did never hate
him more after, but loved him ever after, and gave Tristram many
great gifts; for every estate loved him, where that he went.

8.4

*How Sir Marhaus came out of Ireland for to ask truage of Cornwall,
or else he would fight therefore.*

Then it befell that King Anguish of Ireland sent unto King Mark of
Cornwall for his truage, that Cornwall had paid many winters. And all
that time King Mark was behind of the truage for seven years. And
King Mark and his barons gave unto the messenger of Ireland these
words and answer, that they would none pay; and bade the messenger go unto his King Anguish, and tell him we will pay him no truage,
but tell your lord, an he will always have truage of us of Cornwall, bid
him send a trusty knight of his land, that will fight for his right, and
we shall find another for to defend our right. With this answer the
messengers departed into Ireland. And when King Anguish understood the answer of the messengers he was wonderly wroth. And
then he called unto him Sir Marhaus, the good knight, that was nobly
proved, and a Knight of the Table Round. And this Marhaus was
brother unto the queen of Ireland. Then the king said thus: Fair brother, Sir Marhaus, I pray you go into Cornwall for my sake, and do battle for our truage that of right we ought to have; and whatsomever ye
spend ye shall have sufficiently, more than ye shall need. Sir, said
Marhaus, wit ye well that I shall not be loath to do battle in the right
of you and your land with the best knight of the Table Round: for I
know them, for the most part, what be their deeds; and for to
advance my deeds and to increase my worship I will right gladly go
unto this journey for our right.

So in all haste there was made purveyance for Sir Marhaus, and
he had all things that to him needed; and so he departed out of
Ireland, and arrived up in Cornwall even fast by the Castle of Tintagil.
And when King Mark understood that he was there arrived to fight for
Ireland, then made King Mark great sorrow when he understood that
the good and noble knight Sir Marhaus was come. For they knew no
knight that durst have ado with him. For at that time Sir Marhaus was
called one of the famousest and renowned knights of the world. And
thus Sir Marhaus abode in the sea, and every day he sent unto King
Mark for to pay the truage that was behind of seven year, other else to
find a knight to fight with him for the truage. This manner of message

Sir Marhaus sent daily unto King Mark.

Then they of Cornwall let make cries in every place, that what knight would fight for to save the truage of Cornwall, he should be rewarded so that he should fare the better term of his life. Then some of the barons said to King Mark, and counselled him to send to the court of King Arthur for to seek Sir Launcelot du Lake, that was that time named for the marvelloust knight of all the world. Then there were some other barons that counselled the king not to do so, and said that it was labour in vain, becasue Sir Marhaus was a knight of the Round Table, therefore any of them will be loath to have ado with other, but if it were any knight at his own request would fight disguised and unknown. So the king and all his barons assented that it was no bote to seek any knight of the Round Table. This mean while came the language and the noise unto King Meliodas, how that Sir Marhaus abode battle fast by Tintagil, and how King Mark could find no manner knight to fight for him. When young Tristram heard of his he was wroth, and sore ashamed that there durst no knights in Cornwall have ado with Sir Marhaus of Ireland.

8:5

How Tristram enterprized the battle to fight for the truage of Cornwall, and how he was made knight.

Therewithal Tristram went unto his father, King Meliodas, and asked him counsel what was best to do for to recover Cornwall from truage. For, as meseemeth, said Sir Tristram, it were shame that Sir Marhaus, the queen's brother of Ireland, should go away unless that he were foughten withal. As for that, said King Meliodas, wit you well, son Tristram, that Sir Marhaus is called one of the best knights of the world, and Knight of the Table Round; and therefore I know no knight in this country that is able to match with him. Alas, said Sir Tristram, that I am not made knight; and if Sir Marhaus should thus depart into Ireland, God let me never have worship: an I were made knight I should match him. And sir, said Tristram, I pray you give me leave to ride to King Mark; and, so ye be not displeased, of King Mark will I be made knight. I will well, said King Meliodas, that ye be ruled as your courage will rule you. Then Sir Tristram thanked his father much. And then he made him ready to ride into Cornwall.

In the meanwhile there came is messenger with letters of love from King Faramon of France's daughters unto Sir Tristram, that were full piteous letters, and in them were written many complaints of love; but Sir Tristram had no joy of her letters nor regard unto her. Also she sent him a little brachet that was passing fair. But when the king's daughter understood that Sir Tristram would not love her, as the book saith, she died for sorrow. And then the same squire that brought the letter and the brachet came again unto Sir Tristram, as after ye shall hear in the tale.

So this young Sir Tristram rode unto his eme, King Mark of

Cornwall. And when he came there he heard say that there would no knight fight with Sir Marhaus. Then yede Sir Tristram unto his eme and said: Sir, if ye will give me the order of knighthood, I will do battle with Sir Marhaus. What are ye, said the king, and from whence be ye come? Sir, said Tristram, I come from King Meliodas that wedded your sister, and a gentleman wit ye well I am. King Mark beheld Sir Tristram and saw that he was but a young man of age, but he was passingly well made and big. Fair sir, said the king, what is your name, and where were ye born? Sir, said he again, my name is Tristram, and in the country of Liones was I born. Ye say well, said the king; and if ye will do this battle I shall make you knight. Therefore I come to you, said Sir Tristram, and for none other cause. But then King Mark made him knight. And therewithal, anon as he had made him knight, he sent a messenger unto Sir Marhaus with letters that said that he had found a young knight ready for to take the battle to the uttermost. It may well be, said Sir Marhaus; but tell King Mark I will not fight with no knight but he be of blood royal, that is to say, other king's son, other queen's son, born of a prince or princess.

When King Mark understood that, he sent for Sir Tristram de Liones and told him what was the answer of Sir Marhaus. Then said Sir Tristram: Sithen that he saith so, let him wit that I am come of father side and mother side of as noble blood as he is: for, sir, now shall ye know that I am King Meliodas' son, born of your own sister, Dame Elizabeth, that died in the forest in the birth of me. O Jesu, said King Mark, ye are welcome fair nephew to me. Then in all the haste the king let horse Sir Tristram, and armed him in the best manner that might be had or gotten for gold or silver. And then King Mark sent unto Sir Marhaus, and did him to wit that a better born man than he was himself should fight with him, and his name is Sir Tristram de Liones, gotten of King Meliodas, and born of King Mark's sister. Then was Sir Marhaus glad and blithe that he should fight with such a gentleman. And so by the assent of King Mark and of Sir Marhaus they let ordain that they should fight within an island nigh Sir Marhaus' ships; and so was Sir Tristram put into a vessel both his horse and he, and all that to him longed both for his body and for his horse. Sir Tristram lacked nothing. And when King Mark and his barons of Cornwall beheld how young Sir Tristram departed with such a carriage to fight for the right of Cornwall, there was neither man nor woman of worship but they wept to see and understand so young a knight to jeopardy himself for their right.

8:7
Sir Tristram fought against Sir Marhaus and achieved his battle, and how Sir Marhaus fled to his ship.

And then Sir Marhaus avised Sir Tristram, and said thus: Young knight, Sir Tristram, what dost thou here? me sore repenteth of thy courage, for wit thou well I have been assayed, and the best knights of this land have been assayed of my hand; and also I have matched with the best knights of the world, and therefore by my counsel return again unto thy vessel. And fair knight, and well-proved knight, said Sir Tristram, thou shalt well wit I may not forsake thee in this quarrel, for I am for thy sake made knight. And thou shalt well wit that I am a king's son born, and gotten upon a queen; and such promise I have made at my uncle's request and mine own seeking, that I shall fight with thee unto the uttermost, and deliver Cornwall from the old truage. And also wit thou well, Sir Marhaus, that this is the greatest cause that thou couragest me to have ado with thee, for thou art called one of the most renowned knights of the world, and because of that noise and fame that thou hast thou givest me courage to have ado with thee, for never yet was I proved with good knight; and sithen I took the order of knighthood this day, I am well-pleased that I may have ado with so good a knight as thou art. And now wit thou well, Sir Marhaus, that I cast me to get worship on thy body; and if that I be not proved, I trust to God that I shall be worshipfully proved upon thy body, and to deliver the country of Cornwall for ever from all manner of truage from Ireland for ever.

When Sir Marhaus had heard him say what he would, he said then thus again: Fair knight, sithen it is so that thou castest to win worship of me, I let thee wit worship may thou none lose by me if thou mayest stand me three strokes; for I let thee wit for my noble deeds, proved and seen, King Arthur made me Knight of the Table Round.

Then they began to feutre their spears, and they met so fiercely together that they smote either other down, both horse and all. But Sir Marhaus smote Sir Tristram a great wound in the side with his spear, and then they avoided their horses, and pulled out their swords, and threw their shields afore them. And then they lashed together as men that were wild and courageous. And when they had stricken so together long, then they left their strokes, and foined at their breaths and visors; and when they saw that that might not prevail them, then they hurtled together like rams to bear each other down. Thus they fought still more than half a day, and either were wounded passing sore, that the blood ran down freshly from them upon the ground. By then Sir Tristram waxed more fresher than Sir Marhaus, and better winded and bigger; and with a mighty stroke he smote Sir Marhaus upon the helm such a buffet that it went through his helm, and through the coif of steel, and through the brain-pan, and the sword stuck so fast in the helm and in his brain-pan that Sir Tristram pulled thrice at his sword or ever he might pull it out from his head; and there Marhaus fell down on his knees, the edge of Tristram's sword left in his brain-pan. And suddenly Sir Marhaus rose grovelling, and thew his sword and shield from him, and so ran to his ships and fled his way, and Sir Tristram had ever his shield and his sword.

And when Sir Tristram saw Sir Marhaus withdraw him, he said:

Ah! Sir Knight of the Round Table, why withdrawest thou thee? thou dost thyself and thy kind great shame, for I am but a young knight, or now I was never proved, and rather than I should withdraw me from thee, I had rather be hewn in an hundred pieces. Sir Marhaus answered no word but yede his way sore groaning. Well, Sir Knight, said Sir Tristram, I promise thee thy sword and thy shield shall be mine; and thy shield shall I wear in all places where I ride on mine adventures, and in the sight of King Arthur and all the Round Table.

8:19
How King Mark sent Sir Tristram for La Beale Isoud toward Ireland, and how by fortune he arrived into England.

Then when this was done King Mark cast always in his heart how he might destroy Sir Tristram. And then he imagined in himself to send Sir Tristram into Ireland for La Beale Isoud. For Sir Tristram had so praised her beauty and her goodness that King Mark said that he would wed her, whereupon he prayed Sir Tristram to take his way into Ireland for him on message. And all this was done to the intent to slay Sir Tristram. Notwithstanding, Sir Tristram would not refuse the message for no danger nor peril that might fall, for the pleasure of his uncle, but to go he made him ready in the most goodliest wise that might be devised. For Sir Tristram took with him the most goodliest knights that he might find in the court; and they were arrayed, after the guise that was then used, in the goodliest manner. So Sir Tristram departed and took the sea with all his fellowship. And anon, as he was in the broad sea a tempest took him and his fellowship, and drove them back into the coast of England, and there they arrived fast by Camelot, and full fain they were to take the land.

And when they were landed Sir Tristram set up his pavilion upon the land of Camelot, and there he let hang his shield upon the pavilion. And that same day came two knights of King Arthur's, that one was Sir Ector de Maris, and Sir Morganor. And they touched the shield, and bade him come out of the pavilion for to joust, an he would joust. Ye shall be answered, said Sir Tristram, an ye will tarry a little while. So he made him ready, and first he smote down Sir Ector de Maris, and after he smote down Sir Morganor, all with one spear, and sore bruised them. And when they lay upon the earth they asked Sir Tristram what he was, and of what country he was knight. Fair lords, said Sir Tristram, wit ye well that I am of Cornwall. Alas, said Sir Ector, now am I ashamed that ever any Cornish knight should overcome me. And then for despite Sir Ector put off his armour from him, and went on foot, and would not ride.

9:38
How Mark was sorry for the good renown of Sir Tristram. Some of Arthur's knights jousted with knights of Cornwall.

Now will we speak, and leave Sir Tristram, Sir Palomides, and Sir Dinadan in prison, and speak we of other knights that sought after Sir Tristram many divers parts of this land. And some yede into Cornwall; and by adventure Sir Gaheris, nephew unto King Arthur, came unto King Mark, and there he was well received and sat at King Mark's own table and ate of his own mess. Then King Mark asked Sir Gaheris what tidings there were in the realm of Logris.[12] Sir, said Sir Gaheris, the king reigneth as a noble knight; and now but late there was a great jousts and tournament as ever I saw any in the realm of Logris, and the most noble knights were at that jousts. But there was one knight that did marvellously three days, and he bare a black shield, and of all knights that ever I saw he proved the best knight. Then, said King Mark, that was Sir Launcelot, or Sir Palomides the paynim. Not so, said Sir Gaheris, for both Sir Launcelot and Sir Palomides were on the contrary party against the Knight with the Black Shield. Then it was Sir Tristram, said the king. Yea, said Sir Gaheris. And therewithal the king smote down his head, and in his heart he feared sore that Sir Tristram should get him such worship in the realm of Logris wherethrough that he himself should not be able to withstand him. Thus Sir Gaheris had great cheer with King Mark, and with Queen La Beale Isoud, the which was glad of Sir Gaheris' words; for well she wist by his deeds and manners that it was Sir Tristram. And then the king made a feast royal, and to that feast came Sir Uwaine le Fise de Roy Ureine, and some called him Uwaine le Blachemains. And this Sir Uwaine challenged all the knights of Cornwall. Then was the king wood wroth that he had no knights to answer him. Then Sir Andred, nephew unto King Mark, leapt up and said: I will encounter with Sir Uwaine. Then he yede and armed him and horsed him in the best manner. And there Sir Uwaine met with Sir Andred, and smote him down that he swooned on the earth. Then was King Mark sorry and wroth out of measure that he had no knight to revenge his nephew, Sir Andred.

So the king called unto him Sir Dinas,[13] the Seneschal, and prayed him for his sake to take upon him to joust with Sir Uwaine. Sir, said Sir Dinas, I am full loath to have ado with any knight of the Round Table. Yet, said the king, for my love take upon thee to joust. So Sir Dinas made him ready, and anon they encountered together with great spears, but Sir Dinas was overthrown, horse and man, a great fall. Who was wroth but King Mark! Alas, he said, have I no knight that will encounter with yonder knight? Sir, said Sir Gaheris, for your sake I will joust. So Sir Gaheris made him ready, and when he was armed he rode into the field. And when Sir Uwaine saw Sir Gaheris' shield he rode to him and said: Sir, ye do not your part. For, sir, the first time ye were made Knight of the Round Table ye sware that ye should not have ado with your fellowship wittingly. And pardie, Sir Gaheris, ye knew me well enough by my shield, and so do I know you by your shield, and though ye would break your oath I would not break mine; for there is not one here, nor ye, that shall think I am afeard of you, but I durst right well have ado with you, and yet we be sisters' sons. Then was Sir Gaheris ashamed, and so therewithal every knight went their way, and Sir Uwaine rode into the country.

Then King Mark armed him, and took his horse and his spear, with a squire with him. And he rode afore Sir Uwaine, and suddenly at a gap he ran upon him as he that was not ware of him, and there he smote him almost through the body, and there left him. So within a while there came Sir Kay and found Sir Uwaine, and asked him how he was hurt. I wot not, said Sir Uwaine, why nor wherefore, but by treason I am sure I gat this hurt; for here came a knight suddenly upon me or that I was ware, and suddenly hurt me. Then there was come Sir Andred to seek King Mark. Thou traitor knight, said Sir Kay, an I wist it were thou that thus traitorly has hurt this noble knight thou shouldst never pass my hands. Sir, said Sir Andred, I did never hurt him, and that I will report me to himself. Fie on you false knight, said Sir Kay, for ye of Cornwall are nought worth. So Sir Kay made carry Sir Uwaine to the Abbey of the Black Cross, and there he was healed. And then Sir Gaheris took his leave of King Mark, but or he departed he said: Sir king, ye did a foul shame unto you and your court, when ye banished Sir Tristram out of this country, for ye needed not to have doubted no knight an he had been here. And so he departed.

12   *From* **Beunans Meriasek by Radolphus Ton (1504)**

[*Here the Duke of Cornwall shall parade saying*]

I am Duke of Cornwall:
  as was my father before me,[1]
and high lord in the country
  from Tamar to Land's End.
I live now, without a lie,
  at Castle-an-Dinas,
    in Pydar,[2] certainly,
And in the High Territory
I have another castle,
  called Tintagel:
    that is my chief dwelling-seat.

13   *From* **Itinerary by John Leland (c.1540)**

[Tintagel] castle hath been a marvellous strong and notable fortress, and almost *situ loci inexpugnabile*,[1] especially for the dungeon that is on a great and terrible crag environed with the sea, but having a drawbridge from the residue of the castle on to it. The residue of the buildings and castle be sore weather-beaten and in ruin, but it hath been a large thing. The castle had by likelihood three wards whereof two be worn away with gulfing in of the sea, in so much that it hath made there almost an isle, and no way is to enter into it now but by long elm trees laid for a bridge. So that now without the isle runneth only a gatehouse, a wall, and a false bray digged and walled. In the isle remain old walls, and in the east part of the same, the ground being lower, remaineth a wall embattled, and men alive saw therein postern door of iron. There is in the isle a pretty chapel of St. Ulette *alias* Uliane, with a tomb on the left side. There is also in the isle a well, and nigh by the same is place hewn out of the stony ground to the length and breadth of a man. Also there remaineth in the isle a ground quadrant walled as it were a garden plot; and by this wall appear the ruins of a vault. The ground of this isle now nourisheth sheep...

Also about Camelford, are certain old mines, wrought in times past, but of what metal it is now unknown. Within a mile about that poor village south runneth the river that goeth into the Severn Sea at Padstow, and it is the greatest river on the north side of Cornwall, and is called in the common speech there, Dunmere,[2] and in the king's grant of privilege to the Canons of Bodmin and the burgess of the same town, Alan, it may fortune for Alaune. Some histories call it Camlan.[3] By this river Arthur fought his last field, in token whereof people find there in ploughing bones and harness.

14   *From* **A Herring's Tail by Richard Carew (1598)**

I sing the strange adventures of the hardy snail,
Who durst (unlikely match) the weathercock assail:
A bold attempt, at first by fortune flattered
With boot, but at the last to bale abandoned.
Help, sportful Muse, to tune my gander-keaking[1] quill,
And with ink blottles of sad merriments it fill.

With drum of clapped wings, and with the shrilly blast
Of his throat trumpet, Chanticleer,[2] now third and last,
Had sounded a discharge unto the welkin watch,
To leave their stand, and give their shot, and quench their
    match.
And dame Aurora now, faithful ambassadress
Of the new born day and of the night's decease,
The purple violets and crimson roses, cull'd
In Paradise, had from her fragrant chaplet pull'd,
And strew'd before Dan Phoebus'[3] feet: and now gan he
With peacock-priding rays, th' awaked worldé's glee,
To climb the eastern hills, and with light skips to play
Between the wrinkles of the furrow-faced sea:
When rested Lymazon thrusteth his fenceless head
Out at his doorless house, and with eye measured
How far he climbed had, how far he had to climb,
What guess proportion plots to cunning toil and time:

Whcro, whiles he humbleth sight to the disdained ground,
More than his hope could crave lie his achievement
    found…
So Lymazon goes on, and climbs the haughty tower,
Haught more than that which Cæsar's ashes did
    embower,
Or those of Pharaöhs, who with ambitious strife
By their death houses deem'd to overlie their life.

Fame says, when Uther to the fair Igerna's bed
Made way on carcass of her husband slaughtered,
She, causer of the fact not partner of the guilt,
Washt with her tears the blood by other's hand yspilt,
And sought with price of borrow'd merits to enrich
Her either mate, who did, and suffered too much,
Tintagel was the place where she exchanged loves,
Tintagel was the place where to both their behoves
She rears a stately house, where lowly monks may haunt,
For their souls' requiem sad spells to chat and chaunt:
Whose cells environed a temple rare of frame,
For substance rare, more rare for form that deckt the
    same:
But rarest for the steeple, which with wonder rose
In that huge temple's waste, and wonder overgrows.
The foot whose large assize this giant body bare
Were squarey-faced stones, with sides, outlayed square:
Marble stones, the sides, rule (king of measure) scann'd
Three hundred broad to stretch, high fifty foot to stand;
Within, a labyrinth of wenlace thwarting ways
By searchers' errors blaz'd the craftsman ready praise…

So long and long it lay, even in the ruins fair,
Till Merlin, son of fiend,[4] and of their arts[5] the heir,
With ever daring voice, measu'd to whispering charms
His cursed kin from lowest deep by fluttering swarms
Up calls, and with his finger dipp'd in guiltless blood
A snaky circle twines, which ugly fenced stood,
With characters of uncouth note, and willing penn'd
That damned troop, who press'd th' enjoin'd service
    attend…

The work was done, the workmen gone, Merlin content.
And in the centre of this labyrinth he plac'd
A sumptuous tomb, and centre of that tomb he grac'd
With Igraine's hating loves, conjoin'd in equal rest,
Who erst a divers state, whom now one fate possesst.

15   From **The Survey of Cornwall by Richard Carew (1602)**

Not far from [Bottreaux Castle], Tintagel, more famous for his antiquity than regardable for his present estate, abutteth likewise on the sea; yet the ruins argue it to have been once no unworthy dwelling for the Cornish princes. The cement wherewith the stones were laid resisteth the fretting fury of the weather better than themselves. Half the buildings were raised on the continent and the other half on the island, continued together (within men's remembrance) by a drawbridge, but now divorced by the downfallen steep cliffs on the farther side, which though it shut out the sea from his wonted recourse, hath yet more strengthened the late island for in passing thither you must first descend with a dangerous declining, and then make a worse ascent by a path, as everywhere narrow, so in many places through his stickleness occasioning, and through his steepness threatening, the ruin of your life with the failing of your foot. At the top, two or three terrifying steps give you entrance to the hill, which supplieth pasture for sheep and conies.[1] Upon the same I saw a decayed chapel, a fair spring of water, a cave, reaching once, by my guide's report, some far way underground, and (which you will perhaps suspect of untruth) an hermit's grave hewn out in the rock, and serving each body's proportion for a burial. But if that in Wales carry an equal verity, the miracle will soon reap credit, for this is so sloped inwards at both ends that any tall stature shall find room by a little bending, as the short in the bottom by extending.

The farthest point of this hill is called Black Head, well known to the coasting mariners. The high cliffs are by seas inaccessible round abouts, saving in one place towards the east where they proffer an uneasy landing place for boats, which being fenced with a garetted wall, admitteth entrance through a gate, sometimes of iron, as the name yet continuing expresseth, and is within presently commanded by a hardly climbed hill. Under the island runs a cave thorough which you may row at full sea, but not without a kind of horror at the uncouthness of the place...

It is not laid up amongst the least vaunts of this castle, that our victorious Arthur was here begotten by the valiant Uther Pendragon upon the fair Igerna, and that without taint of bastardy, said Merlin, because her husband died some hours before...

One, collecting the wonders of Cornwall, rhymed touching this as followeth:

> Tintagel in his ruins vaunts,
>   Sometimes the seat of kings,
> And place which worthy Arthur bred,
>   Whose praise the Breton sings,
> A bridge these buildings joined, whom now
>   The fallen cliffs divorce,

Yet strengthen'd so, the more it scorns
  Foes' vain attempting force.
There, cave above, entry admits,
  But thoroughfare denies,
Where that beneath alloweth both,
  In safe, but ghastly wise.
A spring there wets his head, his foot
  A gate of iron guards;
There measure due to each one's length
  The hermit's grave awards.

The Prophecy:

Ewra teyre a war meane Merlyn
Ara Lesky Pawle Pensanz ha Newlyn

[*They shall land on the Rock of Merlin*
Who shall burn Paul, Penzance and Newlyn]

16 *From* **The Lives of the Saints by Nicholas Roscarrock (c.1620)**

Geffry Monmouth, 1.9 c8, and after him Floriligus, a 522 Jonsonne in Hist Eccl, 1, 5 c 47 & 1 6 c. 11 & 19, writeth that Sct Piran was the chaplyne of king Arthur who made him the 8 Archb. of Yorke after Sct Sampson flying from thence to Dole in little Brittan[1] to avoyde persequution about the year 520, fore when the king coming to Yorke to keepe his Christenmasse, hee found the Archb. fledd, churches defaced and all confounded, which he indevoured to repare and remedy and made Piran Arch. there. After king Arthurs death Sct Piran liued a solitary life, giuing over his Archbishoprike about the yeere 503, at a place in Cornwall wher ther was a church or chapple erected to him and bearing his name and wher he was buryed, being called Sct Pirans in the sand.

17 *From* **Merlin's Prophecies and Predictions by Thomas Heywood (1651)**

I   Arthur, the sonne of Uter-Pendragon and Igerna, succeded his father in the Principality, therefore called *The Bore of Cornwall* because begot and borne in that country and of a Cornish duchesse. Hee as a great planter and supporter of religion and the Christian faith: for all our British chronologers report of him. His conquests were many, and some of them miraclous. By the islands of the ocean are meant *Ireland, Island* [Iceland] and *Scotland*, and the *Orcades*, *Gotland*, *Norway* and *Dacia*, all of which are called Provincial Islands, which he broght under the obedience of his sceptre. By the planting of the flowre de Lyces, in his own garden, is likewise intended his conquest of France.

> The Lion next of Justice shall appear,
> Who gains the Celtick[1] towers shall ladders reare,
> And cause the Lily like the aspen shake
> Whose rore shall all the Islands serpents quake.

> A Cornish Eagle clad in plumes of gold
> (Borrowed from others) shall on high behold
> what best can please him to maintain his pride.
> Whose painted feathers shall the Goat misguid:
> who at length aiming to surprise the Beare,
> Him shall the rowzed beast in pieces teare.

18   *From* **The Dutchesse of Cornwall's progresse to see the Land's end & to visit the mount by Nicholas Boson (c.1665)**

They fell upon this facetious project having the Dean of Burrian of their faction who drew up a Cornish petition against Harry the Hermitt representing unto her Highness what grounds they had to suspect him to be witch, whereof so much was found in an old Tinnen box amidst the ruins of King Arthur's castle in old Brittish characters,[1] hardly preserved from the Injury of the moths. Here followeth.

Rag an Arlothas an wolas Kernow.
Dreth gwz Kibmias Benigas, Why ra Cavas dreeu an gwas Harry ma Poddrack broas.
1 Kensa, vrt an hagar auall iggeva gweell do derevoll warneny Keniffer termen drerany moas durt pedden an wolas do sillan &c.
2 Nessa, vrt an skauoll Crackan codna iggeva setha war en crees an aules ewhall heb drogi veeth.
3 Tregya, vrt an Gurroll iggeva gweell gen askern skooth davas, &c.
To the Dutchess of the Dominion of Cornwall.
By your sacred leave your Highness shall find that this fellow Harry is a great witch.
1 Because of the many dangerous storms he hath risen upon us betwixt Silly & Land's end for no other reason but because (as he pretends) our wives would not pay him their tyth eggs, although it is to be suspected he hath more from them than is his due, the tyth belonging to the Dean of Burrian.
2 That almost all the day long he sits in a cliff of a Rock called there Harry an Pader, in an accessible stupendious cliff, where it is impossible for any to come but himself without breaking their necks.

3 That they had many times seen him come foorth out of his cave called Tull pedden penwith, into the open ocean upon a bone of a shoulder of mutton untill they had warn'd all the inhabitants of those parts to pierce a hole in that bone as soon as the flesh was eaten off &c.

19 The History of King Arthur, and his Progenitors by William Hals (c.1736)

After the death of Ambrosius Aurelius, *Anno Dom*. 497, succeeded to the dominion of Britain, some say his brother, others a Briton, named Uter, alias Uter Pendragon; that is to say, in British, the terrible, or dreadful, head, or chief Dragon: So called, as our Historians tell us, from a direful, bloody, or red Dragon, portrayed in the banners of war, with a golden head; as it is to this day borne in our imperial standards of war, in memory doubtless of the red dragon mentioned in Merlin's Prophesy; by which the British nation is figured. For his paternal coat of Armour, as Upton saith, was – *In a field vert, a plain cross argent; in the dexter quarter the images of the Blessed Virgin Mary, holding the images of her Blessed Son in her right hand proper*. He likewise gave for his cognizance of *Britain*, – D'Or, *deux Dragons Verd*, *Corones de Gowles*, *Coutreles*, or endorsed.

Which prince, about the fourth year of his reign, having had divers notable victories over his enemies the Saxons, killing Pascentius, the Son of Hengist, and Gwillimoore King of Ireland, taken Octa and another son of Hengist, and Cossa his nephew, prisoners, and routed their Forces, he resolved, the Easter after, to make a King of triumphal feast and solemnity for the principal nobility, gentry, and soldiers of his kingdom; and ordered that their wives and daughters should also be invited to his Court, to congratulate his victories against his Pagan enemies. Now, this feast was to be kept at Caer-segont, *i.e. the City or Castle of Conquest or Victory*, afterwards called (by the Saxons) Sell-cester, *i.e. great Castle*, now Win-chester; as much to say, the overcoming, conquering, or winning Castle; as before: The very place where the Emperor Constantine put on the purple robes, in order to his dignity.

Among the other princes and confederates who attended this Solemnity, Gorth-lois, or Gorth-louis (*i.e. purple back, or spear*) Prince, King, or Earl of Cornwall, with Igerna his lady, graced the same with their presence. And twas observable, that, in this great Assembly, the said Lady, for beauty, port and mien, exceded all the Ladies then present. With whole unparallel'd demeanor and charms King Uter was so much taken and delighted, or intoxicated rather, that for several days, he omitted all other the most necessary affairs of his Kingdom, in order to enjoy her company. Yea, so violent was his affection that he could not restrain or curb his passion; but kissed and courted her openly even in the sight of her Lord and others.

Whereupon Gorthlois was so possess'd with jealousy, that he took the first opportunity (without leave taken of the King or his nobility), together with his Duchess and Servants, and posted from Winchester towards his own Country of Devon and Cornwall. He had not been long gone but notice thereof was brought to the King, who it in so sill a part, by reason of his inordinate affection to his Lady, that forthwith he sent messengers after him, to let him know that he had further occasion to use his counsel about affairs of the nation.

But Gorthlois so highly prized his Lady, who by this artifice he foresaw would be expos'd to the King's lust, that he sent back positive answer, that he would not come. At which return the King grew more enraged, and sent the Prince[1] of Cornwall word, that if he persisted in his obstinacy, he would invade his Country, and beat his towns and castles about his ears. But in vain were his menaces, for Gorthlois return'd him word, that he was, as his predecessors time out of mind had been, a free Prince, and owned him neither homage or allegiance. Nevertheless, as his countryman, he acknowledged himself his ally and confederate against all foreign opposers, and would keep his articles of agreement: But if Uter was not contented with this answer, but would forcibly invade his Country and property, he would endeavour to keep and preserve the same against him and his adherents. Whereupon King Uter denounced hostility against him, and sent him defiance as an enemy, and set things in a posture of war against him. Neither was Gorthlois less solicitous to keep his Country and Dutchess from Uter's possession, or indeed vile usurpation. In brief therefore, as foresaid, King Uter having raised a great army of soldiers, under pretence of chastising the pride and contempt of Gorthlois, marched with them towards his territories, which extended as far as Axminster. Where he no sooner arrived, but he falls a plundering of the Country, and burning the houses of the inhabitants; with the terror whereof some fled away, and others submitted to his mercy. Gorthlois being then at his chief palace and castle of Caer-Iske[2] *i.e. the Fish Castle, or City situated in the Fish River*, now called Exe, as the City is Exeter: And hearing of this affrightment and revolt of the people on the east part of his dominions, and fearing the cowardice of his citizens of Caer-Iske, he quitted the same upon Uter's approach with his army, and retired with his Lady, and posted themselves in this Castle of Dundagell: where he left his Dutchess, himself retiring to Demeliock-Castle, now in St.Udye, or St.Kewe.[3] Where his army lay entrenched within a trebble-wall'd fortification of earth, still extant, and retaining its name. Wherein he had laid up sufficient provision and ammunition for his camp and soldiers. And there also he was promised to receive assistance of soldiers from one of the five kings of Ireland, which daily was expected.

King Uter, understanding of Gorthlois's departure from Caer-Iske, soon marched with his army into Cornwall, and laid siege to the Castle of Dameliock (that is to say the house or place of skirmish, battle or hazard of war); and no sooner approached the lines but he sent a herald, or trumpet, to Gorthlois, demanding the surrender of himself and Castle on mercy. Gorthlois, rewarding the trumpet, return'd answer, 'That he gave King Uter no just cause of war, or for breaking the league, or invading his Country, and wasting the same in such barbarous manner. But especially, he being a free Prince, neither could nor would betray his trust, or give up his dominions and subjects to an unjust invader.' At which answer King Uter was so much enraged, that he gave order for a straight siege of the castle, and forthwith made many violent assaults by storm in several places thereof. But he was stoutly repulsed, and driven back by the besieged. In this manner, with various success, for several days, the siege and war continued, which occasioned the many camps, fortifications, and intrenchments, in those parts called Castle Killy Biry, Castle Kynock, &c.

Whereupon King Uter, being more desirous to batter the chastity of Gorthlois's Lady Igerne, and to vanquish her than shed blood, or take the Castle of Demeliock, thought of nothing more than how to gratify his unlawful lust. In order to which he was so vain as to enquire whether the said lady was within the said castle, and where she was in so good a state of health as when he saw her at Caersegont? To which questions answer was made, that fame reported nothing to the contrary as to her health; but as for her person, that was not in Dameliock Castle, but kept in a much more secure place, within the impregnable fort of Dundagell. Then enquiring farther of a deserter what manner of place that was, he was told that it was a place munified by art and nature, and so narrow entrance over the sea and rocks by a draw-bridge, that three armed men at once would keep out his whole army, maugre all their skill and strength. At the relation of which circumstances King Uter seem'd mightily dismayed, so that his countenance changed through anguish and perplexity of mind: which put him into such great anxiety as as Ahab for want of Naboth's Vineyard, David for Bathsheba, and Nero for Sabina Poppaea, other men's wives.

So powerful an agent is irregular and dishonest love, or lust, that it can disturb the minds and senses of the greatest monarchs, as well as the meanest vassals, and precipitate them not only into unjust, but mad and foolish actions, which men not tainted with the contagion of such amours are asham'd to act, see or hear of.

King Uter Pendragon, in this extremity, as not being able to reduce Dameliock Castle by storm; nor if he could, would that redress his grief, by procuring the sight of Igerna, resolves upon this expedient: to dislodge part of his soldiers and troops from Demeliock, and march with them to Dundagell in order to try the fortune of war in both places. But as soon as he came in sight thereof, the same appeared more formidable, tremendous, and invincible than what fame had spoken of it. For in those days the wit and force of man could not oblige that Castle to surrender, unless through bribery or treachery of its defendants; for that the same could neither be scaled, batter'd or starved, it having always on the island sheep, rabbits and fish about its rocks and water. And to think of forcing it by storm would be but a foolish project of imagination; the same being an island, surrounded by the sea, and lofty towering rocks, where neither ship nor boat could swim or approach with safety but in one place (as aforesaid) and that in fair weather only. Besides, to think of reducing it by famine would be as vain an attempt; for that it was told him, Gorthlois on notice of this war has stored it with great quantities of provision, and had more coming from Ireland; besides water, the natural produce of island, fish, sheep, goats, rabbits and fowls, there abounding for the inhabitants relief, as aforesaid.

The confederation of which put Pendragon into greater sadness and perplexity of mind, considering the charge and fatigues of war, the stain of his honour in these unsuccessful attempts; but chiefly for that he could not satisfy his concupiscence on the fair Igerna; which made him slave to his senses, and hurried him into these difficult and dangerous enterprizes; which for that cause he had undertaken. Whereupon he grew sickly, and took his bed, his physicians despairing of his life. When it happen'd (as historians tell us) that one Urfan of Richardock, a place near Dameliock or Dundagell, one of King Uter's cabinet-council, advised him to send into Wales for the old British Prophet Merlin, and try whether he could do that by his magic art which neither the art of courage or men of war could effect. Whereupon Pendragon sent for the prophet; who, when arriv'd to his camp, was made acquainted with the premises, and immediately bid the King to be of good comfort, for that he doubted not but in short time he would introduce him into the company of Igerna, without further bloodshed or hostility.

The King gladly heard this discourse, and promised to follow any expedient he should prescribe in order to enjoy the Lady; and further assured him of great reward in case his project succeeded. Whereupon Merlin ordered the King; with whom in secret manner he went towards the draw-bridge gate of Dundagell Castle; where making a noise, the sentinel demanded in the dark, who they were? Merlin, being transformed into the shape of Bricot, a servant who waited on Gorthlois, and lay in his bed-chamber, made answer, that his Duke Gorthlois escaped from the siege of Demeliock, was at the gate for entrance. The sentinel, apprehending he heard the very voice of Bricot, and seeing at some distance two persons talking together, the one King Uter metamorphos'd into the shape of Duke Gorthlois, and another, viz. Urfan of Richardock, transformed into the shape of Jordan of Dundagell, let down the draw-bridge, and so gave them opportunity to enter into the insular castle aforesaid, where he had further confirmation of the identity or reality of their persons by their speech and apparel, as far as the night would permit him. Whereupon he joyfully conducted King Uter to Igerna's chamber; who, in bed, not discovering the fraud, gladly received him for her Lord. When that very night betwixt them was begotten that valiant, noble, and religious Prince Arthur, who for his brave, or sacinorous, and heroic achievements, made his name glorious in his days, as it is still the paragon of ours.

Now, as King Uter was vigorous and amorous that night with the Dutchess Igerna, so his soldiers were as careful and valiant in the siege of Dameliock castle, which then they again stormed with their scaling-ladders, but were as stoutly driven back by the besieged. Whereupon Duke Gorthlois resolving no longer to be thus cooped up, or confined in walls or trenches, but either to conquer or die, the next morning sallied forth with a party of soldiers, and assaulted his enemies in their quarters by surprize. But alas! the success was not answerable to his courage and resolution; for King Uter's men were all in a readiness to receive his charge and onset; so that in the brunt of the first encounter, Gorthlois was kill'd on the spot, his party slain or routed, and all that were taken in arms put to the sword. The castle of Dameliock yielded on, condition of life, (though some say otherwise) the plunder to the King's soldiers.

Early the same morning, before King Uter and the Dutchess were out of the chamber, or had put on their wearing apparel, to the great astonishment of the porter, sentinel, and the garrison, a messenger arrived at Dundagell gate, giving full account of this tragic fact. But when he was admitted to the Dutchess's bed-chamber, and saw, as he verily believed, Duke Gorthlois in her company, he could hardly credit his own report, especially since the Dutchess Igerna being of the same opinion. But alas! so unavoidable a thing is fortune, or fate, the Prophet Merlin then began to uncharm and dissolve his former spells and incantations, so that King Uter appear'd no longer as Gorthlois Duke of Cornwall, but sole Monarch of Britain, his companion not Jordan of Dundagell, but Urfan of Richardock, and the third not Bricot, but Merlin the Prophet, to the admiration of all the spectators.

Thereupon the King took leave of the Dutchess, and posted to his army, then in possession of Dameliock Castle, and ordered search to be made for the body of the Duke; where at length it was found, in common soldier's apparel, extreme bloody, mangled and cut. Whereupon, he call'd for an embalmer, who forthwith dislodged his brains, eyes, and bowels, and placed in the room thereof salt and aromatic spices, to prevent putrefaction, 'till a military interment could be prepared for him; which a month after was splendidly provided, the King and Dutchess being chief mourners. When a few days after King Uter married Igerna, the Dutchess; by whom (as aforesaid) he had a son named Arthur, and a daughter named Amye.[4]

Lastly, 'tis observed by our annalists upon the foregoing history, that after this bloody war and unjust fact of King Uter, he never had any tolerable success against his Saxon enemies; but in many battles was worsted by them. And finally, some of them understanding of a good spring or well of water, whereof he usually drank, they secretly conveyed poison into the same, so that afterwards the King, drinking his customary draught thereof, very soon with intolerable pains died, in the 15th Year of his reign, and the flower of his age, *Anno Dom.* 515: Fulfilling that saying in the sacred writings, the same measure that ye meet shall be measured to you again, brimful and running over. So that as King Uter drank the waters of another man's cistern, afterwards he was unjustly, or rather justly, poison'd with the waters of his own fountain. So that I shall conclude this history in the words of St. Paul, *O the Height of the Wisdom and the Knowledge of God! How unsearchable are his judgments, and his ways past finding out!*

After the death of King Uter Pendragon, his son and heir Arthur, begotten as aforesaid, succeeded to his dominion of Britain, *Anno Dom.* 515; but others say, 518. He is therefore rightly named by some authors Arthur Mab-Uter Pendragon; viz. Arthur the son of Uter Pendragon. Which name Arthur is derived from the British Arthou, a good or sharp-pointed weapon. But Mr. Camden ignorantly tells us, Arthur signifies an iron hammer to break the teeth of Lions, by his leave, *un Morhual Horne the tarthas as Dense Lyons* is an iron hammer to break the teeth of lions. Of this King Arthur long before his birth had Merlin prophesied to King Vortigerne thus:

That the Boar of Cornwall shall bring aid, and shall tread the necks of his enemies under his feet; the islands of the ocean shall be subject to his power; and his famous acts shall be food to those that do relate them; six of his lineage shall sway the scepter, &c. See a particular book written by the author of his volume, call'd A Translation and Explanation of Merlin's Prophecy, originally written in British and Latin by Galfridus Monmouthensis.[5]

King Arthur no sooner succeeded to his father's dominion, but he applied himself with great piety and religion to administer law and justice to his people, the best expedients to establish a tottering scepter. In the next place, he took care to fortify and strengthen himself with soldiers and arms against his Saxon enemies; a mighty and warlike people, then possest of the greatest part of this Kingdom by the late misfortunes of his father, and other princes, in battle with them; so that only Wiltshire, Devon, Dorset, Cornwall, and Wales, made up his dominion. Against these King Arthur drew into the field a mighty army of soldiers, and after eleven pitch'd battles against them, overthrew their whole armies, and obtained the total dominion of this kingdom, and confin'd the Saxons, on condition of tribute and submission, only to the kingdom of Kent. And recorded it is by Annalists, that in one of those battles which King Arthur had with them, he girded himself with an approved sword, called *Callib-burne;*[6] a contraction of (the British Greek) Chalybs, Steel, (for a sword) and burn; as much to say, a sword of burning steel; with which one day he slew, with his own hands, eight hundred Saxons. It seems, this weapon was like Goliath's sword wrapped in the Ephod,[7] there was no sword like it. And thus, according to Merlin's prophecy, did the Boar of Cornwall bring help and assistance, and tread Britain's enemies under his feet.

But no sooner was this land settled in peace at home, than plots and designs from abroad were laid to disturb the tranquility thereof. For at that time the Romans, having made a peace with their enemies the Vandalls,[8] sent messengers to King Arthur, demanding 3000 l. per Ann. Tribute, (a prodigious sum in those days!) many years in arrear, according to the agreement Julius Caesar made with King Cassibellan, and was still due to the Senate:[9] At which demand King Arthur was so distasted, that he sent away the messengers in scorn, and prohibited any Roman ever after to come into this land upon that account; especially for that the Romans for many years had voluntarily quitted, or forsaken, the Government thereof: so that the Britons had neither their protection nor aid against their Saxon or other enemies. When these messengers returned to Rome, this contempt of King Arthur's was very ill resented by the Senate; who thereupon unanimously voted a War against him. And accordingly a great army was raised in order to conquer and reduce this land, which arrived here under the conduct of Lucius, their Prince or Emperor (as historians tell us) together with ten kings, his confederates and auxiliaries.

Against these King Arthur advanced with a mighty host, and gave them battle; after a sharp and bloody conflict, the Roman Emperor Lucius was slain, (his body afterwards sent to Rome) the whole Roman army routed, and the greatest part of them put to the sword. And those whose lives he spared he made his Feodors and Vassals; from whence in all probability first sprung the original of knight service tenure of lands in this kingdom; for a Feodary was an Officer belonging to the court of wards and liveries, who survey'd the value of Knight-service lands. And in like manner thence Vassalage tenure of land, viz. that of a Vassal, or Villain, who is a tenant in fee on condition.

But alas! notwithstanding King Arthur's good fortune in this island against the Romans, he was not contented therewith, but resolved to be further revenged upon them for this wrong bloodshed and indignity; and, for preventing any such invitation for the future, to make a descent upon the Roman territories in Gaul, especially for that from thence the Romans were assisted with great numbers of soldiers, under Lucius, to invade his kingdom of Britain. Whereupon, King Arthur with a considerable fleet of ships, and great army of soldiers, landed in Normandy, then called Neustria, and summoned the people either to come and submit to his scepter or give him battle. In which contest they were totally overthrown, routed or slain. So that soon after the province of Normandy submitted to his mercy, cast down armour, and payed tribute. Whereupon he gave to Gaius his Taster the Earldom of Andegavum (now Angers), and to Bedverus, his Cup-bearer, the Dukedom of Normandy, for their good services. In memory of which Donations, it grew to be a custom amongst the Kings of France for many ages after, to make their tasters and cup-bearers Earls of Andegavum and Normandy.

After this victory, King Arthur dislodged his force, and advanced further into the Roman Gaulish provinces; and subdu'd by conquest to his scepter Flanders, Burgundy, Aquitain, and Andegavum (and, as some tell us, Poland), and obliged those people to pay him an annual tribute; according as Merlin had predicted of him, that the Gaulish forests he should possess, and that the House of Romulus should tremble at his wrath. After these victories, he returned safe into Britain. And then also by his fleet and army returned to his dominion Scotland, Ireland, Iceland, Gothland, Noramy, Dacia; and made them all tributary. Which also was foretold by Merlin, in these words: *the islands of the ocean shall be subject to his power*.

When, after he had established peace in all those lands, and returned to Britain, he instituted an honourable order of Knighthood, called the Knights of the Round Table (the most ancient order of Knighthood in the world): Chiefly to promote self-denial, and prevent differences amongst his nobility, and gentry, or soldiers, who had well deserved of him and his country, for their good services at home and abroad: that so no occasion of dispute might arise without procedence, in merit, antiquity, valour, wealth, honour, or nobility, amongst them; for that all the knights of this his Order were alike and equal in those respects in his esteem, and might sit down indifferently at the Table; go in and out of the house, or church, field, or market, before each other as they came, without exception: It being a hallow'd rule amongst them, that the highest seat at the court, senate, church, or Table, did no more argue the worth, value, religion, valour, or prudent conduct of a man, than the precedence of a military officer did prove him more valiant than his soldiers. The place of meeting of those knights was at Winchester aforesaid, where they assembled yearly at Pentecost or Whitsuntide.

He gave the same religious Christian Coat-Armour as was given by his father, which I have blazon'd before. And in testimony of his thirteen victories over so many crowned head he bore also, in a field azure, thirteen imperial crowns, or (as Upton tells us).

Lastly; – After this Prince had thus vanquish'd his open enemies, had restored the Christian religion, eclipsed by the Saxons, ordained this useful Order of Knighthood, and done all the good offices a just, pious, and religious King could do to his subjects, he was, at last, as many others, ungratefully dealt with by his own people; who, at the instigation of his discontented cousin Mordred, on the Roman Pictish Title, confederated with the Saxons, as against a bastard, and rose a great army in Cornwall in opposition to his power. Against whom King Arthur marched with his army, and gave them battle at a place near Camelford. Where, though he obtained the victory, and Mordred was slain, yet in that battle Arthur received his mortal wounds: so that, soon after, in order to a cure, he retir'd to the Vale of Avallan (*i.e. the Apple Valley*)[10] near Glastenbury, Somerset; where he lies bury'd. In Memory of this his Victory over Mordred, Mr. Carew tells us, that in his time, there was extant a stone, of ancient erection, in the place where the battle was fought, bearing the name of Arthur.

20 *From* **Cornubia: A Poem in Five Cantos by George Woodley (1819)**

Yet, ere we leave the bleak, impressive shore,
Attend! my muse; and let thy song display
The spot, where, rudely pil'd in masses hoar,
Tintagel's moss-clad fragments slow decay:
The theme may well awhile thy flight delay,
For deep it stands combin'd with tales of yore;
And how the Briton fought in former day,
To keep the fierce invader from the shore;
With feasts now only known in legendary lore.

And here, if ancient tales may be believ'd,
That val'rous King, the British Worthy hight,
His mystic birth and wondrous pow'rs receiv'd
To fit him as the most celebrious knight
(Gentle in courtesy and fierce in fight)
Of those - the glory of chivalric days –
Who round his festive board maintain'd their right,
And sought their noblest monuments to raise,
By daring deeds of arms, transcending modern praise!

The philosophic Merlin, – whose deep ken
Of Nature's secret laws, – whose counsels sage,
Excited superstitious dread in men
Rear'd him to his charge; – a humble page,
Long time he trod the vale in menial guise,
Till martial fame awoke his gen'rous rage;
To joust or tournament the stripling flies,
Till Britain's crown fulfils his high-wrought destinies.

Long were the task his matchless deeds to tell,
To show the wonders of his valour wrought,
To point the fields where vanquish'd Saxons fell
And rued the day when they with Arthur fought; –
Another theme is mine; yet oft as Thought
On those dread piles revolves, long-vanish'd years
(Before the view in soft connexion brought)
Dimly reveal the hero; – he appears:
And Arthur's fame in ev'ry sighing breeze hears.

Nor distant is the spot, if right I seem,
Where, – lawless love and civil strife to quell, –
To save, at once, his kingdom and queen,
The monarch in the lap of Vict'ry fell.
Cambula's[1] stream (as old traditions tell)
Witness'd the memorable, dire affray;

Yet though the Fates had sounded Arthur's knell,
Stern Justice rul'd on that fateful day,
And Mordred's rebel-blood did well his crimes repay.

But haply, those who glide in yonder bark,
While fresh'ning breezes urge them on their way, –
Though Arthur's lofty turrets here they mark,
Did ne'er the records of his acts survey;
Nor aught have heard of that eventful day,
When bold Cornubia's[2] chieftain, to repel
A monarch's lawless fires, – in dread array
Cloth'd those huge piles; – bade the loud battle swell,
And ah! too bravely good, here fearless fought and fell.

21   *From* **The Fabulous History of Cornwall by Thomas Hogg (1827)**

Prince Arthur:
Placed 'neath Sir Hector's guardian care,
    By Merlin's counsel sage,
Young Arthur's virtues opened fair,
    Like morning suns on age.

When shepherds drove their bleating flocks,
Safe from wild cliffs, or headlong rocks,
    As wintry torrents roared,
Would Arthur wish he were a man,
To save the nation, in the van,
    From Saxon foes, abhorred.

Of would he, when fierce tempests blew,
His way, to heath-crowned hill, pursue;
    And o'er the main, below,
Would view the billowy mountains rise;
Would, as they sunk, with straining eyes,
    Observe the waves of snow:

Then, down to Merlin's cave[1] he'd hie;
And, whilst the winds rushed whistling by,
    His withered hand, would squeeze,
And ask, if tents, on battle fields,
Where warriors fight with spears and shields,
    Wave, white, like storm-tossed seas.

When Merlin would, the tale, prolong,
For captive queens, how giants strong,
    Their swords in combat, clashed,

His ardent mind glowed at each stroke;
Young thunders, round th' horizon, broke,
    And embryon lightnings flashed.

When squadron'd fairies, clothed in green,
    Their bridles ringing shrill,
Galloped, as scarcely to be seen,
    Around the laughing hill.

When martial shouts came on the gale,
He longed for helm; he longed for mail,
    Impatient of control:
Sir Hector's care, or Merlin's art,
As soon might stay the flying dart,
    As curb young Arthur's soul. –

As circling suns fulfilled their round,
And years rolled swiftly on,
    Pendragon, whom brave Britons owned,
The bulwark of the throne,
Now sleeps in death; – the silent place
    Beholds him, of the royal race.

The last; while whelming bands
    Of stern invaders round the shore,
Secure, the flag of conquest bore,
    And colonised the lands.

Disjointed factions vainly strove,
Long to obtain the people's love,
    By some pretending heir;
And long the realm, 'midst bloodshed, groaned;
Whilst this was crowned; or that, dethroned,
    By sword and falchion² bare.

Sir Tristrem:
Sir Launcelot, too, confessed his shame,
On hearing brave Sir Tristrem's name:
    Then, bleeding, both down kneeled;
Exchange their swords; warm friends, embraced;
Grieved, they should, blood, impassioned, waste;
    Then leave the purpling field.

They went through copse, and flowery lands,
Where, now, Lanhydrock's mansion³ stands;
    And, crossing Fawy's⁴ dale;
They climb the steep redoubt-ascent,

Whence warriors oft have, arrows, sent,
   Foes, ranged below, t' assail.

The courts they enter; – Guenever
Sees clotted blood, their greaves, besmear:
   Their welling wounds, she bathed;
And dressed them with her lily hands;
Brought mollients,[5] and the staying bands,
   With kind attention, swathed.

Sir Tristrem, welcomed, then, she greets;
Recounts the valour and the feats,
   Emblazoning his renown;
His worship meek; his gentle heart;
His dexterous skill, at lance or dart,
   In chace, or hunting-down:

She hopes, he'll, when their wounds are healed,
   With son her cares, repay;
And strike the harp to glory's field,
   And warriors in array.

Fame, busy, to king Marc, reports,
Sir Tristrem, in Restormel[6] courts,
   The tranquil hours enjoys: –
His murderous ire, the news excites: –
He leaves Tintagel with two knights;
   Two trusty squires, employs,
To stab him in Guenever's bower;
   Or intercept his way,
That dragged within his ruthless power,
   Unknown, he might him slay.

Mild twilight's latest glimmerings fail,
when entered they the dewy vale,
   By Fawy's murmuring stream:
The harp's mellifluous cadence falls
Soft from Restormel's sounding halls,
   Commixed with Cynthia's beam.[7]

Merlin and the Woodcutter:
None mourns Isolde and Tristrem more
Than Merlin: –– by Tintagel shore,
   In melancholy's gloom he strayed;
As solace for his poignant grief,
Love kindly flies with prompt relief,
   Instead of magic's feebler aid.

Vivienne,[8] a damsel he had taught
Enchantment, his fond glances, caught:
    He, ardent, supplicates her hand:-
To give his cheek a fresher bloom,
The woods of Moray[9] waft perfume;
    His silver beard, the breezes fanned.

"My parents," she, dissembling, said,
"Oppose; – that they no more upbraid,
    "Instruct me, how I safely may,
"Them, lull to sleep; effectual, bar
"Suspicion; – soft as beam of star,
    "Then swift pursue thy welcome way."

Enraptured, from his wisend cell,
He hastens with a sovereign spell:–
    Inconscious seated in her bower,
She with it, in oblivion, steeps,
Through night, his sense; and faithless, keeps
    Him in her unrelenting power.

When he awoke in morning's beam,
She said, "await me, by the stream
    "Remurmuring to the hoarse cascade,
"Where honey-suckles scent the air,
"And mountain-ash, and beeches fair,
    "Coruscant, form a sylvan glade."

Far through the glooms of Moray wood,
With th' enchantress, he, his way, pursued;
    Perfidious, in a dripping cave,
She, him, confined: – no ancient roll
Records, escaping her control,
    He has ever burst the ruthless grave.

Tintagel's prophet, thus betrayed,
Through years, his spirit, unallayed,
    In solemn warnings, frequent, rose:
Scared shepherds, still, in moonless night,
Start at the sound; see glimmering light
    That, from his dreary dwelling, flows.

The deepening snow, and frost severe,
A poor wood-cutter filled with fear;
    The scanty bread, his family eat,
Upon his daily toil, depends:
He, shivering, to the forest, wends,
    Through drifted wreaths, and pelting sleet.

The biting cold benumbs his hands;
'Midst tinkling ice he pallid stands;
   Deep in the snow his hatchet falls;
A moan he utters at the loss; –
Whilst ruin, want, his thoughts, engross,
   "Merlin!" – a voice behind him calls.

He looked; and hears, in deeper tone,
"Treasure lies hid 'neath yonder stone;[10]
   "After one year, thou do return." –
His wife, soon as he met her eye,
"Left work? – the starving children cry;
   "There is no bread, nor means to buy,
"Nor stick within the door to burn."

The stone from its position rolled,
They find a sum of glittering gold: –
   His sudden riches to conceal,
The woodman, daily, faggots, cut;
Nor alters, in his humble hut,
   His mean attire, or homely meal.

A manored land he saw for sale;
Rank on his family to entail,
   The wide inheritance he bought: –
When poor, him, friends nor parents owned;
The lordly gate, now, daily, moaned,
   As fawning crowds, acquaintance, sought.

The year expired; unseen he rode,
To wait at Merlin's lone abode: –
   "Speak, firm my lasting promise stands."
'Honours I beg to rich domain;
'Undignified, unknown, remain,
   'Devoid of title, manored lands.'

"It shall be granted, as is prayed;
"Humble, as when thy hatchet strayed,
   "Return within twelvemonth's space."
Raised to a judge, he now presides;
Grave, worshipful, weighs, and decides,
   Impartial, each debated case.

At th' appointed time, again he stood;
While Merlin questions from the wood,
   "What wish unsatisfied remains?"
'Could I behold my daughter wed

'A peer; my son, a canon made,
  'My heart, the highest bliss, attains.'

"'Tis granted: – come on th' annual day,
"If wish remain still to convey:" –
  Now shrinks his worship from the task;
He approached the wood in haughty pride;
Shouts, 'irksome 'tis far to ride;
  'No favour more have I to ask.'

"Away! – the honours I conferred,
'From arrogance, should have deterred;
  "For deep ingratitude, returned,
"Shalt thou a scanty pittance gain,
"'Midst drifted snow, and falling rain:–
  "Away! – by Moray's prophet, spurned."

His fortunes sink: – his faded eye
Beholds the canon, countess, die;
  The payment of his land, withheld;
The arm of power, him, dispossessed:
Nor, longer, robes of power invest
  The Justice whom remorse expelled.

Reduced to poverty, he sought
The hamlet where, he whilom, wrought:
  O'erwhelmed with weight of years and shame;
His palsied hand, worn hatchet, took;
Lopped leafless branches, by the brook,
  To feed his lonely cottage-flame.

22   The Sisters of Glen Nectan by Robert Stephen Hawker (c.1831)

It is from Nectan's[1] mossy steep,
The foamy waters flash and leap:
It is where shrinking wildflowers grow,
They love the nymph that dwells below.

But wherefore in this far-off dell,
The reliques of a human cell?
Where the sad stream and lonely wind
Bring man no tidings of his kind.

"Long years agone:" the old man said,
'Twas told him by his grandsire dead;
"One day two ancient sisters came:
None there could tell their race or name;

"Their speech was not in Cornish phrase,
Their garb had signs of loftier days;
Slight food they took from hands of men,
They withered slowly in that glen,

"One died – the other's sunken eye
Gushed till the fount of tears was dry;
A wild and withering thought had she,
'I shall have none to weep for me.'

"They found her silent at the last,
Bent in the shape wherein she passed:
Where her lone seat long used to stand,
Her head upon her shrivelled hand."

Did fancy given this legend birth?[2]
The grandame's tale for winter hearth:
Or some dead bard, by Nectan's stream,
People these banks with such a dream.

We know not: but it suits the scene,
To think such wild things here have been:
What spot more meet could grief or sin
Choose, at the last to wither in?

23   *From* **Scilly and its Legends by H.J. Whitfeld (1852)**

Lethowsow,[1] or the Lionesse:
> Once upon a time, long centuries ago not only

"Ere William led his Norman horde
    To plunder o'er the main.
And the brave Saxon's patient sword
    Had yet expelled the Dane."

but far back in those shadowy annals, which are at once so perplex-
ing and so fascinating; through which we love

"that glance to cast
That lifts the veil and lives amid the past.
To read high tales of virtue and of crime
Robed in the dread magnificence of time.
When error's beauteous mist forbids to scan
The stern sad outlines of primeval man."[2]

Long, long centuries ago, ere the Raven standard flew over our Isle;
ere Hengist and Horsa came in as allies, and remained as masters;

ere Britain ceased to belong to the British, the events occurred, which I have embodied in this following legend

Those who have pored over the old romances of chivalry, and especially the goodly tomes of Syr Thomas Maleor, know well the state of things that existed during the reign of King Arthur. There is a charm in those rude days, an inexpressible charm, against which we struggle in vain. We see Arthur of Britain, drawing his good sword Excalibur from the enchanted stone, and Merlin, the Great Wizard, and the Round Table of Camelot, with its unrivalled knights. As they feast in hall, their forms rise up before us. We see Sir Kaye, the seneschal, whose high qualities were tarnished by his love for scornful jests; and Sir Bors de Ganis; and the noble Ector de Maris; and Sir Caradoc, the husband of the fairest and most virtuous dame; and Sir Tristram, who loved too well the lady of his uncle, the false King Mark; and Lancelot of the Lake, the peerless warrior, over whose dead body it was said so beautifully, – "He was the kindest man that ever struck with sword; and he was the goodliest person that ever rode among the throng of knights; and he was the meekest man, and the gentlest, that did ever eat in hall among ladies; and he was the sternest knight to his mortal foe, that ever laid lance in rest." At the head of the board is Arthur, every inch a king, with his majestic presence, and his kindly smile. Nor was there wanting beauty at that royal banquet. Queen Guenever was there, regal in all respects save one, with her bright train. "Alas! that those so lovely should shrink before the ordeal of virtue, and that one only of their number should dare to pledge the enchanted cup of gold, and to wear the embroidered robe."

In the days of my tale, the "terrors of Tintagel's spear" were yet existing, though the sway of the great monarch approached its close. Arthur was holding high court in his Castle of Tintagel, and around him were gathered his paladins, diminished indeed in numbers by long and bloody war, but still presenting an array that had never yet known reverse or defeat. The king was there, as usual, and at his right hand sat the queen, but the brow of Arthur was sad, and grew dark, when he marked the glances that passed between Guenever and Sir Lancelot. The spirit of the assembled knights was not what it was. There were among them empty seats; and they could not but remember that those places were not always void by death, but that even in that gallant company, treason had stolen in, and seduced some of those deemed the bravest and the best. High among the gathered nobles was an ominous gap, caused by absence of Prince Mordred, and rumour spoke of evil designs, entertained by him against his kinsman and benefactor, even to the levying of open war. However, though changed from the frank courtesy and merriment of other days, the scene was, to the careless eye, splendid, and even gay. There was no lack of mirth, and song. Brave men whispered their homage to no unwilling ears; and soft cheeks waxed rosy, and wore a brighter charm, as the feast went on; and the royal brow of Arthur grew relaxed and lost its wrinkles, as he jested with the maidens of the queen; and though all was not as once it was, there was over all a semblance of enjoyment, and careless bravery, that deceived the eye. If it were a counterfeit, it was a successful one. To those who did not look below the surface, the glory of the Round Table was untarnished, and the gaiety of its knights unimpaired.

When the feast was over, Arthur arose from his throne, and, taking in his hand a golden cup, pledged his guests as of yore. But when he lifted the chalice to his lips, a shudder passed over him, and he cast it from him with an action of horror and disgust. "It is not wine," he exclaimed, "it is blood. My father Merlin is among us, and there is evil in the coming days. Break we up our Court, my peers! It is no time for feasting, but rather for fasting and for prayer."

As he spoke he glanced anxiously and bitterly at the vacant stall of his cousin Mordred. It was no longer unfilled. A shadowy form seemed darkly to rest upon it. There was no distinct figure, no bodied phantom, but a vast dim likeness of something terrible and strange. A cloudy spirit brooded over the traitor's seat. The assembly broke up in ghastly silence. They departed speechless and awestruck. They went to pray against the ills to come.

These came, alas, too soon! Next morning arrived a weary post, with tidings of the revolt of Mordred. Then followed, day after day, fresh disasters. Foes banded together and friends fell off. All whom the high handed king had put down and repressed, all from whom he had wrung ill gotten spoils, all with whom in fair fight he had contended for mastery, all false friends whom he had thought to buy with benefits, now leagued together against him. Single malcontents formed a band, and bands united swelled into an army. It advanced, with Mordred at its head, to strike a blow for the throne of Britain. All the while, Arthur lay still at Tintagel, and gave no sign of life. Perhaps he had lost somewhat of his early vigour. Perhaps he wished to give time to his enemies to declare themselves, that he might know on whom at last to rely. Perhaps he lingered in an agony of proud doubt, and indecision. But perhaps also, and it was most like the stout warrior, he disdained to show any apprehensions of a foe that he despised. Taking counsel only of his own kingly heart, he remained tranquil and undisturbed in his hold, looking down from thence upon the storm, as it came to a head in the plain below, and waiting for the proper hour to sally forth and scatter it.

It was still no child's play. The game was for an empire and battles were to decide the cast. Nor were the players ill-matched; nor was it an "impar congressus Achilli."[3] Those whom he was to meet in the coming war, were no longer rude Pagans or Soldans,[4] clad in barbaric arms. They were the flower of his own chivalry, headed by a prince of his own blood. Together they had ridden through many a bloody field, and not a few of the champions opposed to him had slept under the same cloak, after a day of common danger. They had been trained beneath his experienced eye, and had learned the art of war under the guiding of his leading-staff. Many a one of them could say, in the expressive language of Scripture. "Remember how thou and I rode together after Ahab," and old times must surely have touched their hearts, when they saw in their front that banner, under which they had been so long victorious, and that well known leader, with his sad, yet imperial glance, and his hair of silver sable, and his look, telling rather of sorrow than of years.

But rebellion has no shame. It grows more bitter for its very base-ness, and fiercer for the badness of its cause. The array of Mordred pressed onwards in still increasing numbers. The land of Cornwall, never too friendly to Arthur, was alive with foes. They marched upon Tintagel, sternly but slowly, for they had an instinctive dread of the old chief, as he lay grimly in his fastness, his renowned knights with-in its halls, his veteran levies around them, and in the centre of the whole, himself, a host, calm, unshaken, and resolute. They prepared to beard the lion in his den, but it was with secret misgivings that they did so, and many a heart that knew no other fear, faltered on its approach. And still Arthur never moved. It seemed as if he did not deign to parley with his revolted subjects. Their advanced guards and scouts might be decried from the donjon tower of the castle, but no movement followed the discovery. The main body was even seen, but the King lay stern and still.

Suddenly, at day-break one morning, the great bell of the fortress rang out a stirring peal, and before the barbican the trumpets sound-ed to horse, and all was bustle, and waving of pennons, and mar-shalling to arms. And in a short time, Arthur rode out from the gate, followed by the mighty, who still adhered to him. There filed onwards the most renowned of his followers, Sir Lancelot, and Sir Tristram, Sir Banyan, and Sir Bor, Sir Ector, and Sir Cote mal taillé, Sir Caradoc, and Sir Percival, without a stain. They were the Fathers of the war, the chosen of Britain. They were men who

> "Would scorn, amid the reel of strife,
> To yield one step for death or life."

And now, unconquerable, in proud defiance, they went forth to do battle for God and their king. Alone at their head was Arthur, with a brow of marble, collected and self-possessed. As he passed on, he issued his commands from time to time, but his words were brief and stern, and he never looked back. Men thought that the shade of Merlin held communion with him. And so went forth Arthur to his last of fields.

The next evening, a band of warriors was seen urging their weary steeds across the wild heaths that were common in Cornwall. Their course was in the direction of Cassiteris, and of that fair wide tract of country, called in the Cornish tongue, "Lethowsow." Their numbers were formidable, amounting to several hundreds, but they were in no mood nor condition for resistance, as was shown by their hacked armour, and torn surcoats, and, in many instances, by the blood that welled from their unstaunched wounds. They hurried, for life and death, over the wastes before them. Not a word was spoken. Now and then a straggler fell to the rear from sheer exhaustion, but his absence in the disordered ranks was unmarked. Sometimes they paused for a few minutes at a brook or spring, suffered their horses to take a hasty drink, tightened the saddle-girths, and were gone. Their pace, as may be supposed, was not too quick, but they made some progress, and when, as darkness fell, they drew their reins, and prepared to encamp for the night, it was after thirty miles sped over rough and broken roads. Glory had apparently little to do with that tumultuous disarray. Yet these jaded riders, flying before the face of their pursuer, were all that remained of the chivalry of Britain. Arthur lay dead upon the plain; the banner that had covered his breast, until all was lost, was now borne, torn and bloody, in the van. The survivors of that dreadful day were fleeing for their lives, and Mordred thundered upon their rear.

They arose in the morning, and bouned them again for flight. Veterans as they were, the mere hardship of a rough ride and an unbroken fast was a trifle: they recked little of either. But disgrace and defeat were new and strange evils. These were the true bitterness of death. Nor could they altogether comprehend them, nor believe them as yet to be a sad and stern reality. They could attribute the dishonour that had tarnished their arms to no particular cause: there was no apparent reason for their fall. The stars in their courses had fought against them, and palsied their stout arms, and made their skill and valour vain. They brooded over these things as they rode on. They did not ponder deeply, for the recent shock had confused and rendered dull their ideas, but thoughts like these floated unconsciously through their brain. Arthur of Britain had gone down, and the best lances in the world were flying for their lives, with a conquering foe in hot chase after them.

The course of these waking visions was interrupted by the notes of a trumpet, which followed them with a prolonged wail through the air. Then it came louder, and yet more loud. They halted for a moment, and looked back. The veteran warriors could not brook to fly. They had submitted to misfortune: they could no longer bear disgrace. As they gazed, the air became radiant with the reflected light of steel, as shields, and morions, and lances, gleamed fitfully from the brow of a distant hill. It was the glimmering of the pursuer's arms. Should they make a stand and die? Should they condescend to purchase life by a farther retreat? There was the traitor, the murderer of his kinsman and sovereign. Should they not breathe their chargers, and await his coming, and strike one stroke for revenge?

While they paused, gloomy and irresolute, and gazed steadily at the advancing forces, there seemed to come between them a shadowy dimness, that assumed gradually the form of a gigantic figure. It was like a mountain mist, but yet it wore the shape and aspect of humanity. There was a likeness in its awful lineaments, a resemblance to one honoured and long departed, which the aged knights recognised at once! It was the awful ghost of Merlin! Like a sullen cloud, but yet instinct with the principle of life, it upreared its huge outlines between the spoilers and their prey, terrible in its indistinctness and with a supernatural and spiritual grandeur, rather felt than seen. It was a gulf between the two parties, impassable as that between the Egyptians and the flying Hebrews, and it troubled the following host, and checked them in their headlong speed. And so the chase continued. Sullenly the fugitives retired to the refuge they had chosen, and as sullenly did Mordred follow, hating those he had injured, hunting them to the death, and restrained only in his vindictive career by the clouded aspect of that dusky barrier, which he dared not brave.

By the side of the road, not far from the spot wherein after the days the piety of Athelstan founded the college and church of St. Buryan, there dwelt a holy hermit. In his poor cell one of the knights, whose wounds were mortal, laid down and departed from life. As the hermit knelt and prayed by this body, Mordred rode up. His face was pale as death, and was rendered still more ghastly by a blue livid wound, that traversed his whole forehead, and was lost amid his hair, matted and soaked with blood. He dismounted and entered the hut. The hermit and the dead man were its only tenants, save him. He looked upon the face of the corpse. It was the face of an early comrade of his own. The same blood ran in the veins of each of their mothers. He turned gloomily away and signed the sign of the cross, involuntarily, upon his breast. The hermit sighed, when he beheld the action. "Alas," said he to Mordred, "thou hast in one day done more evil, than all thy ancestry have ever in their whole lives done of good. The crown of Arthur is upon thy brow, but the brand of Cain is there also. Go on, thou traitor to God and man." And Mordred smote him angrily with his gauntlet. "Go on," added the recluse, "thy course is wellnigh done. The shadow of a mighty one is brooding over thee. Go on, and die." And Mordred mounted his horse and urged it furiously forward. But the animal refused to obey the spur. The power of that dread spirit was before him. It had far more terrors for the charger than bit or steel. The avenging spectre would not give place to man's wrath. After a long and ineffectual struggle, the might of the unearthly prevailed. The ghastly chase was resumed, with the same dogged sullenness as before.

And now Mordred reached a lofty slope, from which, more clearly than he had hitherto been able to do, he could see his retiring enemies. They were already at a very considerable distance, upon that winding road which then led over the fertile tract of country called in Cornish "Lethowsow," or, in after-days, "the Lionesse." They were so far in advance that he could only follow their course by catching, at intervals, the gleaming of their arms. Around him was that fair land, now so long lost and forgotten, from the bosom of which men for ages had dug mineral wealth, upon which were seen no fewer than one hundred and forty stately churches, and whose beauty and fruitfulness have been the theme of many a romantic lay. Broken sunlight floated over its soft glades. It never looked so grandly glorious as on that hour of its fate. As Mordred pressed on, full of one thought alone, already in imagination hemming in to slaughter, or driving into the waves, his enemies, his attendants and followers began to be sensible of change in the atmosphere, of a something oppressive and horrible, though he himself perceived it not. Huge battlemented clouds, tinged with lurid red, hung over the horizon. The air became sultry and choking. A tremulous and wavy motion shook the ground at intervals. A low sound, like distant thunder, moaned around. The soldiers of his train drew closer together, awe-struck and terrified. But Mordred heard only the evil voice of his own passions. The war of the elements gave unmistakeable signs of its awaking. But Mordred perceived it not.

At last, amid a silence that might be felt, so dreadful was it, and so dull – that fearful shade, which had hitherto gone before him, and restrained his madness, suddenly itself stopped. It assumed a definite shape. It was the form of Merlin, the Enchanter. But it was even more terrible than Merlin, for it united the unearthly glare of the spectre with the grandeur of the inspired man. Right in Mordred's path, face to face, did the avenger stand. They remained for a few seconds, motionless, frowning upon each other. Neither spake, save with the eye. After those few seconds, the great wizard raised his arm. Then there ensued a confused muttering, a sound, as though the foundations of the great deep were broke up. Soon the voice of the subterranean thunder increased, and the firm soil beneath their feet began to welk and wave, and fissures appeared upon the surface, and the rock swelled like the throes of a labouring sea.[5] With wild cry of agony, the band of pursuers became in turn the pursued. They wheeled and rushed away in headlong flight. But it was in vain. The earth, rent in a thousand fragments, in the grasp of that earthquake, upheaved its surface convulsively, gave one brief and conscious pause, and then, at once, sank down for ever beneath the level of the deep. In a moment, a continent was submerged, with all its works of art, and piety, with all its living tribes, with all its passions, and hopes, and fears. The soldiers of Mordred were whirled away in the stream created by that sudden gulf, which even now flows so violently over its prey below. Last of all, Mordred remained, as it were fascinated and paralyzed, gazing at the phantom with a look in which horror struggled with hate, and which was stamped with scorn and defiance to the end. That morning had dawned upon as bright a scene as ever met the eye. At evening, there was nought from what was then first termed the Land's-end, to St. Martin's head, but a howling and boiling wilderness of waves, bearing here and there upon its bosom a fragment from the perished world beneath or a corse tossed upon the billows, over which sea birds wheeled and screamed.

The remnant that was preserved reached in safety Cassiteris,[6] called afterwards Silura, and now Scilly. There the wicked ceased to trouble, and the weary were at rest. In their island home, upon which still the sea encroaches daily, they dwelt securely. From St. Martin's height, on their arrival, they saw the catastrophe that overwhelmed their enemies, and, dismounting, knelt upon the turf, and thanked God for their deliverance. They never more sought the Britain of their hope and fame. It would have been a changed and a melancholy home for them. Arthur was in his tomb, at Glastonbury. Guenever was dead. The Round Table was broken and its best knights perished or dispersed. Their work was done. In the Isles of Scilly, thus miraculously severed from the main land, and, as it were set apart for their sakes, they lived, and there they died. In after days their children raised a stately religious house, at Tresco, over their bones. But their memory gradually faded away and was forgotten. Sometimes on a clear day there may be seen the remains of walls or buildings under the sea. Sometimes fishermen bring up relics of other times, and men wonder at them and speculate upon their cause, and use. Strangers make pilgrimages to Scilly, and marvel whether it ever exceeded its present limits. But the account of its isolation is remembered only as a confused dream; it is a mystery, an old world tale; a fragment of which, like a portion of a wreck, floats about, here and there, in the visions of the past.

Such is the legend of the Lionesse.

Menavawr and the Eastern Isles

We landed on the Arthurs, there being three of that name. On Great and Middle Arthur, are several barrows, one very large and capable of containing many persons. The remains of inclosures are visible, but there is now nothing living but lop-eared rabbits and rats. Where we embarked I fancied that I could trace the outline and materials of an antique pier (Arthur's quay). The walls too appeared to be very old, almost, as it seemed to me, connected with the circle and barrows. It is really painful to see these vestiges of life and labour, like the dead bones spoken of by the prophet, once instinct with life.

There is nothing remarkable in any of the other rocks, except their picturesque roughness and form, and the fine contrast of the surf, flashing over the blue deep, upon the grey stones and bright bays of sand. From them you emerge into the great ocean. The light-ship on the ridge called the Seven Stones is before you. On a clear day you can see the Land's-end, and you may lie in the stern of your boat, and muse about Lyonesse.

24 *From* **Idylls of the King by Alfred, Lord Tennyson (1856–1874)**

The prince and warrior Gorloïs, he that held
Tintagil castle by the Cornish sea,
Was wedded with a winsome wife, Ygerne:
And daughters had she borne him, – one whereof,
Lot's wife, the Queen of Orkney, Bellicent,
Hath ever like a loyal sister cleaved
To Arthur, – but a son she had not borne.
And Uther cast upon her eyes of love:
But she a stainless wife to Gorloïs,
So loathed the bright dishonour of his love,
That Gorloïs and King Uther went to war:
And overthrown was Gorloïs and slain.
Then Uther in his wrath and heat besieged
Ygerne within Tintagil, where her men,
Seeing the mighty swarm about their walls,
Left her and fled, and Uther enter'd in,
And there was none to call to but himself.
So, compass'd by the power of the King,
Enforced she was to wed him in her tears,
And with a shameful swiftness: afterward,
Not many moons, King Uther died himself,
Moaning and wailing for an heir to rule
After him, lest the realm should go to wrack.
And that same night, the night of the new year,
By reason of the bitterness and grief
That vext his mother, all before his time
Was Arthur born, and all as soon as born
Deliver'd at a secret postern-gate
To Merlin, to be holden far apart
Until his hour should come; because the lords
Of that fierce day were as the lords of this,
Wild beasts, and surely would have torn the child
Piecemeal among them, had they known; for each
But sought to rule for his own self and hand,
And many hated Uther for the sake
Of Gorloïs. Wherefore Merlin took the child,
And gave him to Sir Anton an old knight
And ancient friend of Uther; and his wife
Nursed the young prince, and rear'd him with her own;
And no man knew. And ever since the lords
Have foughten like wild beasts among themselves,
So that the realm has gone to wrack: but now,
Ths year, when Merlin (for his hour had come)
Brought Arthur forth, and set him in the hall,
Proclaiming, 'Here is Uther's heir, your king,'

A hundred voices cried, 'Away with him!
No king of ours! a son of Gorloïs he,
Or else the child of Anton, and no king,
Or else baseborn.' Yet Merlin thro' his craft,
And while the people clamour'd for a king,
Had Arthur crown'd; but after, the great lords
Banded, and so brake out in open war.'

'And there I saw mage Merlin, whose vast wit
And hundred winters are but as the hands
Of loyal vassals toiling for their liege.

'And near him stood the Lady of the Lake,
Who knows a subtler magic than his own –
Clothed in white samite,[1] mystic, wonderful.
She gave the King his huge cross-hilted sword,
Whereby to drive the heathen out: a mist
Of incense curl'd about her, and her face
Wellnigh was hidden in the minster gloom;
But there was heard among the holy hymns
A voice as of the waters, for she dwells
Down in a deep; calm, whatsoever storms
May shake the world, and when the surface rolls,
Hath power to walk the waters like our Lord.

'There likewise I beheld Excalibur
Before him at his crowning borne, the sword
That rose from out the bosom of the lake,
And Arthur row'd across and took it – rich
With jewels, elfin Urim,[2] on the hilt,
Bewildering heart and eye – the blade so bright
That men are blinded by it – on one side,
Graven in the oldest tongue of all this world,
"Take me," but turn the blade and ye shall see,
And written in the speech ye speak yourself,
"Cast me away!" And sad was Arthur's face
Taking it, but old Merlin counsell'd him,
"Take thou and strike! the time to cast away
Is yet far-off." So this great brand the king
Took, and by this will beat his foemen down.'

Then rose the King and moved his host by night,
And ever push'd Sir Mordred, league by league,
Back to the sunset bound of Lyonesse –
A land of old upheaven from the abyss
By fire, to sink into the abyss again;

Where fragments of forgotten peoples dwelt,
And the long mountains ended in a coast
Of ever-shifting sand, and far away
The phantom circle of a moaning sea.
There the pursuer could pursue no more,
And he that fled no further fly the King;
And there, that day when the great light of heaven
Burn'd at his lowest in the rolling year,
On the waste sand by the waste sea they closed.
Nor ever yet had Arthur fought a fight
Like this last, dim, weird battle of the west.
A deathwhite mist slept over sand and sea:
Whereof the chill, to him who breathed it, drew
Down with his blood, till all his heart was cold
With formless fear, and ev'n on Arthur fell
Confusion, since he saw not whom he fought.
For friend and foe were shadows in the mist,
And friends slew friend not knowing whom he slew;
And some had visions out of golden youth,
And some beheld the faces of old ghosts
Look in upon the battle; and in the mist
Was many a noble deed, many a base,
And chance and craft and strength in single fights,
And ever and anon with host to host
Shocks, and the splintering spear, the hard mail hewn,
Shield-breakings, and the clash of brands, the crash
Of battleaxes on shatter'd helms, and shrieks
After the Christ, of those who falling down
Look'd up for heaven, and only saw the mist;
and shouts of heathen and the traitor knights,
Oaths, insults, filth, and monstrous blasphemies,
Sweat, writings, anguish, labouring of the lungs
In that close mist, and cryings for the light,
Moans of the dying, and voices of the dead.

   Last, as by some one deathbed after wail
Of suffering, silence follows, or thro' death
Or deathlike swoon, thus over all that shore,
Save for some whisper of the seething seas,
A dead hush fell; but when the dolorous day
Grew drearier toward twilight falling, came
A bitter wind, clear from the North, and blew
The mist aside, and with that wind the tide
Rose, and the pale King glanced across the field
Of battle: but no man was moving there;
Nor any cry of Christian heard thereon,
Nor yet of heathen; only the wan wave
Brake in among dead faces, to and fro

Swaying the helpless hands, and up and down
Tumbling the hollow helmets of the fallen,
And shiver'd brands that once had fought with Rome,
And rolling far along the gloomy shores
The voice of days of old and days to be.

Then spake King Arthur to Sir Bedivere,
And whiter than the mist that all day long
Had held the field of battle was the King:

'Hearest thou this great voice that shakes the world,
And wastes the narrow realm whereon we move,
And beats upon the faces of the dead,
My dead, as tho' they had not died for me? –
O Bedivere, for on my heart hath fall'n
Confusion, till I know not what I am,
Nor whence I am, not whether I be King.
Behold, I seem but King among the dead.'

———————————

Then murmur'd Arthur, 'Place me in the barge.'
So to the barge they came. There those three Queens
Put forth their hands, and took the King, and wept.
But she, that rose the tallest of them all
And fairest, laid his head upon her lap,
And loosed the shatter'd casque, and chafed his hands,
And call'd him by his name, complaining loud,
And dropping bitter tears against a brow
Striped with dark blood: for all his face as white
And colourless, and like the wither'd moon
Smote by the fresh beam of the springing east;
And all his greaves and cuisses dash'd with drops
Of onset; and the light and lustrous curls –
That made his forehead like a rising sun
High from the daïs-throne – were parch'd with dust;
Or, clotted into points and hanging loose,
Mix'd with the knightly growth that fringed his lips.
So like a shatter'd column lay the King;
Not like that Arthur who, with lance in rest,
From spur to plume a star of tournament,
Shot thro' the lists at Camelot, and charged
Before the eyes of ladies and of kings.

Then loudly cried the bold Sir Bedivere:
'Ah! my Lord Arthur, whither shall I go?
Where shall I hide my forehead and my eyes?
For now I see the true old times are dead,
When every morning brought a noble chance,

And every chance brought out a noble knight.
Such times have been not since the light that led
The holy Elders with the gift of myrrh.
But now the whole Round Table is dissolved
Which was an image of the mighty world,
And I, the last, go forth companionless,
And the days darken round me, and the years,
Among new men, strange faces, other minds.'

    And slowly answer'd Arthur from the barge:
'The old order changeth, yielding place to new,
And God fulfils himself in many ways,
Lest one good custom should corrupt the world.
Comfort thyself: what comfort is in me?
I have lived my life, and that which I have done
May He within himself make pure! but thou,
If thou shouldst never see my face again,
Pray for my soul. More things are wrought by prayer
Than this world dreams of. Wherefore, let thy voice
Rise like a fountain for me night and day.
For what are men better than sheep or goats
That nourish a blind life within the brain,
If, knowing God, they lift not hands of prayer
Both for themselves and those who call them friend?
For so the whole round earth is every way
Bound by gold chains about the feet of God.
But now farewell. I am going a long way
With these thou seëst – if indeed I go
(For all my mind is clouded with a doubt) –
To the island-valley of Avilion;
Where falls not hail, or rain, or any snow,
Not ever wind blows loudly; but it lies
Deep meadow'd, happy, fair with orchard lawns
And bowery hollows crown'd with summer sea,
Where I will heal me of my grievous wound.'

    So said he, and the barge with oar and sail
Moved from the brink, like some full-breasted swan
That, fluting a wild carol ere her death,
Ruffles her pure cold plume, and takes the flood
With swarthy webs. Long stood Sir Bedivere
Revolving many memories, till the hull
Look'd one black dot against the verge of dawn,
And on the mere the wailing died away.

    But when that moan had past for evermore,
The stillness of the dead world's winter dawn

Amazed him, and he groan'd, 'The King is gone.'
And therewithal came on him the weird rhyme,
'From the great deep to the great deep he goes.'

Whereat he slowly turn'd and slowly clomb
The last hard footstep of that iron crag;
Thence mark'd the black hull moving yet, and cried,
'He passes to be King among the dead,
And after healing of his grievous wound
He comes again; but – if he comes no more –
O me, be yon dark Queens in yon black boat,
Who shriek'd and wail'd, the three whereat we gazed
On that high day, when, clothed with living light,
They stood before his throne in silence, friends
Of Arthur, who should help him at his need?'

Then from the dawn it seem'd there came, but faint
As from beyond the limit of the world,
Like the last echo born of a great cry,
Sounds, as if some fair city were one voice
Around a king returning from his wars.

Thereat once more he moved about, and clomb
Ev'n to the highest he could climb, and saw,
Straining his eyes beneath an arch of hand,
Or thought he saw, the speck that bare the King,
Down that long water opening on the deep
Somewhere far off, pass on and on, and go
From less to less and vanish into light.
And the new sun rose bringing the new year.

25   The Quest of the Sangraal[1] by Robert Stephen Hawker (1863)

Ho! for the Sangraal![2] vanished vase of heaven!
That held, like Christ's own heart, an hin[3] of blood!
Ho! for the Sangraal! ... How the merry shout,
Of reckless riders on their rushing steeds,
Smote the loose echo from the drowsy rock
Of grim Dundagel:[4] throned along the sea!

"Unclean! unclean! ten cubits and a span,
Keep from the wholesome touch of human-kind:
Stand at the gate, and beat the leper's bell,
But stretch not forth the hand for holy thing, –
Unclean, as Egypt at the ebb of Nile!"
Thus said the monk: a lean and gnarlèd man;

His couch was on the rock, by that wild stream
That floods, in cataract, Saint Nectan's kieve:
One of the choir, whose life is Orison![5]
They had their lodges in the wilderness, –
Or built them cells beside shadowy sea,
And there they dwelt with Angels, like a dream:
So they unrolled the volume of the Book,
And filled the fields of the Evangelist
With antique thoughts, that breathed of Paradise!

Uprose they for the quest! the bounding men,
Of the siege perilous, and the granite ring!
They gathered at the rock: yon ruddy tor, –
The stony depth where lurked the demon-god,
Till Christ, the mighty Master, drave him forth.

There stood the knights! stately, and stern, and tall;
Tristan; and Perceval; Sir Galahad:
And he, the sad Sir Lancelot of the lay:
Ah me! that logan of the rocky hills,
Pillared in storm, calm in the rush of war,
Shook, at the light touch of his lady's hand!

See! where they move, a battle-shouldering kind!
Massive in mould, but graceful: thorough men:
Built in the mystic measure of the Cross: –
Their lifted arms the Transome: and their bulk,
The Tree, where Jesu stately stood to die!
Thence came their mastery in the field of war: –
Ha! one might drive battalions – one alone!

See now, they pause; for in their midst, the King!
Arthur, the Son of Uter, and the Night.
Helmed with Pendragon: with the crested Crown:
And belted, with the sheathed Excalibur,
That gnashed his iron teeth, and yearned for war!
Stern was that look: high natures seldom smile:
And in those pulses beat a thousand kings.
A glance! and they were hushed: a lifted hand, –
And his eye ruled them like a throne of light!
Then, with a voice that rang along the moor –
Like the Archangel's trumpet for the dead –
He spake – while Tamar sounded to the sea.

"Comrades in arms! mates of the table-round!
Fair sirs, my fellows in the bannered ring, –
Ours is a lofty tryst! this day we meet,

Not under shield, with scarf and knightly gage,
To quench our thirst of love in ladies' eyes:
We shall not mount to-day that goodly throne,
The conscious steed, with thunder in his loins,
To launch along the field the arrowy spear: –
Nay, but a holier theme, a mightier quest –
'Ho! for the Sangraal, vanished vase of God!'

"Ye know that in old days, that yellow Jew,
Accursèd Herod; and the earth-wide judge,
Pilate the Roman: doomster for all lands –
Or else the Judgement has not been for all, –
Bound Jesu-Master to the world's tall tree,
Slowly to die…
Ha! Sirs, had we been there,
They durst not have assayed their felon deed, –
Excalibur had cleft them to the spine! –
Slowly He died, a world in every pang,
Until the hard centurion's cruel spear
Smote His high heart: and from that severed side,
Rushed the red stream that quenched the wrath of
    Heaven!

"Then came Sir Joseph, hight of Arimathèe,[6]
Bearing that awful vase, the Sangraal!
The vessel of the Pasch,[7] Shere Thursday night:
The selfsame Cup, wherein the faithful Wine
Heard God, and was obedient unto Blood!
Therewith he knelt and gathered blessèd drops
From his dear Master's Side that sadly fell,
The ruddy dews from the great tree of life:
Sweet Lord! what treasures! like the priceless gems
Hid in the tawny casket of a king, –
A ransom for an army, one by one!
That wealth he cherished long: his very soul
Around his ark: bent as before a shrine!

"He dwelt in Orient Syria: God's own land:
The ladder foot of heaven – where shadowy shapes
In white apparel glided up and down!
His home was like a garner, full of corn
And wine and oil; a granary of God!
Young men, that no one knew, went in and out,
With a far look in their eternal eyes!
All things were strange and rare: the Sangraal,
As though it clung to some ethereal chain,
Brought down high Heaven to earth at Arimathèe!

"He lived long centuries! and prophesised.
A girded pilgrim ever and anon:
Cross-staff in hand, and folded at his side,
The mystic marvel of the feast of blood!
Once, in old time, he stood in this dear land,
Enthralled: – for lo! a sign! his grounded staff
Took root, and branched, and bloomed, like Aaron's rod:[8]
Thence came the shrine, the cell; therefore he dwelt,
The vassal of the vase, at Avalon!

"This could not last, for evil days came on,
And evil men: the garbage of their sin
Tainted this land, and all things holy fled.
The Sangraal was not: on a summer eve,
The silence of the sky brake up in sound!
The tree of Joseph glowed with ruddy light:
A harmless fire, curved like a molten vase,
Around the bush, and from the midst, a voice:
Thus hewn by Merlin on a runic stone: –
Kirioth: el : Zannah: aulohee: pedàh:[9]

"Then said the shuddering seer – he heard and knew
The unutterable words that glide in Heaven,
Without a breath or tongue, from soul to soul –

"The land is lonely now: Anathema:[10]
The link that bound it to the silent grasp
Of thrilling worlds is gathered up and gone:
The glory is departed; and the disk
So full of radiance from the touch of God!
The orb is darkened to the distant watch
Of Saturn and his reapers, when they pause,
Amid their sheaves, to count the nightly stars.

"All gone! but not for ever: on a day
There shall arise a king from Keltic loins,
Of mystic birth and name, tender and true;
His vassals shall be noble, to a man:
Knights strong in battle till the war is won:
Then while the land is hushed on Tamar side,
So that the warder upon Carradon[11]
Shall hear at once the river and the sea –
That king shall call a Quest: a kindling cry:
'Ho! for the Sangraal! vanished vase of God!'

"Yea! and it shall be won! a chosen knight,
The ninth from Joseph in the line of blood,
Clean as a maid from guile and fleshly sin –

He with the shield of Sarras;[12] and the lance,
Ruddy and moistened with a freshening stain,
As from a severed wound of yesterday –
He shall achieve the Graal: he alone!

"Thus wrote Bard Merlin on the Runic hide
Of a slain deer: rolled in an aumry chest.

"And now, fair Sirs, your voices: who will gird
His belt for travel in the perilous ways?
This thing must be fulfilled: – in vain our land
Of noble name, high deed, and famous men;
Vain the proud homage of our thrall, the sea,
If we be shorn of God: – ah! loathsome shame!
To hurl in battle for the pride of arms:
To ride in native tournay, foreign war:
To count the stars; to ponder pictured runes: –
And grasp great knowledge, as the demons do –
If we be shorn of God: – we must assay
The myth and meaning of this marvellous bowl:
It shall be sought and found: – "
                    Thus said the King.

Then rose a storm of voices; like the sea,
When Ocean, bounding, shouts with all his waves!
High-hearted men: the purpose and the theme,
Smote the fine chord that thrills the warrior's soul
With touch and impulse for a deed of fame.
Then spake Sir Gauvain, counsellor of the King –
A man of Pentecost for words that burn: –

"Sirs! we are soldiers of the rock and ring:
Our table-round is earth's most honoured stone;
Thereon two worlds of life and glory blend!
The boss upon the shield of many a land:
The midway link with light beyond the stars!
This is our fount of fame! let us arise,
And cleave the earth like rivers: like the streams
That win from Paradise their immortal name:
To the four winds of God! casting the lot.

"So shall we share the regions! and unfold
The shrouded mystery of those fields of air.

"Eastward! the source and spring of life and light!
Thence came, and thither went, the rush of worlds,
When the great cone of space[13] was sown with stars!
There rolled the gateway of the double dawn,

When the mere God shone down a breathing man
There, up from Bethany, the Syrian Twelve[14]
Watched their dear Master darken into day!
Thence, too, will gleam the Cross, the arisen wood.[15]
Ah, shuddering sign one day of terrible doom!
Therefore the Orient is the home of God.

"The West! a Galilee: the shore of men!
The symbol and the scene of populous life:
Full Japhet[16] journeyed thither, Noe's son,
The prophecy of increase in his loins,
Westward[17] Lord Jesus looked His latest love –
His yearning Cross along the peopled sea,
The innumerable nations in His soul:
Thus came that type and token of our kind,
The realm and region of the set of sun,
The wide, wide West: the imagined zone of man.

"The North! the lair of demons,[18] where they coil,
And bound, and glide, and travel to and fro:
Their gulph, the underworld, this hollow orb,
Where vaulted columns curve beneath the hills
And shoulder us on their arches: there they throng;
The portal of their pit, the polar gate;
Their fiery dungeon mocked with northern snow:
Their doom and demon haunt a native land,
Where dreamy thunder mutters in the cloud,
Storm broods, and battle breathes, and baleful fires
Shed a fierce horror o'er the shuddering North!

"But thou! O South Wind, breathe thy fragrant sigh:
We follow on thy perfume, breath of heaven!
Myriads, in girded albs, for ever young,
Their stately semblance of embodied air,
Troop round the footstool of the Southern Cross[19] –
Their pentacle of stars: the very sign
That led the Wise Men towards the Awful Child,
Then came and stood to rule the peaceful sea!
So, too, Lord Jesu from His mighty tomb
Cast the dear shadow of His red right hand,[20]
To soothe the happy South: the Angels' home!

"Then let us search the regions! one by one,
And pluck this Sangraal from its cloudy cave!"

So Merlin brought the arrows: graven lots,
Shrouded from sight within a quivered sheath,
For choice and guidance in the perilous path,

That so the travellers might divide the lands.
They met at Lauds, in good Saint Nectan's coll,
For fast, and vigil, and their knightly vow:
Then knelt, and prayed, and all received their God.

"Now for the silvery arrows, grasp and hold!"

Sir Lancelot drew the North: that fell domain,
Where fleshly man must brook the airy fiend –
His battle-foe, the demon: ghastly war!
Ho! stout Saint Michael[21] shield them, knight and knave!

The South fell softly to Sir Perceval's hand:
Some shadowy Angel breathed a silent sign:
That so that blameless man, that courteous knight,
Might mount and mingle with the happy host
Of God's white army in their native land!
Yea, they shall woo and soothe him, like the dove.

But hark! the greeting! – "Tristan for the West!"
Among the multitudes, his watchful way:
The billowy hordes beside the seething sea;
But will the glory gleam in loathsome lands?
Will the lost pearl shine out among the swine?
Woe, father Adam, to thy loins and thee.

Sir Galahad holds the Orient arrow's name:
His chosen hand unbars the gate of day!
There glows that heart, filled with his mother's blood,
That rules in every pulse, the world of man;
Link of the awful Three, with many a star.
O! blessèd East! 'mid visions such as thine,
'Twere well to grasp the Sangraal, and die.

Now feast and festival in Arthur's hall:
Hark! stern Dundagel softens into song!
They meet for solemn severance, knight and king:
Where gate and bulwark darken o'er the sea.
Strong men for meat, and warriors at the wine:
They wreak the wrath of hunger on the beeves, –
They rend rich morsels from the savoury deer, –
And quench the flagon like Brun-guillie[22] dew!
Hear! how the minstrels prophesy in sound.
Shout the King's waes-hael, and Drink-hael the Queen!

Then said Sir Kay, he of the arrowy tongue,
"Joseph and Pharaoh! how they build their bones!
Happier the boar were quick than dead to-day."

The Queen! the Queen! how haughty on the dais!
The sunset tangled in her golden hair:
A dove amid the eagles: Gwennivar!
Aishah! what might is in that glorious eye!
See their tamed lion from Brocelian's glade,[23]
Couched on the granite like a captive king:
A word – a gesture – or a mute caress –
How fiercely fond he droops his billowy mane,
And wooes, with tawny lip, his lady's hand!

The dawn is deep: the mountains yearn for day!
The hooting cairn is hushed: that fiendish noise,
Yelled from the utterance of the rending rock,
When the fierce dog of Cain barks from the moon.

The bird of judgement chants the doom of night:
The billows laugh a welcome to the day,
And Camlan ripples, seaward, with a smile.

"Down with the eastern bridge! the warriors ride,
And thou, Sir Herald, blazon as they pass!"
Foremost sad Lancelot, throned upon his steed,
His yellow banner, northward, lapping light:
The crest, a lily, with a broken stem,
The legend, **Stately once and ever fair**;
It hath a meaning, seek it not, O King!

A quaint embroidery Sir Perceval wore;
A turbaned Syrian, underneath a palm,
Wrestled for mastery with a stately foe,
Robed in a Levite's[24] raiment, white as wool:
His touch o'erwhelmed the Hebrew, and his word,
Whoso is strong with God shall conquer man,
Coiled in rich tracery round the knightly shield.
Did Ysolt's delicate fingers weave the web,
That gleamed in silken radiance o'er her lord?
A molten rainbow, bent; that arch in heaven,
Which leads straightway to Paradise and God;
Beneath, came up a gloved and sigilled hand,
Amid this cunning needlework of words,
**When toil and tears have worn the westering day,
Behold the smile of fame! so brief: so bright**.

A vast Archangel floods Sir Galahad's shield,
Mid-breast, and lifted high, an Orient cruse,
Full-filled, and running o'er with numynous light,
As though it held and shed the visible God;

Then shone this utterance as in graven fire,
I thirst! O Jesu! let me drink and die!

So forth they fare, King Arthur and his men;
Like stout quaternions of the Maccabee:[25]
They halt, and form at craggy Carradon;
Fit scene for haughty hope and stern farewell.
Lo! the rude altar; and the rough-hewn rock:
The grim and ghastly semblance of the fiend:
His haunt and coil within that pillared home,
Hark, the wild echo! did the demon breathe,
That yell of vengeance from the conscious stone?

There the brown barrow curves its sullen breast,
Above the bones of some dead Gentille's soul:
All hushed – and calm – and cold – until anon
Gleams the old dawn – the well-remembered day –
Then may you hear, beneath that hollow cairn,
The clash of arms: the muffled shout of war;
Blent with the rustle of the kindling dead!

They stand – and hush their hearts to hear the King.

Then said he, like a prince of Tamar-land,
Around his soul, Dundagel and the sea –

"Ha! Sirs – ye seek a noble crest to-day,
To win and wear the starry Sangraal,
The link that binds to God a lonely land.
Would that my arms went with you, like my heart!
But the true shepherd must not shun the fold:
For in this flock are crouching grievous wolves,
And chief among them all, my own false kin.
Therefore I tarry by the cruel sea:
To hear at eve the treacherous mermaid's song –
And watch the wallowing monsters of the wave, –
'Mid all things fierce, and wild, and strange, alone!

"Ay! all beside can win companionship:
The churl may clip his master beneath the thatch,
While his brown urchins nestle at his knees:
The soldier give and grasp a mutual palm,
Knit to his flesh in sinewy bonds of war:
The knight may seek at eve his castle-gate,
Mount the old stair, and lift the accustomed latch,
To find, for throbbing brow and weary limb,
That paradise of pillows, one true breast:

But he, the lofty ruler of the land,
Like yonder Tor, first greeted by the dawn,
And wooed the latest by the lingering day,
With happy homes and hearths beneath his breast,
Must soar and gleam in solitary snow!
The lonely one is, evermore, the King.
So now farewell, my lieges, fare ye well,
And God's sweet Mother be your benison!
Since by grey Merlin's gloss, this wondrous cup
Is, like the golden vase in Aaron's ark,
A fount of manha for a yearning world,
As full as it can hold of God and heaven:
Search the four winds until the balsam breathe,
Then grasp, and fold it in your very soul!

"I have no son, no daughter of my loins,
To breathe, 'mid future men, their father's name:
My blood will perish when these veins are dry.
Yet I am fain some deeds of mine should live –
I would not be forgotten in this land:
I yearn that men I know not, men unborn,
Should find, amid these fields, King Arthur's fame!
Here let them say, by proud Dundagel's walls –
They brought the Sangraal back by his command,
They touched these rugged rocks with hues of God:
So shall my name have worship, and my land!

"Ah! native Cornwall! throned upon the hills:
Thy moorland pathways worn by Angel feet,
Thy streams that march in music to the sea
'Mid Ocean's merry noise, his billowy laugh!
Ah me! a gloom falls heavy on my soul –
The birds that sun to me in youth are dead;
I think, in dreamy vigils of the night,
It may be God is angry with my land –
Too much athirst for fame: too fond of blood;
And all for earth, for shadows, and the dream
To glean an echo from the winds of song![26]

"But now, let hearts be high: the Archangel held
A tournay with the fiend on Abarim,
And good Saint Michael won his dragon-crest!

"Be this our cry! the battle is for God!
If bevies of foul fiends withstand your path –
Nay, if strong Angels hold the watch and ward,
Plunge in their midst, and shout, 'a Sangraal!'"

He ceased; the warriors bent a knightly knee,
And touched with kiss and sign, Excalibur;
Then turned, and mounted for their perilous way!

That night Dundagel shuddered into storm –
The deep foundations shook beneath the sea:
Yet there they stood, beneath the murky moon,
Above the bastion, Merlin and the King.
Thrice waved the sage his staff, and thrice they saw
A peopled vision throng the rocky moor!

First fell a gloom, thick as a thousand nights –
A pall that hid whole armies, and beneath
Stormed the wild tide of war; until on high
Gleamed red the dragon, and the Keltic glaive
Smote the loose battle of the roving Dane!
Then yelled a fiercer fight: for brother blood
Rushed mingling; and twin dragons fought the field!

The grisly shadows of his faithful knights
Perplexed their lord: and in their midst, behold!
His own stern semblance waved a phantom-brand,
Drooped, and went down the war: – then cried the King,
"Ho! Arthur to the rescue!" and half drew
Excalibur – but sank, and fell entranced!
A touch aroused the monarch: and there stood
He, of the billowy beard and Awful eye,
The ashes of whole ages on his brow,
Merlin the bard: son of a demon-sire!
High, like Ben Amram[27] at the thirsty rock,
He raised his prophet staff: that runic rod,
The stem of Igdrasil[28] – the crutch of Raun –
And wrote strange words along the conscious air.

Forth gleamed the east, and yet it was not day:
A white and glowing horse outrode the dawn;
A youthful ride ruled the bounding rein,
And he, in semblance of Sir Galahad shone:
A vase he held on high; one molten gem,
Like massive ruby or the chrysolite:
Thence gushed the light in flakes; and flowing, fell
As though the pavement of the sky brake up,
And stars were shed to sojourn on the hills,
From grey Morwenna's stone to Michael's tor,
Until the rocky land was like a heaven.

Then saw that the mighty quest was won:
The Sangraal swooned along the golden air:

The sea breathed balsam, like Gennesaret:[29]
The streams were touched with supernatural light:
And fonts of Saxon rock, stood, full of God!
Altars arose, each like a kingly throne,
Where the royal chalice, with its lineal blood,
The glory of the presence, ruled and reigned.
This lasted long: until the white horse fled,
The fierce fangs of the libbard in his loins:
Whole ages glided in that blink of time,
While Merlin and the King, looked, wondering, on.
But see! once more the wizard-wand arise,
To cleave the air with signals, and a scene.

Troops of the demon-north, in yellow garb,
The sickly hue of vile Iscariot's hair,
Mingle with men, in unseen multitudes!
Unscared, they throng the valley and the hill;
That which held God was gone: Maran-atha:[30]
The Awful shadows of the Sangraal, fled!
Yet giant-men arose, that seemed as gods –
Such might they gathered from the swarthy kind:
The myths were rendered up: and one by one,
The fire – the light – the air – were tamed and bound
Like votive vassals at their chariot-wheel!

The shrines were darkened and the chalice void:
Then learnt they war: yet not that noble wrath,
That brings the generous champion face to face
With equal shield, and with a measured brand,
To peril life for life, and do or die!
But the false valour of the lurking fiend -
To hurl a distant death from some deep den:
To wing with flame the metal of the mine:
And so they rend God's image, reck not who!

"Ah! haughty England! lady of the wave:"
Thus said pale Merlin to the listening King:
"What is thy glory in the world of stars?"
"To scorch and slay: to win demoniac fame,
In arts and arms; and then to flash and die!
Thou art the diamond of the demon-crown,
Smitten by Michael upon Abarim,
That fell; and glared, an island of the sea!
Ah! native England! wake thine ancient cry;
Ho! for the Sangraal! vanished vase of heaven,
That held, like Christ's own heart, an hin of blood!"
He ceased; and all around was dreamy night:
There stood Dundagel, throned: and the great sea,

Lay, a strong vassal at his master's gate,
And like a drunken giant, sobbed in sleep!

26 *From* Popular Romances of the West of England: The Drolls, Traditions, and Superstitions of Old Cornwall by Robert Hunt (1865)

Arthur Legends:

The scarcity of traditions connected with King Arthur is not a little remarkable in Cornwall, where he is said to have been born, and where we believe him to have been killed. In the autumn of last year (1863) I visited Tintagel and Camelford. I sought with anxiety for some stories of the British King, but not one could be obtained. The man who has charge of the ruins of the castle was very sorry that he had lent a book which he once had, and which contained many curious stories, but he had no story to tell me.

We hear of Prince Arthur at the Land's End, and of his fights with the Danes in two or three other places. Merlin, who may be considered as especially associated with Arthur, has left indications of his presence here and there, in prophetic rhymes not always fulfilled;[1] but of Arthur's chieftains we have no folklore. All the rock markings, or rock peculiarities, which would in West Cornwall have been given to giants, are referred to King Arthur in the eastern districts.

Jack the Giant Killer and Thomas Thumb – the former having been his tutor, in his own especial calling, to King Arthur's only son, and the latter the king's favourite dwarf – are, except in story-books, unknown. Jack Hornby – if he ever lived near the Land's End, unless he is the same with "Little Jack Horner", – has been so long a stranger, that his name is forgotten.

The continuance of a fixed belief in the existence of Arthur is easily explained. The poets and the romance writers have made the achievements of a British chieftain familiar to all the people; and Arthur has not only a name, but a local habitation, given to him equally in Scotland, England, Wales and Ireland.

Mr Campbell[2] in his "West Highland Tales", gives a "Genealogy Abridgment of the very ancient and noble family of Argyle, 1779". The writer says this family began with Constantine, grandfather to King Arthur; and he informs us that Sir Moroie Mor, a son of King Arthur, of whom great and strange things are told in the Irish Traditions – who was born at Dumbarton Castle, and who was usually known as "The Fool of the Forest" – was the real progenitor of "Mac Callen Mor". From this Moroie Mor was derived the mighty Diarmaid, celebrated in many a Gaelic lay – "to whom all popular traditions trace the Campbell clan".

"Arthur and Diarmaid," writes Mr Campbell, "primeval Celtic worthies, whose very existence the historian ignores, are thus brought together by a family genealogist."

"Was the Constantine grandfather to Arthur one of the five tyrants named by Gildas?"[3] – I quote from Camden and Milton,

Constantinus, son of Cador, Duke of Cornwall, Arthur's half-brother by the mother's side, "a tyrannical and bloody king".

Aurelius Conanus, who "wallowed in murder and adultery".

Vortipore, "tyrant of Dimeta".

Cuneglas, "the yellow butcher".

Maglocunes, "the island dragon".

It is curious to find a Scotch genealogist uniting in one bond the Arthur of Dundagel and the ancestors of the Argyles of Dumbarton.

May we not after this venture to suggest that, in all probability, the parish of Constantine (pronounced, however, *Cus-ten-ton*[4]), between Helstone and Penryn, may derive its name from this Constantinus, rather than from the first Christian emperor?

Again, the family of Cossentine has been often said to be offsets from Constantine, the descendant of the Greek emperors, who was buried in Landulph Church. Seeing that the name has been known for so long a period in Cornwall, may not this family rather trace their origin up to this Constantine the Tyrant?

The Battle of Vellan-Druchar:[5]

The Sea Kings,[6] in their predatory wanderings, landed in Genvor Cove, and, as they had frequently done on previous occasions, they proceeded to pillage the little hamlet of Escols. On one occasion they landed in unusually large numbers, being resolved, as it appeared, to spoil many of the large and wealthy towns of Western Cornwall, which they were led to believe were unprotected. It fortunately happened that the heavy surf on the beach retarded their landing, so that the inhabitants had notice of their threatened invasion.

That night the beacon-fire was lit on the chapel hill, another was soon blazing on Castle-an-Dinas, and on Trecobben. Carn Brea promptly replied, and continued the signal-light which also blazed lustrously that night on St Agnes Beacon. Presently the fires were seen on Belovely Beacon, and rapidly they appeared on the Great Stone, on St Bellarmine's Tor, and Cadbarrow, and then the fires blazed out on Roughtor and Brownwilly, thus rapidly conveying intelligence of war to Prince Arthur and his brave knights, who were happily assembled in full force at Tintagel to do honour to several native Princes who were at that time on a visit to the King of Cornwall. Arthur, and nine other kings, by forced marches, reached the neighbourhood of the Land's End at the end of two days. The Danes crossed the land down through the bottoms to the sea on the northern side of the promontory, spreading destruction in their paths. Arthur met them on their return, and gave them battle near Vellan-Druchar. So terrible was the slaughter, that the mill was worked with blood that day. Not a single Dane of the vast army that had landed escaped. A few had been left in charge of the ships, and as soon as they learned the fate of their brethren, they hastened to escape, hoping to return to their own northern land. A holy woman, whose name has not been preserved to us, "brought home a west wind" by cmp tying the Holy Well against the hill, and sweeping the church from the door to the altar. Thus they were prevented from escaping, and were all thrown by the force of a storm and the currents either on the rocky shore, or on the sands, where they were left high and dry. It happened on the occasion of an extraordinary spring-tide, which was yet increased by the wind, so that the ships lay high up on the rocks, or on the sands; and for years the birds built their nests in the masts and rigging.

Thus perished the last army of Danes who dared to land upon our western shores.

King Arthur and the nine kings pledged each other in the holy water from St Sennen's Well, they returned thanks for their victory in St Sennen's Chapel and dined that day on the Table-men.

Merlin, the prophet, was amongst the host, and the feast being ended, he was seized with the prophetic afflatus, and in the hearing of all the host proclaimed –

> "The northmen wild once more shall land,
> And leave their bones on Escol's sand.
> The soil of Vellan-Druchar's plain
> Again shall take a sanguine stain;
> And o'er the mill-wheel roll a flood
> Of Danish mix'd with Cornish blood.
> When thus the vanquish'd find no tomb,
> Expect the dreadful day of doom."[7]

Arthur at the Land's End:

Bolerium, or *Bellerium*, is the name given by the ancients to the Land's-End. Diodorus writes Belerium; Ptolemy, Bolerium. Milton adopts this name in his 'Lycidas' and leads his readers to infer that it was derived from the Giant Bellereus. It is quite possible that in Milton's time the name of one of the numerous giants who appear to have made the Land's-End district their dwelling-place, might have still lived in the memories of men. Certain it is no such giant is remembered now.

In a map of Saxon England we find the Land's-End called Penrithrteort, and in some early English books this promontory is named *Penrhin-guard* and *Penrlien-gard*, said to signify the 'head-land of blood'. The old Cornish people called this promontory 'Pen-von-las' the 'End of the 'Earth', hence we derive the name of Land's-End. May not this sanguinary name have been derived from a fact, and that actually several battles were fought by the Britons under the command of Arthur, with the Saxons or the Danes, in this neighbourhood? We have not far off the *Field of Slaughter*, 'Bollait', where the ancient people of Cornwall made their final stand against the Saxons. On this field flint arrow-heads have frequently been found. the tradition of Vellan-Druchar, which is but one of several I

115

had heard of a similar character, points to the same idea. Arthur, according to one story, held possession of Trereen Castle for some time. Another castle on the north coast is said to have been occupied by him. An old man living in Pendean once told me that the land at one time 'swarmed with giants, until Arthur, the good king, vanished them all with his cross-sword'.[8]

Traditions of the Danes in Cornwall:

The Danes are said to have landed in several places around the coast, and have made permanent settlements in some parts. We have already spoken of the battle of Vellan-Druchar. In Sennen Cove there was for a long period a colony of red-haired people, – indeed, I am informed some of them still live on the spot, – with whom the other inhabitants of the district refused to marry. Up to a very recent period, in several of the outlying villages, a red-haired family was 'looked down' upon. 'Oh, he or she is a red-haired Daäne,' was a common expression of contempt.

There are several hills which bear the names of Danes' Castles – as Castle-an-Dinas,[9] near Penzance, and another in St. Columb. Another very remarkable earthwork in Perran-Zabula (*Caer-Dane*) is described by Hals.

Eventually the Danes are said to have made permanent settlements in Cornwall, and to have lived on friendly terms with the Britons.

The Danes and the Cornish are reported to have concentrated their forces to oppose Egbert the Saxon. In 835 the combined body are reported to have met, and fought a pitched battle on Hengistendane (now Hengistondown), near Callington. The Cornish were so totally routed, that Egbert obliged the Danes to retire to their ships, and passed a law "that no Briton should in future cross the Tamar, or set foot on English ground, on pain of death".

In 997 the Danes, sailing about Penwrith-steort, landed in several places, foraged the country, burnt the towns, and destroyed the people.

Many of the traditions which are given in different parts of these volumes have much of the Danish element in them.

King Arthur in the Form of a Chough:

I quote the following as it stands: –

"In Jarvis's translation of 'Don Quixote', book ii. chap v., the following passage occurs: –

'Have you nor read, sir,' answered Don Quixote, 'the annals and histories of England, wherein are recorded the famous exploits of King Arthur, whom, in our Castilian tongue, we always call King Artus; of whom there goes an old tradition, and a common one, all over that kingdom of Great Britain, that this king did not die, but that, by magic art, he was turned into a raven; and that, in the process of time, he shall reign again and recover his kingdom and sceptre, for which reason it cannot be proved that, from that time to this, any Englishman has killed a raven?'

"My reason for transcribing this passage is to record the curious fact that the legend of King Arthur's existence in the form of a raven was still repeated as a piece of folk-lore in Cornwall about sixty years ago. My father, who died about two years since, at the age of eighty, spent a few years of his youth in the neighbourhood of Penzance. One day he was walking along Marazion Green with his fowling-piece on his shoulder, he saw a raven in the distance, and fired at it. An old man who was near immediately rebuked him, telling him that he ought on no account to have shot at a raven, for that King Arthur was still alive in the form of that bird. My father was much interested when I drew his attention to the passage which I have quoted above.

"Perhaps some of your Cornish or Welsh correspondents may be able to say whether the legend is still known among the people of Cornwall or Wales.

Edgar MacCulloch.
"Guernsey"

I have been most desirous of discovering if any such legend as the above exists. I have questioned people in every part of Cornwall in which King Arthur has been reported to have dwelt or fought, and especially have I inquired in the neighbourhood of Tintagel, which is reported to have been Arthur's stronghold. Nowhere do I find the raven associated with him, but I have been told that bad luck would follow the man who killed a Chough, for Arthur was transformed into one of these birds.

The Cornish Chough:
The tradition relative to King Arthur and his transformation into a raven, is fixed very decidedly on the Cornish Chough, from the colour of its beak and talons. The –
"Talons and beak all red with blood"
are said to mark the violent end to which this celebrated chieftain came.

Slaughter Bridge:
Historians and poets have made the world familiar with King Arthur. We know how Merlin deceived, by his magic, the beautiful Igerna, so that she received King Uter as her husband. We know also that Uter Pendragon died, and that his son, by Igerna, reigned as King of Britain. How Arthur ruled, and how he slaughtered all the enemies of Britain, is told in the chronicles. But even at Tintagel all is silent respecting the king or his celebrated Round Table.

"In the days of King Arthur the Mount of Cornwall was kept by a monstrous giant", is familiar to us all; and it is curious to find a tradition that the extirpation of these Titans was due to Arthur and Christianity, as already related. At Slaughter Bridge I heard the story, but it did not sound like a tradition; the true native character was not in the narrative, – that in 824 the Cornish and Saxons fought so bloody a battle that the river ran red with blood. On Slaughter Bridge Arthur is said to have killed his nephew, Modred, but that, previously to this last fight, Modred wounded his uncle with a poisoned sword, nearly in front of Worthyvale House. A single stone laid over a stream, having some letters cut on its lower surface, is believed to mark the exact spot where Arthur received his death-wound.

Camelford and King Arthur:

At the head of this river Alan is seated Camelford, otherwise written Galleford, a small town. It was formerly called Kambton, according to Leland, who tells us that "Arthur, the British Hector", was slain here, or in the valley near it. He adds, in support of this, that "pieces of armour, rings, and brass furniture for horses are sometimes digged up here by the countrymen; and after so many ages, the tradition of a bloody victory in this place is still preserved." There are also extant some verses of a Middle Age poet about "Camels" running with blood after the battle of Arthur against Modred.

"Camulus is another name of the god of war, occurring in two of Gruter's inscriptions."

Seeing that Arthur's great battles were fought near this town, and on the banks of the river, may not the names given to the town and river be derived from Camulus?

> "O'er Cornwall's cliffs the tempest roar'd,
> High the screaming sea-mew soar'd;
> On Tintagel's topmost tower
> Darksome fell the sleety shower;
> Round the rough castle shrilly sung
> The whirling blast, and wildly flung
> On each tall rampart's thundering side
> The surges of the tumbling tide:
> When Arthur ranged his red cross ranks
> On conscious Camlan's crimson'd banks."
> *The Grave of Arthur* – Wharton.

In a Welsh poem it is recited that Arthur, after the battle of Camlan in Cornwall, was interred in the Abbey of Glastonbury, before the high altar, without any external mark. Henry II, is said to have visited the abbey, and to have ordered that the spot described by the bard should be opened. We are told that at twenty foot deep they found the body deposited under a large stone, with Arthur's name inscribed thereon.

Glastonbury Abbey is said to have been founded by Joseph of Arimathea, in a spot anciently called the island or valley of Avolmia or Avolon.

Bale, in his "Acts of English Votaries", attests to the finding of the remains of Arthur: –

"In Avallon, anno 1191, there found they the flesh bothe of Arthur and of hys wyfe Guenever turned all to duste, wythin theyr coffines of strong oke, the bones only remaynynge. A monke of the same abbeye, standyng and behouldyng the fine broydinges of the wommanis heare as *yellow as golde* there still to remayne. As a man ravysched, or more than halfe from his wyttes, he leaped into the graffe, xv fote depe, to have caugte them sodenlye. But he fayled of his purpose. For so soon as they were touched they fell all to powder."

Dameliock Castle:

The ancient British castle once stood in savage grandeur a rival to Tintagel. Its ruins, which can scarcely be traced, are in the parish of St. Tudy. Here Gothlois of the Purple Spear, Earl of Cornwall, fortified himself against Uter Pendragon's soldiery, and here he was slain. Gothlois, or Gothlouis, was the husband of Igerna, who was so cruelly deceived by Uter, and who became the mother of Arthur.

Carlian in Kea:

One of the most celebrated of Arthur's knights, Sir Tristram, is said to have been born in this parish. A traditions of this is preserved in the parish, but it is probably derived from the verses of Thomas of Erceldoune, better known as Thomas the Rhymer.

Temple Moors:

The parish of Temple in 1851 had a population of 24. Yet once the Knights Templar built a church here; and with the purposes of civilising the inhabitants of the moor in the midst of which it was founded, they secured for their temple some special privileges. "Many a bad marriage bargain," says Tonkin, "is there yearly slubbered up; and grass widows with their failings put to lie-in and nurse here." "Send her to Temple Moors," implied that any female requiring seclusion might at one time secure it under the charge of these Christian knights in this their preceptory, and be returned to the world again, probably, in all respects, a better woman. At all events, the world, being in ignorance, did not repudiate the erring sister.

Stories linger over this wilderness of mixed good and evil. The church, which was consecrated to the great cause of saving sinners, has perished. No stone remains to tell us where it stood; and to "send her to Temple moors", is to proclaim a woman an outcast from society.

King Arthur's Stone:

In the western part of Cornwall, all the marks of any peculiar kind found on the rocks are referred either to the giants or the devil. In the eastern part of the county such markings are almost always attributed to Arthur. Not far from the Devil's Coit in St. Columb on the edge of the Gossmoor, there is a large stone, upon which are deeply-impressed marks, which a little fancy may convert into the marks of four horse-shoes. This is 'King Arthur's Stone', and these marks were made by the horse upon which the British king rode when he resided at *Castle Denis*, and hunted on these moors. King Arthur's beds, and chairs, and caves, are frequently to be met with. The Giant's Coits, – and many traditions of these will be found in the section devoted to the giant romances – are probably monuments of the earliest types of rock mythology. Those of Arthur belong to the period when the Britons were so far advanced in civilisation as to war under experienced rulers; and those which are appropriated by the devil are evidently instances of the influence of priestcraft on the minds of an impressible people.

27   The Buried City by John Harris (1868)

Low lies beneath the watery wave
A city in its watery grave;
And many a chronicler will tell
What once fair Lyonesse befel:
How rose the sea with sullen frown,
And beat the rocky barriers down;
Then roll'd o'er mead and orchard glade,
And home's loved hearth where childhood play'd,
Entombing on its march sublime
Grey stooping age and manhood's prime,
Loved beauty bright and genius rare,
And grief with matted locks and spare,
And tower, and church, and mansion heap,
Within the chambers of the deep;
For which, when rolls the tempest tone,
The rough Land's End sends out its moan.
Amid the rising, flashing spray
A horseman gallops fleet away.
On, on he flies, not looking back,
Dashing the water from his track.
Each side the rising waves he sees,
Which reach even now the horse's knees.
He spurs the brute, and jerks the rein,
And shouts and shouts its name again,
Until with many a spring and bound
He gains at last a higher ground;
And, looking out along the shore,
His precious home is seen no more.
A watery waste is everywhere,
Except a few rocks here and there;
And Perranuthnoe safe from harms
Receives Trelawney[1] to its arms.

28 Dozmare Pool, Cornwall by John Brent (1880)

In one of the wildest districts of Cornwall – a land tree-less, river-less, a level of bog and moor, where, excepting the "Jamaica Inn" and two or three cottages scattered widely over the expanse – is situated a small lake called Dozmare Pool. It lies on a table-land at the base of a hill or tor called Bran Gilly,[1] and is located at a height of about 900 feet above the level of the sea. If the sky be bright, as the traveller approaches it from Launceston he catches from afar a glimpse of the clear, silver water flashing above the dark moorland. The Pool is about a mile in circumference, and of oval shape. Of late years a building has been erected upon its bank, for the purpose of storing ice, when the winter has been inclement enough to have permitted of its being collected from the lake. It is situated about eleven miles from Launceston. The "Jamaica Inn", where tourists often make their rest-ing-places, is about a mile and a half distant from the Pool.

This piece of water is generally considered to be the traditional lake into which Sir Bedivere hurled Arthur's sword, Excalibur, after having twice deceived the dying King when he lay somewhere in the neighbourhood, his life fast ebbing away from the mortal wound he had received in the dreadful battle of Lyonnesse, wherein the greater part of the chivalry of Britain, the Knights of the Round Table, per-ished with him. The loneliness of the spot is well-described in *Morte d'Arthur* of Tennyson, – a place "where no man hath been since the making of the world". Here, arising from the lake as Excalibur flashed through the air in its descent to the waters, was once seen the arm

> "Clothed in white samite, mystic, wonderful,
> That caught him by the hilt and brandished him
> Three times, and drew him under in the mere."

And here it was when Arthur, hither borne by the same Knight, lay on the margin of the lake,

> "There hove in sight a dusky barge,
> Dark as a funeral scarf from stem to stern."[2]

It was filled with stately forms, and amongst them were "three queens with crowns of gold", who, when they beheld the condition of the dying King, set up a cry of agony. They bore off Arthur on their barge, and Sir Bedivere remained long watching them. Of course, the size of the lake is exaggerated, and the reply of the knight to Arthur, after he had concealed the sword in the rushes, that he saw nothing but "the waves wap and the waters wan", as given in the prose *Morte d'Arthur*, is more strictly correct than the poet's allusion to the "water lapping the crag", for there are no crags; the smooth, quiet lake shal-lows up without a bank to its margin of turf and sand. Camelot may be Camelford of the present era; and Lyonesse, whereat Arthur contended with Modred, could not, to make the story consistent; be far distant. The locality where Arthur fell is said, according to some authors, to have been the Slaughter Bridge, in Cornwall, near Tintagel, about one mile from Camelford; and Lyonesse was situated off Scilly, near the Land's End.

We must not look for exactness to the composer of the prose *Morte d'Arthur*, nor even for the smallest knowledge of geography. A strange confusion exists in the localities of the last scenes connected with Arthur and his final disappearance. When Sir Mordred assumes to be king of England, he lands at Dover, "makes a Parliament", and is crowned at Canterbury. All this wears a very modern dress. Arthur, in pursuit of him, arrives at Dover with a great fleet. He fights with Modred on Barham Downs, and the latter being defeated flees to Canterbury. However, Modred is again speedily in arms with a large army, and another battle ensues on a down near Salisbury. In this encounter Modred is slain, and Arthur mortally wounded.

The scene suddenly shifts to the west. We are not informed of the precise locality of the lake over which Morgan le Fay presided, and from which Arthur departed into the Vale of Avilion "to heal him of his grievous wound", but we are led to assume it lay near Camelot, and was in Cornwall. Nevertheless, Avalon, or Avilion, is said by some authorities to have been a submerged island off the coast of Brittany. Mr Whittaker is the great authority for the authenticity of the British Arthur. "The whole island", he says, "in spite of numerous fables, is in traditionary possession of his character, and hundreds are distinguished by his name. The historic Arthur is said to have been the son of Uther Pendragon, a British king, born A.D. 502." Arthur having subdued many nations, and founded the Round Table, died of his wounds in A.D. 542. His tomb, according to Giraldus Cambrensis was discovered A.D. 1189, at Glastonbury, bearing a Latin inscription, "Here lies the famous King Arthur, buried in the Vale of Avalon". Henry II is said to have exhumed the body of the king, who was found buried in the trunk of a tree with his beautiful queen beside him, with her long, flowing hair, bright as gold. The bones of the king were large; his skull exhibited the marks of ten wounds.

I visited the lake on a bright day towards the close of last September, and I felt a contrast to the Kentish scenery with which I am familiar, – the cottage homes and rich corn and hop lands. Of a winter's day, when the sun is obscured, and the bleak wind is sweeping over the moorland, and as we step upon the bog and peat saturated with moisture, and in some places black in hue, with a sparse vegetation around, – a land almost flowerless in summer, – we feel truly the force of the old Kentish epithet, that it is an "ellinge" place, a spot dismally lonesome.

29 *From* **Tristram of Lyonesse by A.C. Swinburne (1882)**

And Iseult rose up where she sat apart,
And with her sweet soul deepening her deep eyes
Cast the furs from her and subtle embroideries
That wrapped her from the storming rain and spray,
And shining like all April in one day,
Hair, face, and throat dashed with the straying showers,
She stood the first of all the whole world's flowers,
And laughed on Tristram with her eyes, and said,
"I too have heart then, I was not afraid."
And answering some light courteous word of grace
He saw her clear face lighten on his face
Unwittingly, with unenamoured eyes,
For the last time. A live man in such wise
Looks in the deadly face of his fixed hour
And laughs with lips wherein he hath no power
To keep the life yet some five minutes' space.
So Tristram looked on Iseult face to face
And knew not, and she knew not. The last time –
The last that should be told in any rhyme
Heard anywhere on mouths of singing men
That ever should sing praise of them again;
The last hour of their hurtless hearts at rest,
The last that peace should touch them, breast to breast,
The last that sorrow far from them should sit,
This last was with them, and they knew not it.
For Tristram being athirst with toil now spake,
Saying, "Iseult, for all dear love's labour's sake
Give me to drink, and give me for a pledge
The touch of four lips on the beaker's edge."
And Iseult sought and would not wake Brangwain[1]
Who slept as one half dead with fear and pain,
Being tender-natured; so with hushed light feet
Went Iseult round her, with soft looks and sweet
Pitying her pain; so sweet a spirited thing
She was, and daughter of a kindly king.
And spying what strange bright secret charge was kept
Fast in that maid's white bosom while she slept,
She sought and drew the gold cup forth and smiled
Marvelling, with such light wonder as a child
That hears of glad sad life in magic lands;
And bare it back to Tristram with pure hands
Holding the love-draught that should be for flame
To burn out of them fear and faith and shame,
And lighten all their life up in men's sight,
And make them sad for ever. Then the knight
Bowed toward her and craved whence had she this

       strange thing
That might be spoil of some dim Asian king,
By starlight stolen from some waste place of sands,
And a maid bore it here in harmless hands.
And Iseult, laughing – "Other lords that be
Feast, and their men feast after them; but we,
Our men must keep the best wine back to feast
Till they be full and we of all men least
Feed after them and fain to fare so well;
So with mine handmaid and your squire it fell
That hid this bright thing from us in a wile:"
And with light lips yet full of their swift smile,
And hands that wist not though they dug a grave,
Undid the hasps of gold, and drank, and gave,
And he drank after, a deep glad kingly draught:
And all their life changed in them, for they quaffed
Death; if it be death so to drink, and fare
As men who change and are what these twain were.
And shuddering with eyes full of fear and fire
And heart-stung with a serpentine desire
He turned and saw the terror in her eyes
That yearned upon him shining in such wise
As a star midway in the midnight fixed.

———————————

… Nor other hand there needed, nor sweet speech
To lure their lips together; each on each
Hung with strange eyes and hovered as a bird
Wounded, and each mouth trembled for a word;
Their heads neared, and their hands were drawn in one,
And they saw dark, though still the unsunken sun
Far through fine rain shot fire into the south;
And their four lips became one burning mouth.

———————————

… Clothed and covered with the nuptial dark
Soft like a bride came Brangwain to King Mark,
And to the queen came Tristram; and the night
Fled, and ere danger of detective light
From the king sleeping Brangwain slid away,
And where had lain her handmaid Iseult lay.
And the king waking saw beside his head
That face yet passion-coloured, amorous red
From lips not his, and all that strange hair shed
Across the tissued pillows, fold on fold,
Innumerable, incomparable, all gold,
To fire men's eyes with wonder, and with love
Men's hearts; so shone its flowering crown above

The brows enwound with that imperial wreath,
And framed with fragrant radiance round the face
    beneath.
  And the king marvelled, seeing with sudden start
Her very glory, and said out of his heart;
"What have I done of good for God to bless
That all this he should give me, tress on tress,
All this great wealth and wondrous? Was it this
That in mine arms I had all night to kiss,
And mix with me this beauty? this that seems
More fair than heaven doth in some tired saint's dreams,
Being part of that same heaven?..."
  So the king mused and murmured; and she heard
The faint sound trembling of each breathless word,
And laughed into the covering of her hair.

  ... Eastward was a strong bright wind begun
Between the clouds and waters: and he said,
Seeing hardly through dark dawn her doubtful head;
"Iseult?" and like a death-bell faint and clear
The virgin voice rang answer – "I am here,"
And his heart sprang, and sank again: and she
Spake, saying, "What would my knightly lord with me?"
And Tristram: "Hath my lady watched all night
Beside me, and I knew not? God requite
Her love for comfort shown a man nigh dead."
  "Yea, God shall surely guerdon it," she said ...

  And high from heaven suddenly rang the lark,
Triumphant; and the far first refluent ray
Filled all the hollow darkness full with day.
And on the deep sky's verge a fluctuant light
Gleamed, grew, shone, strengthened, into perfect sight;
As bowed and dipped and rose again the sail's clear white.
And swift and steadfast as a sew-mew's wing
It neared before the wind, as fain to bring
Comfort, and shorten yet its narrowing track.
And she that saw looked hardly toward him back,
Saying, "Ay, the ship comes surely; but her sail is black."
And fain he would have sprung upright, and seen,
And spoken: but strong death struck sheer between,
And darkness closed as iron round his head:
And smitten through the heart lay Tristram dead.
  And scare the word had flown abroad, and wail
Risen, ere to shoreward came the snowbright sail,
And lightly forth leapt Ganhardine[2] on land,

And led from ship with swift and reverent hand
Iseult: and round them up from all the crowd
Broke the great wail for Tristram out aloud.
And ere her ear might hear her heart had heard,
Nor sought she sign for witness of the word;
But came and stood above him newly dead,
And felt his death upon her: and her head
Bowed, as to reach the spring that slakes all drouth;
And their four lips become one silent mouth.

... And the king
Built for their tomb a chapel bright like spring
With flower-soft wealth of branching tracery made
Fair as the frondage each fleet year sees fade,
That should not fall till many a year were done.
There slept they wedded under moon and sun
And change of stars: and through the casements came
Midnight and noon girt round with shadow and flame
To illume their grave or veil it: till at last
On these things too was doom as darkness cast:
For the strong sea hath swallowed wall and tower,
And where their limbs were laid in woeful hour
For many a fathom gleams and moves and moans
The tide that sweeps above their coffined bones
In the wrecked chancel by the shivered shrine:
Nor where they sleep shall moon or sunlight shine
Nor man look down for ever: none shall say,
Here once, or here, Tristram and Iseult lay:
But peace they have that none may gain who live,
And rest about them that no love can give,
And over them, while death and life shall be,
The light and sound and darkness of the sea.

30 *From* **An Unsentimental Journey through Cornwall by Dinah Craik (1884)**

Our way ran along lonely quiet roads and woods almost as green as when Queen Guinevere rode through them 'a maying', before the dark days of her sin and King Arthur's death.

Here it occurs to me, as it did this day to a practical youthful mind. 'What in the world do people know about King Arthur?'

Well, most people have read Tennyson, and a few are acquainted with the "Morte d'Arthur" of Sir Thomas Malory. But, perhaps I had better briefly give the story, or as much of it as is necessary for the edification of outsiders.

Uther Pendragon, King of Britain, falling in love with Ygrayne, wife of the duke of Cornwall, besieged them in their twin castles of

Tintagel and Terrabil,[1] slew the husband, and the same day married the wife. Unto whom a boy was born, and by advice of the enchanter Merlin, carried away, from the sea-shore beneath Tintagel, and confided to a good knight, Sir Ector, to be brought up as his own son, and christened Arthur. On the death of the king, Merlin produced the youth, who was recognized by his mother Ygrayne, and proclaimed king in the stead of Uther Pendragon. He instituted the Order of the Knights of the Round Table, who were to go everywhere, punishing vice and rescuing oppressed virtue, for the love of God and of some noble lady. He married Guinevere, daughter of King Leodegrance, who forsook him for the love of Sir Lancelot, his bravest knight and dearest friend. One by one, his best knights fell away into sin, and his nephew Mordred raised a rebellion, fought with him, and conquered him at Camelford. Seeing his end was near, Arthur bade his last faithful knight, Sir Bedevere, carry him to the shore of a mere (supposed to be Dozmare Pool) and throw in there his sword Excalibur; when appeared a boat with three queens, who lifted him in, mourning over him. With them they sailed away across the mere to be healed of his grievous wound. Some say that he was afterwards buried in a chapel near, others declare that he lives still in fairy land, and will reappear in latter days, to reinstate the Order of Knights of the Round Table, and rule his beloved England,[2] which will then be perfect as he once tried to make it, but in vain.

31 *From* **Cornish Feasts and Folklore by Margaret A. Courtney (1890)**

Tourists visit West Cornwall to see the Land's End and its fine coast scenery and express themselves disappointed that none of the country people in that district know anything of King Arthur. They forget Uther's heir was washed up to Merlin's feet by a wave at the base of 'Tintagel Castle by the Cornish sea', which is in the eastern part of the county. This castle was built on one of the grandest headlands in Cornwall (slate formation).

The ruins of King Arthur's Castle are most striking. They are situated partly on the mainland and partly on a peninsula, separated by a ravine, once said to have been spanned by a drawbridge connecting the two.

The ascent of this promontory, owing to the slippery nature of the path cut in the friable slate, is far from pleasant; and as there was a stiff breeze blowing when I mounted it, I thought old Norden was right when he said: 'Those should have eyes who would scale Tintagel.' You are, however, amply repaid for your trouble, when you get to the top.

In addition to telling you of the grandeur of the castle in good King Arthur's days, the guides show you some rock basins to which they have given the absurd names of 'King Arthur's cups and saucers.'[1]

Tradition assigns to this king another Cornish castle as a hunting seat, viz. – the old earth-round of Castle-an-dinas near St. Columb from whence it is said, he chased the wild deer on Tregoss Downs.

A dreary drive through slate-quarries takes you from Tintagel to Camelford. Near that town is Slaughter Bridge, the scene of a great battle between King Arthur and his nephew Modred, whom by some writers he is said to have killed on this spot; others have it that Arthur died here of a wound from a poisoned arrow shot by Modred and that, after receiving his death wound at Camelford, he was conveyed to Tintagel Castle, where, surrounded by his knights, he died. All the time, he lay a-dying supernatural noises were heard in the castle, the sea and winds moaned, and their lamentations never ceased until our hero was buried at Glastonbury. Then, in the pauses of the solemn tolling of the funeral bells, sweet voices came from fairy-land welcoming there, from whence one day he will return and again be king of Cornwall.

32 _From_ **The Arthurian Legend by John Rhys (1890)**

Now Malory makes Dame Liones the owner of a Castle Perilous, hard by the Isle of Avallon and he also speaks of a country of Liones and a Castle of Liones. This last is spoken of as not far from Tintagel in Cornwall and the three names of the lady, the castle and the country are probably not to be severed, though Malory suggests, be it marked, no connection between the lady and the castle or the country. The reason for this is probably to be sought in the fact that he, or the authority he followed, had fixed the Isle of Avallon at Glastonbury; but from what has already been said, it will be seen that we are warranted in unmooring it and attaching to it the West Coast of Cornwall; there Dame Liones comes readily by her own in a castle and a country of the same name with herself and lying somewhere under the sea between Lundy and the Isles of Scilly. From that mythic land comes Tristram, just as Gahalt,[1] the haute prince, hails from the Far Away Isles, and Lancelot from the verdant abode of the Lady Lake who was his foster mother. Without dwelling on the probably extreme antiquity of the myths underlying these romances, one may venture to point out that we seem to have evidence, dating from the early Roman occupation of this country, to the equasion of some such a hero as Tristram or Lancelot with the Heracles of classical mythology.

33 **Lyonesse by James Dryden Hosken (1902)**

> The listless tides arise and fall,
>   With murmur of their old distress,
> O'er shadowy tower and knightly hall,
>   Of ancient Lyonesse.

Far down within the changing deep
   That splendid realm unchanging lies
Where many a lord and lady sleep
   'Neath scutcheon'd[1] canopies.

A land of fair romance long lost
   Enchanted held in perfect rest;
All lapped in golden light, and cross'd
   With tincture of the west.

The happy youth, with lute in hand,
   Sings to the maiden in her bower;
And banners hang above the land
   From many a silent tower.

And knights are there in armour dight.
   And white-hair'd minstrels sit serene;
And there is one, that land's delight,
   A solitary Queen.

She dreams of love and olden wars,
   Her maidens lying at her feet:
A moon amid a heaven of stars
   In loveliness complete.

34 *From* Some Possible Arthurian Place-Names in West Penwith by Henry Jenner (1912)

Beyond the isthmus of low-lying land between the northern and the southern seas is a strange and separate hill country, full of memorials of a distant past. On its many round-topped hills there are generally signs of fortresses, some of them in good preservations – Trencrobm, the western Castle-an-Dinas, Chun, Caer Brane, Bartinney, Chapel Carn Brea, and the rest. The map is dotted all over with 'ancient British village', 'stone circle', 'cromlech', and 'barrow'. Often a hill fort on the top, a cromlech on the shoulder of the hill and the remains of a village at the foot are found together. Perhaps the best specimen of this is at Chun, where the castle and cromlech are in good preservation and the foundations of the huts are easily traced. Round the coast are cliff-castles. St. Ives Island, the Gurnard's Head, Bosigran Castle, Kenidjack, Cape Cornwall and Castle Treryn (the Logan), and possibly others, seem to have been fortified headlands. There are 'allées couvertes'[1] at Trewoofe, Chapel Uny, and Pendeen, a considerable number of menhirion, and several stone circles, one of which at Boscawen Ûn, in Buryan parish, is mentioned in an early triad as one of the three principal 'gorsedds' or session places of the Bards of the Island of Britain.[2] And of all these very interesting remains, in which the district is far richer for its size than any other part of Great Britain there are next to no historical traditions. There are observances attached to some of them, which in spite of the modern spirit in education and religion still go on, though they are not easily got at by outsiders. Those who know are not always willing to tell, for example, why little heaps of pebbles are to be found on an altar-shaped stone, or at the foot of a menhir. Such stories as there are seem to be generally connected with piskies and giants and matters of that sort. But if, as is evidently the case some 'fragments of forgotten peoples', pre-Celtic folk like the Bigoudens of Penmarc'h and Pont l'Abbé district of Brittany do still dwell in Zennor, or Morvah and St. Just, there are fragments of forgotten faiths as well, faiths with pre-Celtic magic, black or white, at the bottom of them. And of stories that can be connected with any known history there are very few. Are there any such stories enshrined in place-names? I cannot tell for certain, but it looks rather as if there were.

The district has not as yet been accounted an Arthurian one. There is one Arthurian folk tradition, of which I shall speak presently, and one undoubted Merlin association. But that appears at first sight to be all. But I think I have found a certain number of names which seem to commemorate characters in the Arthurian cycle of romances, and in what may be real Arthurian history. I do not say that this implies that any events connected with Arthur really happened in this district. That would be too large an assertion, and there are other ways of accounting for the fact, if fact it be, that Arthurian names should have been given to these places.

I will take the names more or less by their position.

1. *Bosigran*. This is on the north coast, a short way to the west of Gurnard's Head, which is the modern rather vulgar name of what, as the name of the neighbouring village shows, was once the cliff-castle of Treryn, or, as it is pronounced, Treen. It is a fine headland of granite, at the foot of Carn Galvar, the nearest approach to a real mountain in appearance in the district. Mr. J. B. Cornish, in his account of the embankments and forts of Cornwall in the Victoria County History, doubts whether it was ever a cliff-castle, and thinks that the so-called vallum and trench are only a modern hedge and ditch. He may be quite right but it is only the name with which I am concerned, though it seems to be always called 'Bosigron (or Bosigran) Castle' now. 'Bos' is dwelling-place, house, and 'Igron' or 'Igran', as is common in words beginning with 'bos', may well be a proper name. If so it recalls the name of Arthur's mother, Igraine. 'Igraine' is the Frenchified form of the romances. Geoffrey calls her 'Igerna', and the Welsh form is generally 'Eigyr', or 'Eigr'. The epithet in Bosigran may possibly be connected with the Cornish 'egr', a daisy, or with a Cornish form of the Welsh, 'eigren', a young girl. The Iolo MSS.,[3] a poor authority, mention 'Eigron' as one of the sons of Caw, the father of Gildas, and say that he founded a church in Cornwall, but nothing is known of him, and the church has not been identified. But a name

not far off adds to the possibility of the mother of Arthur being com-
memorated in this name.

2. *Bosworlas*. This is a farm in St. Just, which is in the same district. The husband of Igraine was 'Gorlois', and in composition an initial *g* not infrequently changes to *w*, if, as also happens after 'bos', it
does not change to *c*. 'The House of Gorlois' would therefore be either
'Bos-worlois' or 'Boscorlois.' The former is more likely of the two, if,
as is very probable, the Cornish form of the name was 'Gworlos'. It
has been suggested that the place was originally 'Boswollas', lower
dwelling, and in that case we ought to find a 'Boswartha' somewhere
over against it, for these two names generally go in pairs. But there
does not appear to be any such name near.

3. *Botallack*. This may have a quasi-Arthurian association,
though it belongs, if my conjecture is correct, to what I believe to be
another set of stories, added to the Arthur cycle after the populariza-
tion of the romances in the twelfth century. The father of Tristan has
various names given to him in the romances. The Breton tradition
makes him 'Rioallen', a name wich may be the same as 'Riwallus',
who is identified with Hoel (Ri-Hoellus, King Hoel) who came to
Brittany in 513. The French tradition, in the 'Tristan' of Luces de Gast
and the 'Palamades' of Élie de Borron, makes him 'Meliadus', and
this is the name which Malory represents as 'Meliodas'. But the
Welsh allusions to Tristen in Triads and elsewhere invariably make
him 'Tristan' or 'Drystan ap Tallwch.' There may be soem confusion
here with the name of a king of the 'Gwyddel Ffichti' (Picts), Drust
mac Talargan, who just comes into Welsh history. But Botallack in St.
Just may well be 'the dwelling of Tallack', though not necessarily of
that Tallack or Tallwch, who was the father of Tristan of the
romances. If, as is possible, 'Tallack' is an adjective derived from 'tal',
a brow or front, a word which is common enough in Welsh place-
names, the name is otherwise accounted for, and would be fairly
descriptive, for the place is on the front of a cliff. Also there exists still
a Cornish surname 'Tallack'. It is only the accumulation of Arthurian
names, or of what are possibly such, that would make one see any
reason for including this one.

These are all that the northern part of the peninsular supplies.
Leaving the north coast as we go to the south. On the edge of the district is St. Michael's Mount, which, or its namesake across the sea, it
is not quite clear which, comes into the Arthur story. It was here (or
there) that Arthur fought with the giant, who had carried off the
daughter or 'niece' of Hoel, King (or Duke) of Brittany. But that
derived its present name, not as the romances tell, from a church
founded in honour of St. Michael by Arthur after his victory, but from
the legend of the apparition of the Archangel on the Mount, which,
according to William of Worcester, happened in 710, and seems to
be the 'Michaelis in monte tumba' of October 16 in the Salisbury cal-
endar, though this is disputed, and the day and vision are claimed by
the Breton Mount. In Arthur's time our Mount was certainly 'Dunsul',

'the Mount of the Sun', or, as it continued to be as long as the Cornish lasted, 'Carrack Lûs an Cûs,' 'the Hoar Rock in the Wood'. Just above Penzance station is a hill-fort called 'Lescudjack' or 'Lescaddock'. This is clearly the court of Cadoc'. Cadawg ap Gwynlliw, Abbot of Llancarvan, called 'Doeth' or 'the Wise' is associated with Arthur's knights in late and not very authoritative Triads. The historical St. Cadoc was certainly a contemporary of Arthur, and we know from the his life in Cott. MS., Vesp. A. xiv, that he visited the Mount. Mr. Baring-Gould conjectures (Lives of the British Saints, vol.ii, p.40) that as one of 'the three knights that kept the Holy Grail' he was the original of Sir Galahad. But that is as may be.

I am not going into the question of the submerging Lyonesse in historical times. I know nothing about geology, and it is better to avoid subjects one does not know anything about. I believe in a vague sort of way that granite is an igneous rock, and that a granite country is a 'land of old upheaven from the abyss of fire', but of whether any of it may have 'sunk into the abyss again' in historic times I am no judge. From what some geologists have told me it seems to be against the rules of the game, as at present understood, though there is some difference of opinion. But geological evidence or not to the contrary, there is a persistent tradition of a subsidence in Mount's Bay, its previous state is probably the reason for the Cornish name of the Mount, and, as is well known, trunks of trees have been discovered in the Bay below high-water mark. If any such subsidence did take place within historic times, not perhaps 'by fire' or any volcanic agency, but by the inroad of the sea into low-lying land, and in the usual exaggerated form gave rise to the legend of Lyonesse, the story probably relates to a tract of land or a fringe of coast from Cuddan Point across to Newlyn and Mousehole, and perhaps along the coast towards Lamorna and the Logan. It would not take too much to submerge some more between Penzance and Marazion. It is at Mousehole that we begin to find Arthurian names.

4. *Men Merlin* or *Merlin's Rock*. This is a name about which there is no question, though one does not know how old it is. In the Ordnance Survey maps a rock is marked 'Merlyn Rock' between the south-western end of the town of Mousehole and the cavern called the 'Mouse Hole', but there is reason to suppose that the original 'Men Merlin' was broken up to make the pier. I think Borlase mentions that somewhere. There is an often quoted prophecy in Cornish, which with restored text, for it is generally spelt all anyhow, reads: –

'Y a wra tira Men Merlin,
A wra lesky Paul, Penzans ha Newlyn.'
[*They shall land on the Stone of Merlin,
Who shall burn Paul, Penzance and Newlyn.*]

The fulfilment of the prophecy is supposed to be the Spanish raid of 1595, when all these things were done, but the verses as recorded are in corrupted middle Cornish, and so may be earlier, though popular prophecies which 'come off' are generally written after events. The connection of Merlin with a rock on the coast of Cornwall is certainly much older. There are several stories about the disappearance of Merlin, and there were at least two Merlins, Merddyn Emrys (Merlinus Ambrosius) and Merddyn Wyllt (Merlinus Sylvester or Caledonius). In a Welsh Triad the second of the three disappearances (tri difancoll) of the Island of Britain was that of: – 'Merddyn Bardd Emrys Wledig a'i naw Beirdd cylfeirdd a aethant i'r mor yn y Ty Gwydrin, ac ni bu son i ba le ydd aethant'. Which is, being interpreted, 'Merlin the Bard of Aurelius Ambrosius and his nine fellow Bards, who went to sea in the House of Glass, and there was no report of where they went to'. There would not be, under the circumstances, though conjecture is not difficult. This is certainly Merlinus Ambrosius. In the 'Vita Merlini', where the two Merlins are confused, Merlin flees after the battle of Ardderyd (573) into the 'Nemus Caledonis', the 'Coit Celidon' of Arthur's seventh battle, which is considered to be the great Caledonian Wood, of which Ettrick and Selkirk Forests were a part. Here he lives for some time in a house built for him by his sister Ganieda, the Gwendydd of the 'Afallenau' poem and the dialogue in the Red Book of Hergest. He is visited here by Talgesinus (Taliessin) and the conversation takes place of which I have already spoken. A 'regulus' or chief, called Meldredus, seizes him, and he offends the wife of his captor, who employs some shepherds to kill him. They pursue him with sticks and stones, and he falls dying over a bank of the Tweed, and is impaled on a salmon stake in the water, so that he dies by a combination of three different deaths, which he had prophesied previously for himself. In this story, the latter part of which comes into the prose narrative of the meeting of Merlin and St. Kentigern attached to the 15th century copy of the 'Vita Merlini' in Cott. MS. Titus A. xix., he is much associated with St. Kentigern. The death-story is evidently that of Merlinus Sylvester. There are also two versions of the enchantment, the one by Vivien la Fay under a hawthorn in the forest of Brocéliande, which is well known from the poems of Tennyson and Matthew Arnold, and the other, told by Malory and in a curious alliterative Scottish poem of the 15th century, according to which Merlin is 'closed in a crag on Cornwall coast'. I suppose there is little difficulty in identifying that 'crag' with the 'Men Merlyn' at Mousehole. Further along the coast, near the Logan, there is headland called 'Merthen Point', which seems to give the Welsh form of his name. It was Bagdemagus who found Merlin under the rock and could not get him out, 'for,' as Malory says, 'it was so heavy that a hundred men might not lift it', but it was Gawain who found him in Brocéliande, and the next headland to Merthen is 'Boscawen Point', of which presently.

In the country to the west of Paul there is definite Arthurian tradition. The tale, as told by Bottrell, is to the effect that Arthur fought a battle with the 'Danes' on Vellandruchar Downs and that the slaughter was so great that the mill – 'Vellandruchar' means 'wheel mill' – was turned with blood. The mill was on the stream which divides

Paul from Buryan and eventually flows into Lamorna Cove. Arrow, spear and axe-heads are said to have often been found in the peat moss there, and the neighbourhood is noted for adders. This is a small point, but it is curious to note in passing that it was because a knight was 'stung' by an adder and drew his sword to kill it, that according to Malory and his original the Last Battle of Arthur began, before the other side, who took the sword-drawing for a signal, were ready. There is another battle tradition of Boleigh or Boleit, not far off, and the menhirion and barrows there are popularly supposed to commemorate the slain. The name is said to mean 'the place of slaughter'. It is possible that 'Boladh', which would have that meaning, was the original form, but it might equally well be 'Boleath', milk place, or dairy farm. The name is old, as the 18th century tombstones of Clarice de Boleit in Buryan Church testifies. Here the present story is that the battle was between Athelstan and the Cornish in 936, and it is connected with the foundation of the collegiate church of St. Buryan. But this may well be a modern explanation of the battle tradition. The Anglo-Saxon Chronicle says not a word about any such battle, or about Athelstan penetrating far into Cornwall at all. All we get from the English side is that he drove the Welsh out of Exeter and set the Tamar for their boundary. From what one knows of the Saxon writers they might have claimed a victory which did not happen, but they were very unlikely to omit to mention one which did. I am inclined to connect this tradition with that of the Vellandruchar fight, and to consider it to be part of the same battle. And here it is that I find a whole nest of possible Arthurian names. To continue, –

5. The stream that runs down from Vellandruchar to the Lamorna Valley is as often as not called the *Kemyel* river. Three farms that stretch from Lamorna nearly to Mousehole are 'Kemyel Wartha', or Upper Kemyel, 'Kemyel Cres', or Middle Kemyel, and 'Kemyel Drea', or Home Kemyel, the cliff is 'Kemyel cliff', and the mill in Lamorna Valley is 'Kemyel Mill'. The name has never been satisfactorily explained. It has been said by Bannister to mean the 'honey hedge', but that is not a material out of which hedges are usually constructed. Is it the 'Kemelen' of Giraldus, the 'Camlan' of the continuator of Nennius and the Welsh writers, and the 'Cambula' or Geoffrey? The name is not further off than 'Camel' is.

6. *Rosemodress*. This is a place a little beyond Boleit. It can hardly mean anything else but 'the Heath of Modred', with the common change of *d* to *s*. The usual interpretation, 'the Heath of the Ring', in allusion to the circle called the 'Dawns Myin' or 'the Merry Maidens', will not do at all. 'Moderuy' means a thumb-ring in later Cornish, though the Cottonian Vocabulary translates it 'armilla', a bracelet, and it is not a likely name for the circle of stones. Moreover, the change from 'ruy' to 'res' is too improbable to be regarded. I do not say that it was necessarily called after Arthur's nephew and enemy, for some later person may have borne the name, though it is odd that so discredited a name should have been given to anyone. Still, such

things do happen, and people do get called after very queer characters in history. As I have already mentioned, there are 'Towns of Modred' in the older form, 'Tremodret', in Roche[4] and Duloe.

7. *Boscawen Rose*. This is close to Rosemodress. There is another Boscawen called 'Boscawen Ûn' to the north of Buryan church-town. The first means 'Boscawen on the Heath', the second 'the Dwelling of Elder-trees,' but that would be 'Boscaw', for 'scawen', an elder-tree, is one of those words which form their singular from a collective plural by adding the individualizing syllable 'en'. Still, 'the Dwelling of the Elder-tree' is not an impossible name. But 'bos', a dwelling, is one of those words which sometimes cause 'provection' in composition, and change a broad initial into a thin one. Other prefixes ending in s do the same. Thus we get 'Rospannel' for 'Ros bannel', 'Nanspean' for 'Nans bean'. A b becomes p, a d becomes t, and a g, hard, may become c or k. I do not find a single name in Bannister's Glossary beginning with 'bosg', though there are certainly several which show that this prefix also causes softening of the initial, which in the case of 'Bosworlas', 'Bosworgy' and others, adding a w, and I have not found a case of hardening the initial g, though there are cases with b and d. If this hardening is possible, it may have happened in this case, and 'Boscawen' may be 'Bos-Gawen', which I should have little hesitation in translating 'the Dwelling of Gawain.' I do not profess to decide whether it is called after Arthur's nephew or after someone else of the same name – the proximity to the 'Merry Maidens' would have suited the Gawain of the Round Table right well – or whether it was here that Gawain's ghost appeared to Arthur before the battle, but I do say that the name will bear that meaning. According to William of Malmesbury ('De Gestis Regum', anno 1087) the grave of Walwinus, the nephew of Arthur, who is certainly Gawain, was found in a part of 'Wales' called 'Ros', by which he is generally supposed to mean Rhos in Pembrokeshire. Does he really mean 'Boscawen en Ros', the Dwelling, the last dwelling, of Gawain on the Ros, or Heath? The 'Englynion y Beddau' say that the grave of Gwalchmai, which is the Welsh form of Gawain, is 'in Peyrddon, where the ninth wave flows', wherever that may be.

8. *Roseluken*, or *Roslukem*. This is between Boleit and Rosemodress. It will be remembered that two knights were with Arthur at the last, Bedevere and his brother Lucan. Roseluken is the Heath of Luken, whoever Luken may have been. Was he Lucan?

9. *Tregadgwith*. This name may refer to a battle. It is perhaps 'the Town of the Battle Trees'. 'Cadg' is for 'cas' (the Welsh 'cad'), battle, and 'with' is for 'gwidh' or 'gwedh' (Welsh, 'gwydd'), trees. The word 'cadgwith' comes into place-names elsewhere in Cornwall, either by itself (as in Ruan Minor) or in combination with prefixes. I do not put very much on this interpretation, for there is a Welsh word 'cadwydd' which means 'a bushy or brambly place', though it is not found in Cornish and Breton, and is not very common in Welsh. Words compounded with 'cad' or 'cas', battle, are very common in all three lan-

guages, so 'cadgwith' for 'battle trees', meaning, no doubt, a wood or clump of trees in which a battle took place, is not at all unlikely. This place is between Vellandruchar and Boleit.

10.   *Trevider*. This is to one side of Tregadgwith and Vellandruchar. It might be 'the Town of Bedwyr'. This is to one side of Tregadgwith and Vellandruchar. It might be 'the Town of Bedwyr', the Welsh form of Bedevere's name, or it might be called after Ider or Ederyn ap Nudd, who is called 'Hider' by Geoffrey. He was sent to rescue Gawain, Boso and Guerin, when they were treacherously attacked by Lucius Hiberius. But 'Trevedran', of which presently, may contain the other form of his name. It is never quite easy to decide, in the cases of words beginning with 'Trev', whether the *v* belongs to the prefix or to the epithet, the full and original form of 'tre', a town, being, as in Welsh, 'trev'.

11.   On the other side of Vellandruchar is *Trevorian*. This is either 'Tre Vorian', in which case the personal name with which it is compounded is probably 'Morian' (a name found in 'Englynion y Beddau' and in the 'Gododdin') or 'Trev Orian', which certainly suggests Urien of Rheged, who married 'Morgan la Fay, that was King Arthur's sister'. There is another Trevorian in Sennen.

12.   *Trelew*. This is to the north of Vellandruchar. Bannister suggests 'the sheltered town,' which would do very well, if it did not happen to be on a wind-swept down, close to the appropriately named 'Chy an Gwens', the House of the Wind. If there was even a fair-sized pond there, which there is not, one might suggest 'Tre-Lugh', Lake Town. One has to fall back upon 'Army Town' ('lu', army) or 'Lew's Town'. Now Llew or Lothus was the father of Mordred and Gawain, and the brother of Urien of Rheged. Is Trelew called after him?

13.   *Bojewan*, close by, seems to be 'Bos Ewan', the Dwelling of Ewan. Ewan is not a very uncommon name, but there was a son of Urien[5] of Rheged, the 'Sir Ewaine' of Malory, who bore it, and he was the 'Owain' of the tale of 'Iarlles y Ffynnon' or, as the Red Book of Hergest calls it, 'Owain a Lluned,' the 'Iwaine' of Chrétien de Troyes's 'Chevalier au Lion', and the 'Iweine' of Hartmann von Aue.

14.   *Trevorgans*. This is on the other side of Buryan Churchtown. The personal name in it is, I think, 'Morgans'. The Welsh form of the name would be 'Morgant'. There was a Morgant at whose instigation Urien was killed. He is mentioned in Llywarch Hen's 'Song of Urien' in the Red Book.

15.   *Boskennel*. This is a little to the west of the battle site, due south of Buryan Churchtown. Bannister says it is 'the house on the ascent of the cliff'. Being in the middle of a wide and fairly level down, there seems to be no particular reason to call it so. He also suggests 'Sechnall's dwelling', but I think it is more probably 'Kennal's dwelling'. This is well known as a Cornish surname. Carew mentions 'Dr Kennall the civilian', who was probably John Kennall, D.C.L., Archdeacon of Oxford, as the last great authority on Cornish.

The Welsh equivalent is 'Cynwyl'. According to the 'Culhwch ac Olwen' there were three men who escaped from the battle of Camlan, of whom the third was Cynwyl, 'ef a ysgarwys diwethaf ac Arthur y ar Hengroen y march' (he separated the last from Arthur on Hengroen his horse). The Triads agree about the first two, but make the third not 'Cynwyl Sant' (Cynwyl the saint), but Glewlwyd Gafaelfawr the porter. Cynwyl was the son of Dunawd, son of Pabo, 'the Pillar of Britain'.

16.   *Trevedran* is a little to the south of Boskennal, and its name suggests Edeyrn ap Nudd.

17.   *Trevervyn*, to the west of Trevedran, suggests Erbin, king of Damnonia, the father of that Geraint, who was the hero of the romance of 'Geraint and Enid', and the subject of the well-known elegy by Llywarch Hen. Erbin was the son of Custennan, who is Constantine, identified by Welsh writers and Geoffrey with the usurping emperor who succeeded Gratian Municeps and Marcus. There is another form, 'Treverbyn', near St. Austell. Independently of Arthurian traditions, this is a likely man for Cornish places to be called after, for Cornwall was in his kingdom. But he is made out to have been a near relation, perhaps an uncle, of Arthur.

18.   *Tregonebras*. This is to the north of Buryan in the parish of Sancreed. It is probably 'the Town of Ebras', and 'Goon-Ebras' is the Down of Ebras, whatever or whoever Ebras may be. It is curious to note that in the 'Brut Tysilio' the first person mentioned as having been slain on Arthur's side at Camlan is *'Ebras* vrenin Llychlyn' (Ebras king of Norway). The chronicle in which this occurs is not of any great historical value, for it is really an abridged translation of Geoffrey, pretended to be a translation back into Welsh by Walter Archdeacon of Oxford, of the book which he had once translated from Welsh and given to Geoffrey to found his history on. Its attribution to Tysilio (son of Brochwael, and bishop of St. Asaph in the 7th century) does not date before the publication of the 'Myvyrian Archæology of Wales' (1801) in which the 'Brut' appears. The oldest MS. is in the Book of Basingwerk, 1461. In the original of Geoffrey 'Ebras' is called 'Olbricht, King of Norway', and in the Welsh 'Brut Gruffydd ap Arthur', which is a complete translation, as well as in the intermediate 'Brut y Brenhinoedd', he is called 'Etbrict'. 'Ebras', with its final *s* for the final *t* of the others, looks very like a Cornish form.

There is a field in Dormennack, between Rosemodress and the sea, called 'Tristram's Down' and another called 'Top Tristram'. This can have no allusion to the battle, for Tristram (or Tristan) was not there, but it is Arthurian as far as the romances are concerned. I do not know whether 'Barn Gallek', the edge of Kemyel Cliff, over-looking Lamorna Cove, which is 'Bar an Gallek', the 'summit of the Gallek', whatever Gallek may mean, can be connected with Gallawg ap Llennawg, who in the 'Triads of Arthu and his Men' (Trioedd Arthur ae Wyr) in Hengwrt MS. 536 (circ. 1300) is one of the 'Three Battle Pillars' of Britain, and was one of the four, of whom Urien, Llew and

Arawn were the others, who were put in command of districts recovered by Arthur from the Saxons. Geoffrey calls him 'Galluc of Salisbury'. But it would be only a coincidence of no import that Malory calls Camlan 'Salisbury'. It is said that 'Bosava' in the Lamorna valley is 'Bosaval,' the Place of Apples, which suggests Avalon, but I do not think much can be made of that, for names with the word for 'apple' in them are too likely to be descriptive to build theories on, nor can I go so far as to connect 'Banns' in Buryan, just north of Trevorgans, with King Ban of Benwick, the father of Lancelot, 'Pellas' Down, in Bosfranken, 'Pelles' Croft, in Tresidder, and 'Pillas' Cliff, in Boskenna, with King Pelles 'of the foreign country, and cousin nigh unto Joseph of Arimathie', the keeper of the Grail, whose daughter Elaine, was the mother of Galahad. Or to go further north, one would hardly dare to connect 'Caer Brane' in Sancreed, with either Bran the Blessed, the 'Brons' of the Graal story, or the Bran ap Melleyrn who comes into the Urien Song of Llywarch Hen. 'Pelles' means bare or bald, a likely epithet for a down in that country, and 'Caer Brane' is probably 'Crow's Castle' or 'Ravensburg', though 'Bran' may be a personal name, it certainly comes into the composition of one not far off on the Men Scrifa – Rialo-Bran.

To sum up. There are two battles traditions, which I believe to refer to the same battle. Of the names of 'Men Merlyn' and 'Rosemodress' there is no doubt whatever. 'Danes' in the one tradition is near enough for popular history of the mixed host of Pagans, Picts and Saxon pirates led by Modred. 'Boleit', the Place of Slaughter, if that is its true meaning, might be supposed to be where the battle was hottest, the Heath of Modred might be where Modred was slain, and 'Rosluken' where Lucan died in the singularly unpleasant manner described by Malory. The menhirion and circle have probably nothing to do with any historical battle, though they might be attached to the tradition of one by the unlearned, especially as even the learned are not decided on their age or what they were for. The barrows may be connected with the battle, whenever or whatever it may have been, on which the tradition is based. Then 'Kemyel' may well be 'Camlan', though this is less certain than my interpretation of 'Rosemodress,' and 'Boscawen' may be 'Gawain's Place'. If a certain number of names can be established with reasonable probability, others, which by themselves would not have suggested Arthurian associations, may really have them also. The evidence must needs be cumulative.

The conclusions are sufficiently startling, and I must admit that I have come to them with some reluctance, for they are against all my prejudices on the subject of place-names. The district in which they occur is a very small one – two miles and a half by about a mile and a half – chiefly in Buryan parish, but so some extent in Paul, and I have not found any other district, with the possible exception of Kea, in which I can make out similar etymologies. It may be noted that the name of Arthur himself does not come into any place-names here, whereas in other districts associated with him, his is almost the only name that occurs. This seems to dispose of any connection with the mythological Arthur.

It may be that some of these derivations can be upset by earlier forms of the names. But certainly, not all of them, and least of all 'Rosemodress', which, combined with the battle tradition, was what originally called my attention to the district.

Perhaps it would be wisest to have no theory on the subject of how the names got there, and simply to say that there they appear to be, and neither I nor anyone else can tell why they are there. But there are several possible explanations, between which it is not easy to decide.

1. It is possible that the 'Last Battle of Arthur' really did take place there. This is a very large supposition, for the localities of the events in the career of the historical Arthur must in the present state of our information be largely, if not altogether, a matter of conjecture. There is every reason historically to place many of them, but by no means all, in the neighbourhood of the Roman Walls.

2. There is a familiar process by which folk-tales, traditional legends and even historical narratives of events which happened elsewhere, tend to be localized by tale-tellers in their own districts, and if there should be to start with any similarity of names, other supplementary names are added to complete the identification. Malta and Meleda, off the Dalmatian coast, divide the honour of being St. Paul's 'Melita', and in each there is a 'St. Paul's Bay', answering (more or less) to the description in the Acts, and the places are shown where the events related by St. Luke took place. I believe each island claims to have snakes which commonly behave as St. Paul's viper did. There is a well-known folk-tale, occurring with local variations in the Sanscrit 'Hitopadesa', in a French 13th century story of 'Saint' Gwenifortis, and in several other places, which has actually given a name to a village at the foot of Snowdon, where 'Badd Gelert', the Grave of Gelert, the faithful greyhound, is still shown, and a very slight study of the distribution of folk-tales will supply many more instances. The late Mr. W. Copeland Borlase, in his book on the Irish Dolmens, attempted, apparently with some success to show reason for thinking that the Irish Legends of Partholan, Nemed, the Firbolg, Fomorians and the rest of them, were transferences as to both time and place, and recorded events which happened on the Continent in the early centuries of the Christian era, not in Ireland in the 15th century B.C. In so prosaic a work as the Post Office Directory for 1902, under the parishes of St. Eval and Paul, exactly the same story is told in almost the same words of a party of Royalists taking refuge from the troopers of Fairfax in a 'fogou' still to be seen on an estate called in each 'Trewoofe or Troove'. The measurements of the 'fogous' are exactly the same, and each is said to be surrounded by a triple entrenchment. In each situation is given, one 'in a secluded valley near Porthcothan', the other 'in romantic valley which terminates in Lamorna Cove.' Of course if two sets of Royalists really did hide from

Fairfax in two 'fogous,' each 36 ft. by 6 ft. by 5 ft., in two secluded (or romantic) valleys on estates called Trewoofe or Troove, in two widely separated localities in Cornwall, this is not an instance, but I strongly suspect that both accounts refer to the same story, given by Hals under Buryan (in which Troove manor-house is, though the 'fogou' is in Paul), of which the Levelis of the period was the hero. There is a good modern instance on the borders of Exmoor, which shows what developments of nomenclature may be produced by a thoroughly popular romance. Blackmore built up his 'Lorna Doone' on the slender foundation of a vague local tradition concerning a gang of ordinary robbers. The rest is his own very excellent invention, and he magnified and idealized both scenery and robbers. Yet, though the romance is only about forty years old, a system of place-names founded on it has grown up, and tourists at Lynton and Lynmouth are seriously taken to see the actual places where events, which had no existence outside of Blackmore's imagination, really happened. They are no doubt in most cases the places which he had in his mind, as the Tintagel and Camelford district was probably in Geoffrey's mind, and as it may be that the Buryan district was in the mind of some unknown teller of folk-tales in olden time. The process is so familiar that it is not necessary to go on multiplying instances, and there is no reason to consider that what we have seen going on in our own time, with the influence of Blackmore on Exmoor, with the Prince Charlie legend (for there is plenty of that, besides his real historical career) in the Highlands, and with the influence of Scott in Scotland at large, was improbable with the Arthur story in the Middle Ages.

3. It is possible that at a comparatively late period, after the Arthur legend had settled down into its romance form, some literary-minded landowner, with an enthusiasm for these stories, gave names chosen from them to new houses. As a variant one may conjecture a fashion for Arthurian personal names. We still have the names of Arthur, Gawain, Lionel, Lancelot, Tristan, Perceval and others, which have gone on more or less continuously since the thirteenth and fourteenth centuries. There are also modern revivals, chiefly Tennysonian, such as Enid, Elaine, Ysolt, Vivien and others and the Cornish name 'Jennifer' which is certainly 'Guinevere', is always with us. In Cornwall the names of the hero and heroine of the most certainly Cornish of the romances, 'Tristan (or Tristram)' and 'Ysolt' are found not infrequently in the mediæval parts of pedigrees. 'Tristram' is still not uncommon here. If these names were used, why not others? So it is possible that the places were named after Arthurian characters only at second-hand, that is to say, after owners and occupiers who bore the same names. That some are the names of the less estimable characters, such as Modred, matters very little. After all, the Gawain, Lancelot, Tristan, Guinevere, Ysolt and Vivian of the romances were not precisely saints, though they must have been nicer people to meet than Modred.

The two last suggested theories have one point in common. They suggest the existence of local folk-tales, presumably in Cornish, once well known, but now lost, probably for ever, for they probably were never written down. Judging by the analogy of the folk-tales in other Celtic countries, such as those collected by the later J.F. Campbell of Islay, in the West Highlands, the *form* of a story was constant. It was told by various tellers in exactly the same words. Any variation would be telling it wrong. Therefore, being in Cornish, and no English form being current, the stories would naturally disappear with the cessation of the language. It is, as I have said, the common practice to localize such tales. The one specimen of a Cornish folk-tale that is left, the story of 'John of Chy an Hur', is a common tale all over Europe. It is known as the 'Tale of the Three Advices', and as told in various places is generally localized, and the scene laid in the country in which it is told. Its earliest form is probably that which occurs in the episode of Grimaud, found in some manuscripts of the prose 'Saint Graal' of Robert de Borron. It therefore just touches the Arthurian Cycle. In the Cornish form the hero lives at 'Chy an Hurdh' in St. Levan. He goes east seeking work. On his return he meets with merchants from Treryn, in his own parish, coming from Caresk (Exeter) Fair, goes with them across St. Hilary Downs to Marazion, where adventures happen, and leaves them where their ways divide at 'Kuz karn na Huila' (now Cotnawhilly) in Buryan. The tale survived because John Boson of Newlyn gave it to Lluyd and to Gwavas, to help to teach them Cornish. This particular tale seems to have been circulated in English also, for Bottrell gives a version of it (with a curious touch, found in the Grimaud story, but not in Boson's Cornish, that the villain of the piece is a red-haired man), and some of his other tales look as if there must have once been a Cornish form of them. 'Droll-tellers', as they were called, would go about telling these tales at meetings like those which under the name of 'ceilidh' still take place in the Highlands. The Cornish word 'daralla', a tale, is perhaps the origin of the word 'droll' as applied in Cornwall to a story, unless 'daralla' is a Cornicized version of 'droll', which is less likely, for there is not necessarily anything 'droll' in the ordinary English sense about these tales, and the word as applied in English to a literary composition means a farce or comic interlude. Among these 'darallow' there would naturally be Arthurian stories, either indigenous or borrowed from Wales and Brittany, at first hand perhaps, but also, no doubt, at second-hand through the romances which had become the common property of Europe. It being accepted everywhere that Arthur was a Cornish hero, the droll-tellers would have the more reason for putting the incidents in places known to their audience. If the district that I have been describing was fixed upon as the scene of the 'Last Battle', various points in it would come to be called after the various actors in the story, by the very process that we might have seen actually going on in the 'Lorna Doone' country, or in the 'Lady of the Lake' country around Loch Katrine and the Trossachs. I do not say that this certainly did happen in the Buryan and Paul case, but it seems to commend itself as the best conjectural hypothesis. If it is to be accepted, another point of interest arises. Several of the names incline to the forms in which they appear in the Welsh Arthurian stories and poems, rather than to those which occur in the French, and English romances, which are generally in the Breton form, and some of them seem to be names which are found only in the Welsh. How did that come about? There is no answer to the question at present, but it looks as if some of the so-called 'Mabinogion' of Arthur were known in Cornwall also. Mediæval Celtic Cornwall is very little known to us. Between us and it there is a barrier of a lost language, and perhaps a lost literature as well, for in a change of language, as in moving house, a good many things get broken and lost. But many names do occur in the Breton form, and there is one case in which apparently both forms of the same name of found, for we have 'Men Merlyn' and 'Merthen Point' (cf. Welsh 'Merddyn' or 'Myrddin') not very far apart. The occurence of so many names in this one very small district is also in favour of the localized legend theory, and this seems to me to be the 'lode' that looks the most 'keenly', and I think it may be worth following up, though I do not at present see how we are going to get much more information to go upon. Also I would warn all enquirers, and myself among the number, that it may be taken as a general axiom, to which there are but few exceptions, that when there is a choice between an interpretation of a name which is romantic, historical, mythological or poetical and one which is commonplace and prosaic, the latter, especially if it is at all appropriate and descriptive, is more likely to be correct.

I leave my suggestion at this for the present. I should be very glad to have it tested as much as possible by others. There are several ways of doing this, and one is by finding older forms of the names, which may confirm or upset my suggestion. Another is by trying whether the same thing cannot be done with a number of other places in Cornwall. Whether that would prove or disprove the theory it is not easy to say. But I wish to make it clear that I do not consider the theory as proved, but only as a tentative suggestion that may be worth going into.

35 *From* Legend Land by 'Lyonesse' (1922)

There is a lot of truth mingled with the old legends that tell of the lost land of Lyonesse, a fertile and prosperous country that once extended west from Cornwall as far as the Scillies. According to those old traditions a vast number of villages and 140 churches were overwhelmed on that day, over eight hundred years ago, when the angry sea broke in and drowned fertile Lyonesse, and now, as an old rhyme has it:

> "Beneath Land's End and Scilly rocks
> Sunk lies a town that Ocean mocks."[1]

On that fatal day, November 11, 1099,[2] a mighty storm raged all about our coasts, but the gale was of unparalleled severity in the West. Those who have seen a winter gale blowing across the sea that now flows above the Lost Land will know that it is very easy to believe that those giant angry waves could break down any poor construction of man's hand intended to keep the wild waters in check.

For Lyonesse, they say, was stolen by the sea gradually. Here a bit and there a bit would be submerged after some winter storm, until came this grim November night, when the sea made a clean sweep of the country and rushed, with stupendous speed, across the flat wooded lands until it was brought to a halt by the massive cliffs of what is now the Land's End peninsula.

Today all that is left of the lost land are the beautiful Scilly Islands and the cluster of rocks between the Scillies and Land's End, known as the Seven Stones. These rocks are probably the last genuine bit of old Lyonesse, for their Cornish name is Lethowsow, which was what the old Cornish called Lyonesse. Even now the local fishermen refer to the Seven Stones as "The City," for tradition tells that there was situated the principal town of the drowned land, and stories are told of how on calm days ruined buildings may be discerned beneath the waters near Lethowsow, and that in times past fishing-nets have brought up old weathered domestic utensils from the sea bottom near at hand.

Though in the Scillies you may feel very far away from the great world, quaint, fascinating Penzance, from which you start, is very near – in time – from London. It is only six and a-half hours from Paddington, although over 300 miles have to be traversed in the rail journey.

36 The Famous Tragedy of the Queen of Cornwall at Tintagel in Lyonesse by Thomas Hardy (1923)

Characters

MARK, KING OF CORNWALL
SIR TRISTRAM
SIR ANDRET
OTHER KNIGHTS
SQUIRES
MESSENGER
HERALD
WATCHMAN
RETAINERS, MUSICIANS, ETC.
ISEULT THE FAIR, QUEEN OF CORNWALL
ISEULT THE WHITEHANDED
DAME BRANGWAIN
DAMSEL
THE QUEEN'S ATTENDANTS, BOWERMEN, ETC.
SHADES OF DEAD CORNISH MEN – CHANTERS
SHADES OF DEAD CORNISH WOMEN – CHANTERS
MERLIN

The Time covered by the events is about the Time of representation. The Stage is any large room; round the end of which the audience sits. It is assumed to be the interior of the Great Hall of Tintagel Castle: that the floor is strewn with rushes: that there is an arch in the back-centre (a doorway or other opening may counterfeit this) through which the Atlantic is visible across an outer ward and over the ramparts of the stronghold: that a door is on the left, and one on the right (curtains, screens or chairs may denote these): that a settle spread with skins is among the moveables: that above at the back is a gallery (which may be represented by any elevated piece of furniture on which two actors can stand, in a corner of the room screened off). Should the performance take place in a real theatre, the aforesaid imaginary surroundings may be supplied by imitative scenery. The costumes of the players are the conventional ones of linen fabrics, made gay with knots and rosettes of ribbon, as in the old mumming shows; though on an actual stage they may be more realistic.

Scene 1
Prologue
Enter MERLIN, *a phantasmal figure with a white wand. The room is darkened: a blue light may be thrown on Merlin.*

Merlin
I come, at your persuasive call

To raise up in this modern hall
A tragedy of dire duress
That vexed the Land of Lyonesse:–
Scenes, with their passions, hopes and fears
Sunk into shade these thousand years
To set, in ghostly grave array,
    Their blitheness, blood, and tears,
Feasts, ardours, as if rife today
    Before men's eyes and ears.

The tale has travelled far and wide:–
Yea, that King Mark to fetch his bride,
Sent Tristram; then that he and she
Quaffed a love-potion witlessly
While homeward bound. Hence that the King
    Wedded one heart-aflame
For Tristram! He in dark despair,
Roved recklessly, and wived elsewhere
    One of his mistress' name.

I saw these times I represent
Watched, gauged them as they came and went,
Being ageless, deathless! And those two
Fair women – namesakes – well I knew!
Judge them not harshly in a love
    Whose hold on them was strong;
Sorrow therein they tasted of,
    And deeply, and too long.
                                        Exit.

CHANTERS; SHADES OF DEAD OLD CORNISH MEN,
    SHADES OF DEAD CORNISH WOMEN.
Right and Left in Front.

Chanters: Men *(in recitative)*
Tristram a captive of King Mark
Racked was the Queen with qualm and cark,
Till reached her hand a written line,
That quickened her to deft design.

Chanters: Women
Then, Tristram out, and Mark shut in,
The Queen and Tristram winged to win
Gard Castle, where, without annoy,
Monthswhile they lodged in matchless joy!

Chanters: Men
Anon, when Queen Iseult had homed,

Brittany-wards Sir Tristram roamed
  To greet his waiting wife,
White-handed Iseult, whom the Queen
Has recked not of. But soon, in teen
  And troublous inner strife,
She Tristram of her soul besought
By wringing letters rapid wrought
(The King gone hunting, knowing nought)
  To come again to her
Even at the cost – such was her whim –
Of bringing Whitehands[1] back with him
  In wifely character.

Chanters: Women
There was no answer. Rest she could not;
Then we missed her, days. We would not
  Think where she might have been.
And, having sailed, maybe twice ten
Long leagues, here came she back again,
And sad and listless – just as when
  She went – abides her mien!

Chanters: Men and Women
Hist! ... Lo; there by the nether gate
New comers hail! Oh who should wait
The postern door to enter by,
  The bridge being clearly seen?
The King returned? – But that way; why?
Would he try trap his queen?

Watchman (*crossing without the archway*)
The King's arriving! Ho!

Enter HERALD. *Sounds a trumpet.*
Enter BRANGWAIN.

Scene II
HERALD, BRANGWAIN, AND CHANTERS.

Herald
    The King's at hand!

Brangwain
God's grace, she's home, either from far or near!

Herald
Whither plied she? Many would like to hear!

Chanters: Men and Women
We do not know. We will not know.
She took a ship from the shore below,
 And was gone many days.
By friending winds she's back before him:
Extol God should she and adore Him
 For covering up her ways!

Enter KING MARK *with* SIR ANDRET *and other Knights,
 retinue, and rude music of ram's – horns, crouds, and
 humstrums,* BRANGWAIN *standing aside.*

Scene III
KING MARK, KNIGHTS, RETINUE, ETC., BRANGWAIN,
 AND CHANTERS.

K. Mark
Where is the Queen?

> *Drinks from silver flagon which has been standing on
> the hearth on a brandise. Retinue drink after him
> from the same.*

Brangwain (*advancing*)
 Sir King, the Queen attires
To meet your Majesty, and now comes down.
(*Aside.*) Haply he will not know!

Enter QUEEN ISEULT THE FAIR *attended, and followed
 by the hound* HOUDAIN.

Scene IV
QUEEN ISEULT, KING MARK, KNIGHTS, BRANGWAIN,
 ETC., AND CHANTERS.
 (Q. ISEULT *has dark hair, and wears a crimson robe,
 and tiara or circlet.*)
 MARK *smacks the* QUEEN *on her shoulders in rough
 greeting.*

K. Mark
Why is this brachet[2] in the hall again?

Q. Iseult
I know not how she came here.

K. Mark
 Nay, my wife,
Thou dost know well – as I know women well! –

And know her owner more than well, I reckon,
And that he left the beast to your regard.
  He kicks the dog away.

Sir Andret (*aside to* K. MARK)
Aye, aye, great King, thou speakest wisely on't
This time as ever. Wives dost thrid all through!
  Exeunt severally KNIGHTS, RETINUE, ETC., AND
    BRANGWAIN.

Scene V
KING MARK, QUEEN ISEULT, AND CHANTERS.

Q. Iseult
I've not beheld of late the man you mean;
Maybe, my lord, you have shut him in the dungeon,
As you did formerly!

K. Mark
        You spell me better!
And know he has felt full liberty for long,
And that you would have seen him, and much more,
Had not debarred you one o' those crosses which,
Happily, scotch unlawful lovers' schemes
No less than sanct intents. If that good knight[3]
Dallies in Brittany with his good wife –
So finger-white – to cheer her as he ought,
'Tis clear he can't be here.

Q. Iseult (*with slight sarcasm*)
              'Tis clear you plead
Some what in waste to prove as much. But faith,
      (*petulantly*)
'Twas she, times tiresome, quirked and called to him
Or he would not have gone!

K. Mark
        Ah, know'st thou that!
Leave her alone, a woman lets all out!
Well, I may know things too. I slipped in sly
When I came home by now, and lit on this:
That while I've sued the chase you followed him,
Vanishing on a voyage of some days,
Which you'd fain cloak from me, and have confessed
To no one, either of my people here.

Q. Iseult (*evasively*)
I want to take the air, being qualmed to death.

Surely a queen is dowered with such degree
Of queenship, or what is't to be a queen?
No foot, I swear, set in Brittany,
Or upon soil of any neighbour shore,
'Twixt putting from the cove below these walls
And my return hereto.

K. Mark
   Protests – no more!
You sailed off somewhere, – (so a sea-nath[4] hints me
That heeds the tidings every troubled billow
Wails to the Beeny-Sisters from Pen-Tyre) –
At risk, too, of your life, the ship being small,
And trickful tempests lurking in the skies.
A woman does not raise a mast for nought
On a cockle-shell, even be the sea-signs fair.
But I have scorned to ask the mariners
The course you bore – or north, or south, or what –
It might have been to Brittany, it might not!

Q. Iseult
I have not seen him.

K. Mark
   Well, you might have done't
Each sunrise, noon, or eve, for all the joy
You show in my return, or gladness wont
To a queen shore-reached in safety – so they tell me –
Since you crept cat-like home.

Q. Iseult (*indignantly*)
   I saw him not!
You stifle speech in me, or I'd have launched,
Ere this, the tidings rife. See him no more
Shall I, or you. He's gone. Death darkens him!

K. Mark (*starting*)
So much the better, if true – for us and him!
   (*She weeps.*)
But no. He has died too many many times
For that report to hold! In tilts, in frays,
Through slits and loops, louvres and battlements,
Has he been pierced and arrowed to the heart,
Then risen up again to trouble me!
Sir Andret told, ere Tristram shunned Tintagel,
How he espied you dallying – you and he –
Near the shot-window southward. And I went
With glaive in hand to smite him. Would I had!

Yea, and I should have, had I been sustained.
But not one knight was nigh. – Where are they now?
Whence comes this quietude? – I'll call a council:
What's best to do with him I'll learn thereat,
And then we'll keep a feast. A council! Ho!
                Exit KING MARK.

Scene VI
QUEEN ISEULT AND CHANTERS.
The Queen sits in dejection.

Chanters: Men
  Why did Heaven warrant, in its whim,
  A twain mismated should bedim
  The courts of their encompassment
  With bleeding loves and discontent!
  Who would not feel God favoured them,
  Past wish, in throne and diadem?
And that for all His plaisance they would praise
Him upon earth throughout their deeds and days!

Chanters: Women
  Instead, see King and Queen more curst
  Than beggars upon holt or hurst: –
  A queen! One who each night and morn
  Sighs for Sir Tristram; him gloom-born
  In his mother's death, and reared mid vows
  Of poison by a later spouse:
  In love Fate-haunted, doomed to drink
  Charmed philtres, melting every link
  Of purposed faith! Why wedded he
  King Howel's lass of Brittany?
Why should the wave have washed him to her shore –
Him, prone to love our Queen here more and more?

Chanters: Men and Women
In last misfortune did he well-nigh slay
Unknowingly in battle Arthur! Ay,
Our stainless Over-king of Counties – he
Made Dux Bellorum[5] for his valiancy! –
If now, indeed, Tristram be chilled in death,
Will she, the Queen, care aught for further breath?

Q. Iseult (*musing*)
How little he knows, does Mark! And yet, how much?
Can there be any groundage for his thought
That Tristram's not a ghost? O, no such hope!
My Tristram, yet not mine! Could it be deemed

Thou shouldst have loved me less in many years
Hadst thou enjoyed them? If in Christland now
Do you look down on *her* most, or on *me*?
Why should the King have grudged so fleet a life
Its pleasure, grinned with gall at its renown,
Yapped you away for too great love of me,
Spied on thee through his myrmidons – aye, encloaked
And peeped to frustrate thee, and sent the word
To kill thee who should meet thee? O sweet Lord,
Thou has made him hated; yet he still has life;
While Tristram ... Why said Mark he doubtless lived?
   But he was ever a mocker, was King Mark,
And not far from a coward.

Enter BRANGWAIN

Scene VII
QUEEN ISEULT, BRANGWAIN, AND CHANTERS.

Q. Iseult (*distractedly*)
Brangwain, he hard denies I did not see him!
But he is dead! ... Perhaps not ...
Can it be?

Brangwain
Who doth deny, my Queen? Who is not dead?
Your words are blank to me; your manner strange.

Q. Iseult
One bleeds no more on earth for a full-fledged sin
Than for a callow! The King has found out now
My sailing the south water in his absence,
And weens the worst. Forsooth, it's always so!
He will not credit I've no cause to land
For the black reason – it is no excuse –
That Tristram, knight, had died! – Landed had I,
Aye, fifty times, could he have still been there,
Even there with her. – My Love, my own lost Love!
         (*She bends down.*)

Brangwain
You did not land in Brittany, O Queen?

Q. Iseult
I did not land, Brangwain, although so near.
         (*She pauses.*)
– He had been long with his White-handed one,
And had fallen sick of fever nigh to death;

Till she grew fearful for him; sent for me,
Yea, choicelessly, at his light-headed calls
And midnight repetitions of my name.
Yes, sent for me in a despairing hope
To save him at all cost.

Brangwain
          She must, me thinks,
Have loved him much!

Q. Iseult (*impatiently*)
   Don't speak, Brangwain, but hear me.
Yes: women are so ... For me, I could not bear
To lose him thus. Love, others' somewhile dainty,
Is my starved, all-day meal! And favouring chance
That of the King's apt absence, tempted me;
And hence I sailed, despite the storm-strid air.
What did I care about myself, or aught?
– She'd told the mariner her messenger
To hoist his canvas white if he bore me
On the backward journey, black if he did not,
That, so, heart-ease should reach the knight full quick –
Even ere I landed – quick as I hove in sight.
Yea, in his peril so profound, she sent
The message, though against her. Women are so!

Brangwain
Some are, my lady Queen: some may not be.

Q. Iseult
While we were yet a two-hours' toss from port
I bade them show the sheet, as had been asked,
The which they did. But when we touched the quay
She ran down thither, beating both her hands,
And saying Tristram died an hour before.

Brangwain
But O, dear Queen, didst fully credit her?

Q. Iseult
Aye! Sudden-shaken souls guess not at guile. –
I fell into a faint at the very words. –
Thereon they lifted me into the cabin,
Saying: "She shall not foot this deadly land!"
When I again knew life I was distraught,
And sick with the rough writhing of the bark. –
They had determined they would steer me home,
Had turned the prow, and toiled a long league back;

Strange that, no sooner had they put about,
The weather worsed, as if they'd angered God
By doing what they had done to sever me
Even from my Love's dead limbs! No gleam glowed more,
And the seas sloped like houseroofs all the way.
We were blown north along the shore to Wales,
Where they made port and nursed me, till, next day,
The blinding gale abated: we returned,
And reached by shifts at last the cove below.
The King, whose queries I had feared so much,
Had not come back; came only at my heels;
Yet he has learnt, somewise, that I've been missed,
And doubtless I shall suffer – he's begun it!
Much I lament I put about so soon.
I should have landed, and have gained his corpse.

Brangwain
She is his wife, and you could not have claimed it.

Q. Iseult
But could I not have seen him? How know you?

Brangwain
Nay: she might not have let you even see him:
He is her own, dear Queen, and in her land
You had no sway to make her cede him up.
I doubt his death. You took her word for it,
And she was desperate at the sight of you.
Sick unto death he may have been. But – dead?
        (*Shakes her head.*)
Corpses are many: man lives half-amort;
But rumour makes them more when they run short!

Q. Iseult
If he be not! O I would even condone
His bringing her, would he not come without;
I've said it ever since I've known of her,
Could he but live: yes, could he live for me!
Q. ISEULT *sings sadly to herself,* BRANGWAIN *having
   gone to the back of the hall:*
  Could he but live for me
  A day, yea, even an hour,
  Its petty span would be
  Steeped in felicity
Passing the price of Heaven's held-dearest dower:
Could he but live, could he
But live for me!
   Exit Q. ISEULT, *followed by* BRANGWAIN.

Chanters: Women

Maybe, indeed, he did not die!
Our sex, shame on't, is over prone
To ill conceits that amplify.
Maybe he did not die – that one,
The Whitepalmed, may in strategy
Have but avowed it! Weak are we,
And foil and fence have oft to seek,
Aye, even by guile, if fear so speak!

Chanters: Men

Wounded in Ireland, life he fetched,
In charge of the King's daughter there,
Who healed him, loved him, primed him fair
For the great tournament, when he stretched
Sir Palomides low.

Chanters: Women

      Yet slight
Was King Mark's love for him, despite!
Mark sent him thither as to gain
Iseult, but, truly, to be slain!

Chanters: Men

Quite else her father, who on sight
Was fain for Tristram as his son,
Not Mark. But woe, his word was won!
Alas, should wrong vow stand as right?

Chanters: Women

And what Dame Brangwain did to mend,
Enlarged the mischief! Best have penned
That love-drink close, since 'twas to be
Iseult should wed where promised: wretched she!

Chanters: Men and Women

Yet, haply, Tristram lives. Quick heals are his!
He rose revived from that: why not from this?

Watchman (*without*)
One comes with tidings! – (*to the comer*)
  Bear them to the hall.

Enter a MESSENGER (*at back*), *pausing and looking
    round.* QUEEN ISEULT, *attended, re-enters (at front)
    and seats herself.*

Scene VIII
QUEEN ISEULT, ATTENDANT-LADIES, MESSENGER,
   AND CHANTERS.

Messenger (*coming forward*)
Where is Iseult the Queen?

Q. Iseult
      Here, churl. I'm she.

Messenger
I'm sent here to deliver tidings, Queen,
To your high ear alone.
         Exeunt Attendants.

Q. Iseult (*in strung-up tones*)
      Then voice them forth.
A halter for thee if I find them false!

Messenger
Knight Tristram of the sorry birth is yet
Enrolled among the living, having crept
Out of the very vaults of death and doom!
– His heavy ails bedimmed him numb as night,
And men conceived him wrapt in wakeless rest;
But he strove back. Hither, on swifter keel
He has followed you; and even now is nigh.
   (QUEEN ISEULT *leans back and covers her eyes.*)
Iseult the Pale-palmed, in her jealousy,
With false deliverance feigned your sail was black,
And made him pray for death in his extreme,
Till sank he to a drowse: grey death they thought it,
And bells were bidden toll the churches through,
And thereupon you came. Scared at her crime
She deemed that it had dealt him death indeed,
And knew her not at fault till you had gone.
– When he aroused, and learnt she had sent you back,
It angered him to hot extremity,
And brings him here upon my very stern,
If he, forsooth, have haleness for the adventure.
        Exit Messenger.

Q. Iseult
O it o'erturns! ... "Black" told she! Cheat unmatchable!

Enter BRANGWAIN

Scene IX
QUEEN ISEULT, BRANGWAIN, AND CHANTERS. THEN
KING MARK AND SIR ANDRET.

Brangwain
There stands a strange old harper down below,
Who does not look Sir Tristram, yet recalls him.
   KING MARK *crosses the ward outside the arch.*

K. Mark
(*speaking off, and shading his eyes*)
What traveller's that, slow mounting to the wall,
Scanning its strength, with curious halting crawl,
As knowing not Tintagel's Towers at all?

Watchman (*crossing without*)
'Tis but a minstrel from afar, Sir King,
Harping around for alms, or anything.

Q. Iseult (*starting up*)
It must be he!
SIR TRISTRAM'S *steps heard approaching. He enters,*
   disguised as a harper.

KING MARK (*glancing back casually at* SIR TRISTRAM
   in going off)
Dole him his alms in Christ's name, if ye must,
And irk me not while setting to bowse with these.
   Exit KING MARK *from the outside to the banqueting-*
   hall, followed across the back of the arch by Knights,
   etc., including SIR ANDRET.

Sir Andret (*to himself as he goes*)
That harper struck me oddly! … In his gait –
Well: till the beakers have gone round I'll wait.
     Exit behind the others.

Scene X
QUEEN ISEULT, TRISTRAM, BRANGWAIN, AND
CHANTERS.

Tristram
My Queen and best belov'd! At last again!
   (*He throws off the cloak that disguises him.*)
– Know I was duped by her who dons your name;
She swore the bellied sheeting of your ship
Blotted the wind-wafts like a sable swan;
And being so weak from my long lying there

I sank to senselessness at the wisht words –
So contrary to hope! Whilst I was thus
She sallied out, and sent you home forthwith!
Anon I poured my anger on her head,
Till, in high fear of me, she quivered white.
– I mended swiftly, stung by circumstance,
And rose and left her there, and followed you.
Sir Kay lent aidance, and has come with me.

Brangwain
I'll out and watch the while Sir Tristram's here.
                    Exit BRANGWAIN.

Scene XI
QUEEN ISEULT, TRISTRAM, AND CHANTERS.

Q. Iseult
You've come again, you've come again, dear Love!

Tristram
To be once more with my Iseult the Fair,
          (He embraces the Queen.)
Though not yet what I was in strength and stay,
Yet told have I been by Sir Launcelot
To ware me of King Mark! King Fox he calls him –
Whom I'd have pitied, though he would not yield thee,
Nor let you loose on learning our dire need
Of freedom for our bliss, which came to us
Not of fore-aim or falseness, but by spell
Of love-drink, ministered by hand unseen!

Q. Iseult
Knowing as much, he swore he would not slay thee,
But Launcelot told him no man could believe him,
Whereat he answered: "Anyhow she's mine!"

Tristram
It's true, I fear. He cannot be believed.

Q. Iseult
Yet, Tristram, would my husband were but all!
Had you not wedded her my namesake, Oh,
We could have steered around this other rock –
Trust me we could! Why did you do it, why!
Triumph did he when first I learnt of that,
And lewdly laughed to see me shaken so.

Tristram

You have heard the tale of my so mating her
Twice told, and yet anew! Must I again?
It was her sire King Howel brought it round
In brunt of battle, when I saved his lands.
He said to me: "Thou hast done generously:
I crave to make thee recompense! My daughter,
The last best bloom of Western Monarchy –
Iseult of the White Hand the people call her –
Is thine. I give thee her. O take her then,
The chief of all things priceless unto me!"
Overcome was I by the fiery fray,
Arrested by her name – so akin to yours –
His ardour zeal. I thought: "Maybe her spouse,
By now, had haled my Iseult's heart from me,"
And took the other blindly. That is all.

Q. Iseult

A woman's heart has room for one alone;
A man's for two or three!

Tristram

      Sweet; 'twas but chance!

Q. Iseult (*more softly*)

Yet there may lie our doom! ... I had nerved myself
To bid you come, and bring your wife with you.
But that I did not mean. It was too much;
And yet I said it! ...

Tristram

      Lean ye down, my Love:
I'll touch to thee my very own old tune.
I came in harper-guise, unweeting what
The hazardry of our divided days
Might have brought forth for us!
   He takes the harp. QUEEN ISEULT *reclines.*

Tristram

      Let's meet again to-night, my Fair,
        Let's meet unseen of all;
      The day-god labours to his lair,
        And then the evenfall!

      O living lute, O lily-rose,
        O form of fantasie,
      When torches waste and warders doze
        Steal to the stars will we!

While nodding knights carouse at meat
  And shepherds shamble home,
We'll cleave in close embracements – sweet
  As honey in the comb!

Till crawls the dawn from Condol's crown,
  And over Neitan's Kieve,[6]
As grimly ghosts we conjure down
  And hopes still weave and weave!

Watchman (*crossing without*)
A ship sheers round, and bring up in the bay!
        Re-enter BRANGWAIN.

Scene XII
QUEEN ISEULT, TRISTRAM, BRANGWAIN, AND
    CHANTERS.

Brangwain
My Queen, the shingle shaves another keel,
And who the comer is we fail to guess.
Its build bespeaks it from the Breton coasts,
And those upon it shape of the Breton sort,
And the figure near the prow is white-attired.

Q. Iseult
What manner of farer does the figure show?

Brangwain
My Lady, when I cast eye waterwards
From the arrow-loop, just as the keel ground
Against the popplestones, it seemed a woman's
But she was wimpled close.

Q. Iseult
        I'll out and see.
QUEEN ISEULT *opens the door to the banqueting-hall,
    and stands in the doorway still visible to the
    audience. Through the door comes the noise of
    trenchers, platters, cups, drunken voices, songs, etc.,
    from the adjoining apartment, where* KING MARK *is
    dining with Knights and retainers.*

Voice of K. Mark (*in liquor*)
Queen, whither goest thou? Pray plague me not
While keeping table. Hath the old knave left,
He with his balladry we heard by now
Strum up to thee?

Q. Iseult
I go to the pleasance only,
Across the feasting-hall for shortness' sake,
Returning hither swift.

Voice of K. Mark
Yea, have thy way,
As women will!

Voice of Sir Andret
Aye, hence the need to spy them!
Exeunt QUEEN ISEULT *and* BRANGWAIN *through the
banqueting-hall to the outside of the Castle. Noise of
cups, trenchers, drunken voices, songs, etc.,
resumed, till the door shuts, when it is heard in
subdued tones.*

Scene XIII
TRISTRAM AND CHANTERS. THEN ISEULT THE
WHITEHANDED.

Tristram
(*going and looking seaward through arch*)
A woman's shape in white ... Can it be she?
Would she in sooth, then, risk to follow me?

Chanters: Men
O Tristram, thou art not to find
Such solace for a shaken mind
   As seemed to wait thee here!
Chanters: Women
One seized of right to trace thy track
Hath crossed the sea to win thee back
   In love and faith and fear!

Chanters: Men and Women
From this newcomer wis we pain
Ere thou canst know sweet spells again,
   O knight of little cheer!

Enter ISEULT THE WHITEHANDED. *She has corn-brown
hair, and wears a simple robe.*

Iseult the Whitehanded
I could not help it, O my husband! Yea
I have dogged you close; I could not bear your rage;
And Heaven has favoured me! The sea smiled smooth
The whole way over, and the sun shone kind.
Your sail was eyesome fair in front of me,

And I steered just behind, all stealthfully!
– Forgive me that I spoke untruly to you,
And then to her, in my bruised brain's turmoil.
But, in a way of saying, you were dead;
You seemed so – in a dead drowse when she came.
And I did send for her at your entreaty;
But flesh is frail. Centred is woman's love,
And knows no breadth. I could not let her land,
I could not let her come!

Tristram
    Your speech is nought,
O evil woman, who didst nearly witch
The death of this Queen, saying such of me!

Iseult the White H.
Forgive me, do forgive, my lord, my husband!
I love, have loved you so imperishably;
Not with fleet flame at times, as some do use!
Had I once been unfaithful, even perverse,
I would have held some coldness fitly won;
But I have ever met your wryest whim
With ready-wrought acceptance, matched your moods,
Clasped hands, touched lips, and smiled devotedly;
So how should this have grown up unaware?

  Enter QUEEN ISEULT *and* BRANGWAIN *in the Gallery
   above, unperceived*.

Scene XIV
QUEEN ISEULT, BRANGWAIN, ISEULT THE
  WHITEHANDED, TRISTRAM, AND CHANTERS.

Q. Iseult
What do they say? And who is she, Brangwain?
Not my suspicion hardened into mould
Of flesh and blood indeed?

Brangwain
    I cannot hear.

Tristram
I have no more to say or do with thee;
I'd fade your face to strangeness in my eyes!
Your father dealt me illest turn in this;
Your name, too, being the match of hers!
 Yea thus
I was coerced. I never more can be
Your bed-mate – never again.

Iseult the White H.
        How, Tristram mine?
What meaning mete you out by that to me?
You only say it, do you? You are not,
Cannot be, in true earnest – that I know!
I hope you are not in earnest? – Surely I
This time as always, do belong to you,
And you are going to keep me always yours?
I thought you loved my name for me myself,
Not for another; or at the very least
For the sake of some dear sister or mother dead,
And not, not –
        (*She breaks down*)

Tristram
I spoke too rawly, maybe; mouthed what I
Ought only to have mused. But do you dream
I for a leastness longer could abide
Such dire disastrous lying? – Back to your ship;
Get into it; return by the aptest wind
And mate with another man when thou canst find him,
Never uncovering how you cozened me:
His temper might be tried thereby, as mine!

Iseult the White H.
No, no! I won't be any other's wife!
How can a thing so monstrous ever be?

Tristram
If I had battened in Brittany with thee –

Iseult the White H.
But you don't *mean* you'll live away from me,
Leave me, and henceforth be unknown to me,
O you don't surely? I could not help coming;
Don't send me away – do not, do not, do so!
    (Q. ISEULT *above moves restlessly*.)
Forgive your Iseult for appearing here,
Untoward seem it! For I love you so
Your sudden setting out was death to me
When I discerned the cause. Your sail smalled down:
I should have died had I not followed you.
Only, my Tristram, let me be with thee,
And see thy face. I do not sue for more!

Q. Iseult (*above*)
She has no claim to importune like that,
And gloss her hardihood in tracking him!

Tristram
Thou canst not haunt another woman's house!

Iseult the White H.
O yes I can, if there's no other way!
I have heard she does not mind. I'd rather be
Her bondwench, if I am not good enough
To be your wife, than not stay here at all, –
Aye, I, the child of kings and governors,
As luminous in ancestral line as she,
Say this, so utter my abasement now!
– Something will happen if I go away
Of import dark to you (no matter what
To me); and we two should not greet again!
– Could you but be the woman, I the man,
I would not fly from you or banish you
For fault so small as mine. O do not think
It was so vile a thing. I wish – how much! –
You could have told me twenty such untruths,
That I might then have shown you *I* would not
Rate them as faults, but be much joyed to have you
In spite of all. If you but through and through
Could spell me, know how staunch I have stood, and am,
You'd love me just the same. Come, say you do,
And let us not be severed so again.

Q. Iseult (*above*)
I can't bear this!

Iseult the White H.
          All the long hours and days
And heavy gnawing nights, and you not there,
But gone because you hate me! 'Tis past what
A woman can endure!

Tristram (*more gently*)
          Not hate you, Iseult.
But, hate or love, lodge here you cannot now:
It's out of thinking.
          (*Drunken revellers heard.*)
          Know you, that in that room
Just joining this, King Mark is holding feast,
And may burst in with all his wassailers,
And that the Queen –

Q. Iseult (*above*)
          He's softening to her. Come!
Let us go down, and face this agony!

QUEEN ISEULT *and* BRANGWAIN *descend from the Gallery.*

Iseult the White H.
O, I suppose I must not! And I am tired,
Tired, tired! And now my once-dear Brittany home
Is but a desert to me.
   (Q. ISEULT and BRANGWAIN come forward.)
      – Oh, the Queen!
Can I – so weak – encounter –

Q. Iseult
        Ah – as I thought,
Quite as I thought. It is my namesake, sure!
   (ISEULT THE WHITE H. faints. Indecision.
     BRANGWAIN goes to her.)
Take her away. The blow that bruises her
Is her own dealing. Better she had known
The self-sown pangs of prying ere she sailed!
   BRANGWAIN *carries her out,* TRISTRAM *suddenly assisting at the last moment as far as the door.*

Chanters: Men *(as she is carried)*
   Fluttering with fear,
  Out-tasked her strength has she!
   Loss of her Dear
   Threatening too clear,
  Gone to this length has she!
  Strain too severe!

Scene XV
QUEEN ISEULT, TRISTRAM, AND CHANTERS.

Q. Iseult *(after restlessly watching* TRISTRAM *render aid and return)*
So, after all, am I to share you, then,
With another, Tristram? who, as I count, comes here
To take the Castle as it were her own!

Tristram
Sweet Queen, you said you'd let her come one day!
However, back she's going to Brittany,
Which she should not have left. Think kindly of her,
A weaker one than you!

Q. Iseult
      What, Tristram; what!
O this from you to me, who have sacrificed

Honour and name for you so long, so long!
Why, she and I are oil and water here:
Other than disunite we cannot be.
She weaker? Nay, I stand in jeopardy
This very hour –
    (*Noise of* MARK *and revellers.*)
    Listen to him within!
His peer will pierce your cloak ere long – or would
Were he but sober – and then where am I?
Better for us that I do yield you to her,
And you depart! Hardly can I do else:
In the eyes of men she has all claim to thee
And I have none, yes, she possesses you! –
    (*Turning and speaking in a murmur.*)
– Th' other Iseult possesses him, indeed;
And it was I who set it in his soul
To seek her out! – my namesake, whom I felt
A kindness for – alas, I know not why!
    (*Sobs silently.*)

Chanters: Women
    White-Hands did this,
  Desperate to win again
    Back to her kiss
    One she would miss! –
  Yea, from the Queen again
    Win, for her bliss!

Chanters: Men and Women
    Dreams of the Queen
  Always possessing him
    Racked her yestreen
    Cruelly and keen –
  Him, once professing him
    Hers through Life's scene!

Re-enter BRANGWAIN.

Scene XVI
TRISTRAM, QUEEN ISEULT, BRANGWAIN, AND
    CHANTERS.

BRANGWAIN *stands silent a few moments, till* Q. ISEULT
    turns and looks demandingly at her.

Brangwain
The lady from the other coast now mends.

Q. Iseult (*haughtily*)
Give her good rest. (*Bitterly*) Yes, yes, in sooth I said
That she might come. Put her in mine own bed:
I'll sleep upon the floor!
        Exit BRANGWAIN.

Tristram
        'Tis in your bitterness,
My own sweet Queen, that you speak thus and thus!

  Enter KING MARK *with* SIR ANDRET *to the Gallery,*
  unperceived.

Scene XVII
KING MARK AND SIR ANDRET (*above*): QUEEN ISEULT,
    TRISTRAM, AND CHANTERS.

Sir Andret (*to* K. MARK)
See, here they are. God's 'ounds, sure, then was he
That harper I misdoubted once or twice;
Or must have come while we were clinking cups,
No mischief dreaming!

Tristram
        But, my best-beloved,
Forgo these frets, and think of Joyous Gard!
        (*Approaches her.*)

  Q. Iseult (*drawing back*)
Nay, no more claspings! And if it should be
That these new meetings operate on me
(You well know what I am touching on in this)
Mayhap by year's end I'll not alive,
The which I almost pray for –

K. Mark (*above*)
        Then 'tis so!
Their dalliances are in full gush again,
Though I had deemed them hindered by his stay,
And vastly talked of ties, in Brittany.

Sir Andret
Such is betokened, certes, by their words,
If we but wit them straight.

Tristram
        O Queen my Love,
Pray sun away this cloud, and shine again;

Throw into your ripe voice and burning soul
The music that they held in our aforetime:
We shall outweather this!
      (*Enter* DAMSEL *with a letter.*)
        Who jars us now?

Scene XVIII
QUEEN ISEULT, TRISTRAM, DAMSEL, KING MARK, SIR
    ANDRET, AND CHANTERS.

Damsel (*humbly*)
This letter, brought at peril, noble Knight,
King Mark has writ to our great Over-King –
Aye, Arthur – I the bearer. And I said,
"All that I *can* do for the brave Sir Tristram
That do will I!" So I unscreen this scroll
(A power that chances through a friendly clerk).
In it he pens that as his baneful foe
He hold Sir Tristram, and will wreak revenge
Thrice through his loins as soon as hap may serve.
   KING MARK *descends from Gallery and stands in the*
     background, SIR ANDRET *remaining above.*

Q. Iseult (*aside to* TRISTRAM *with misgivings*)
These threats of Mark against you quail my heart,
And daunt my sore resentment at your wounds
And slights of late! O Tristram, save thyself,
And think no more of me!

Tristram
      Forget you – never!
(*Softly*) Rather the sunflower may forget the sun!
(*To* DAMSEL) Wimple your face anew, wench: go unseen;
Re-seal the sheet, which I care not to con,
And send it on as bid.
      Exit DAMSEL.

Scene XIX
QUEEN ISEULT, TRISTRAM, KING MARK, SIR ANDRET,
    AND CHANTERS.

Tristram
      Sure, Mark was drunk
When writing such! Late he fed heavily
And has, I judge, roved out with his boon knightage
Till evenfall shall bring him in to roost.

Q. Iseult

I wonder! ... (*nestling closer*) I've forebodings, Tristram
    dear;
But, your death's mine, Love!

Tristram

       And yours mine, Sweet Heart! ...
– Now that the hall is lulled, and none seems near,
I'll keep up my old minstrel character
And sing to you, ere I by stealth depart
To wait an hour more opportune for love. –
I could, an if I would, sing jeeringly
Of the king; I mean the song Sir Dinadan
Make up about him. He was mighty wroth
To hear it.

Q. Iseult

  Nay, Love; sadness suits you best ...
Sad, sad are we: we will not jeer at him;
Such darkness overdraws us, it may whelm
Us even with him my master! Sing of love.
       (TRISTRAM *harps a prelude*.)
I hope he may not heel back home and hear!

Tristram (*singing and playing*)

Yea, Love, true is it sadness suits me best!
Sad, sad we are; sad, sad shall ever be.
What shall deliver us from Love's unrest,
And bonds we did not forecast, did not see!

Q. Iseult

Yea, who will dole us, in these chains that chafe,
Bare pity! – O were ye my King – not he!
    (*She weeps, and he embraces her awhile*.)

Tristram (*thoughtfully*)

Where is King Mark? I must be soon away!
   KING MARK, *having drawn his dagger, creeps up*
    behind TRISTRAM.

K.Mark (*in a thick voice*)

He's in his own house, where he ought to be,
Aye, here! where thou'lt be not much longer, man!
   He runs TRISTRAM *through the back with his dagger.*
    QUEEN ISEULT *shrieks*. TRISTRAM *falls,* QUEEN
    ISEULT *sinking down by him with clasped hands.* SIR
    ANDRET *descends quickly from the gallery*.

Tristram (*weakly*)

From you! – against whom never have I sinned
But under sorcery unwittingly,
By draining deep the love-compelling vial
In my sick thirst, as innocently did she! ...
This, when of late you sent me, before
I went to Brittany, to come and help you!
"Fair nephew," said you, "Here upswarm our foes;
They are stark at hand, and must be strongly met
Sans tarriance, or they'll uproot my realm."
"My power," said I, "is all at your command."
I came. I neared in night-time to the gate,
Where the hot host of Sessoines clung encamped;
Killed them at th' entrance, and got in to you,
Who welcomed me with joy. I forth'd again,
Again slew more, and saved the stronghold's fame!
Yet you (*weaker*) requite me thus! You might – have fought
    me!
    (K. MARK *droops his head in silence.*)

Sir Andret

O fie upon thee, traitor, pleading thus!
It profits naught. To-day here sees thee die!

Tristram

O Andret, Andret; this from thee to me –
Thee, whom I onetime held my fastest friend;
Wert thou as I, I would not treat thee so!
    (SIR ANDRET *turns aside and looks down.*)
(*Weaker.*) Fair Knights, bethink ye what I've done for
    Cornwall, –
Its fate was on my shoulder - and I saved it! –
Yea, think in jeopardies I've thrust myself
To fame your knighthood! - daily stretched my arm
For – the weal – of you – all!
            TRISTRAM *dies.*

Q. Iseult

(*springing up, the King standing dazed*)
O murderer, husband called! – possest of me
Against my nature and my pleading tears,
When all my heart was Tristram's – his past wording,
To your own knowledge. Now this mute red mouth
You've gored in my Belovéd, bids me act:
Act do I then. So out you – follow him!
   She snatches KING MARK'S *dagger from his belt and*
     stabs him with it. KING MARK *falls and dies.* QUEEN
     ISEULT *rushes out.* SIR ANDRET*, stooping and*

finding the King dead, follows after the Queen. A few
moments' pause during which the sea and sky
darken, and the wind rises, distant thunder
murmuring. Enter WATCHMAN; *next* BRANGWAIN.

Scene XX
WATCHMAN AND CHANTERS, WITH THE DEAD KING
    AND TRISTRAM; THEN BRANGWAIN.

Watchman
She's glode off like a ghost, with deathy mien;
It seems toward the ledge – yes, she – the Queen.

Brangwain (*entering hurriedly*)
She's over the cliff, and Tristram's brachet with her! ...
What have we here? ... Sir Tristram's body? O!

Chanters: Men
(BRANGWAIN *standing and gradually drooping during*
    their chant)
    Alas, for this wroth day!
  She's leapt the ledge and fallen
    Into the loud black bay,
  Whose waters, loosed and swollen,
    Are spirting into spray!
    She's vanished from the world,
    Over the blind rock hurled;
    And the little hound her friend
    Has made with hers its end!

Chanters: Women
    Alas, for this wroth day!
    Our Tristram, noble knight,
    A match for Arthur's might,
    Lies here as quaking clay.
    This is no falsehood fell,
    But very truth indeed
    That we too surely read!
    Would that we had to tell
    But pleasant truth alway!

Brangwain (*arousing and gazing round*)
Here's more of this same stuff of death.
    Look down –
What see I lying there? King Mark, too, slain?
The sea's dark noise last night, the sky's vast yawn
Of hollow bloodshot cloud, meant murder, then,
As I divined!

Enter ISEULT THE WHITEHANDED, *Queen's Ladies,*
Retainers, Bower-women, and others.

Scene XXI
ISEULT THE WHITEHANDED, BRANGWAIN, QUEEN'S
LADIES, ETC., AND CHANTERS.

Iseult the White H.
I heard her cry. I saw her leap! How fair
She was! What wonder that my brother Kay
Should pine for love of her ... O she should not
Have done it to herself! Nor life nor death
Is worth a special quest.
                (*She sees* TRISTRAM'S *body*.)
                    What's this – my husband?
My Tristram dead likewise? He one with her?
                (*She sinks and clasps* TRISTRAM.)

Chanters: Men and Women
Slain by King Mark unseen, in evil vow,
Who never loved him! Pierced in the back – aye, now,
By sleight no codes of chivalry allow!

Iseult the White H.
And she beholding! *That* the cause wherefor
She went and took her life? He was not hers ...
Yet did she love him true, if wickedly!
  Re-enter SIR ANDRET, *with other Knights, Squires,*
  Herald, etc.

Scene XXII
ISEULT THE WHITEHANDED, BRANGWAIN, SIR
ANDRET, ETC., AND CHANTERS.

Sir Andret (*saturninely*)
Nor sight nor sound of her! A Queen. 'Od's blood,
Her flaws in life get mended by her death,
And she and Tristram sport re-burnished fames!

Iseult the White H.
(*seeing* MARK'S *body*)
And the King also dead? My Tristram's slayer?
Yet strange to me. Then even had I not come
Across the southern water recklessly
This would have shaped the same – the very same.
                (*Turning again to* TRISTRAM)
Tristram, dear husband! O! ...
                (*She rocks herself over him*.)

What a rare beauteous knight has perished here
By this most cruel craft! Could not King Mark
If wronged, have chid him – minded him of me,
And not done this, done this! Well, well; she's lost him,
Even as have I. – This stronghold moans with woes,
And jibbering voices join with winds and waves
To make a dolorous din! ...
      (*They lift her.*)
      Aye, I will rise –
Betake me to my own dear Brittany –
Dearer in that our days there were so sweet,
Before I knew what pended me elsewhere!
These halls are hateful to me! May my eyes
Meet them no more!
      (*She turns to go.*)

Brangwain
      I will attend you, Madam.
  Exit ISEULT THE WHITEHANDED *assisted by*
    BRANGWAIN *and Bowerwomen. Knights, retainers,*
    etc., lift the bodies and carry them out. A dirge by the
    Chanters.

Epilogue

Re-enter MERLIN.
  Thus from the past, the throes and themes
  Whereof I spake – now dead as dreams –
    Have been re-shaped and drawn
  In feinted deed and word, as though
  Our shadowy and phantasmal show
  Were very movements to and fro
    Of forms so far-off gone.

  These warriors and dear women, whom
  I've called, as bidden, from the tomb,
    May not have failed to raise
  An antique spell at moments here?
  – They were, in their long-faded sphere,
  As you are now who muse thereat;
  Their mirth, crimes, fear and love begat
    Your own, though thwart their ways;
  And may some pleasant thoughts outshape
  From this my conjuring to undrape
    Such ghosts of distant days!

37   The Coming of Arthur by John Baragwanath King (1925)

Persons represented:

Uter Pendragon	King of Britain.
Gothlois	Earl of Cornwall.
Bricot	Follower of Gothlois.
Ursan	Follower of Pendragon.
Merlin	A Wizard.
Jubelin	A Disciple of St. Piran.
Alward	Porter of Tintagel.
Igerna	Wife to Gothlois.

Good Spirits, Evil Spirits, Servitors, Henchmen.

Opening scene, – A wild heath before Tintagel. Evening.

After victories over the Saxons, Uter Pendragon celebrates them by a feast at Caersegont. At this gathering the king becomes infatuated with Igerna, wife to the Cornish Earl Gothlois. Fired with jealousy, Gothlois with his duchess and servants leave Caersegont. He refuses to return at the bidding of the lustful king. Knowing this, Pendragon treats Gothlois as his enemy, and with his troops the king invades Cornwall. For greater safety the Cornish Earl sends Igerna to Tintagel Castle while he holds Demeliock against the King and his troops. On learning that Igerna is at Tintagel the King repairs there. Finding it impregnable, one of the king's followers counsels Pendragon to send for Merlin the magician, whose art will enable the lewd King to enter the castle, and obtain his desire with Igerna. The scene opens where Pendragon with impatience awaits the coming of Merlin. Spirits of Evil in the form of witches are first heard in chorus. Later they show themselves. Ursan seeing the King's dejection speaks to his master remindingly.

Song of the Witches:
Far-off thunder growling low,
     Lightning flash of elfin hate;
Speak, ye oracles of woe,
     Read Pendragon's ordered fate.
Blow, ye winds of darkness, blow,
     O'er Atlantic's ebon gloom;
Voice Pendragon's weal or woe,
     Sing for Uter bliss or doom.

Pendragon the fearless now halts on the moor,
     The moor of Richardoc by Cornwall's dark sea;
His war-horse is freighted with armour full sore,
     And Uter Pendragon is sick as can be,
          As Ursan well knows,

And the sickness of it grows.
And as his sore chieftain goes stamping on the ground,

Ursan:
He cries "Mighty Uter, fain well would I see,
Pendragon again, where the battle's crash sound;
Not here where the moor-fowl in terror doth flee;
But in the brave fight,
'Gainst henchman and knight;
But here, my liege lord, thou art held in duress,
Whilst thy henchmen are fretting to be in the fray;
Then arouse thee Pendragon, thy dolour confess
To the presbyter[1] Piran who passed hence to-day,
And will yet anon,
Ere night well is gone."

Jubelin:
"Who calleth on Piran? be it Ursan the bear?"
Cries a voice from the gloom of the hastening day:–
"I, Jubelin, I, from that sainted isle fair,
Am chanting for Piran his joy-bearing lay:–
Ye folk of this land,
Good tidings at hand;
No longer be dumb,
Christ Jesu is come;
Sweet Mary's first born,
Is come to adorn,
This world its true king,
This lay then I sing."

Song of the Witches:
Heighho! what a song to sing,
Take thy cross and chant and go;
Stung by love is Britain's King,
Fired by lust for weal or woe.

Jubelin:
"'Tis the spirit of the night singing dolorous fear,"
Cries Jubelin softly, "But, Uter, take heed;
From the caverns of night rush these forebodings drear;
But glad are the tidings I bring to thy need.
Then list thee, great king,
'Tis glory I sing."

Pendragon:
"Stay, stay!" cries Pendragon, "wist thee now that thy song,
Is one perchance fitting my dolour and gloom?

Get thee hence lest my anger may do thee sad wrong,
By sending another daft wight to his doom!"

Ursan:
"My liege pray beware,"
Cries Ursan the bear.

Witches:
"Ho, ho!" cry the witches appearing in black,
"Pendragon give ear to our cure for thy woe;
This witless forerunner of Piran alack,
Hath nothing to ease thee, or pleasure to show;
Then list to our lay.
Cast dolour away;
Give vent to thy lust,
This life is but bust;
Come darkness thy spell,
Cloak virtue full well;
Come spirits below,
All sprightly and show,
Pendragon the bliss,
That soon will be his."

Jubelin:
"Beware great Pendragon!" cries young Jubelin:–
"These beldames would wreck thee thy now drifting
soul;
This cross I uplift will cleanse thee thy sin;
On this cross Jesu died to make thee well whole,
His life he did give,
That all men might live;
Then look, Britain's king,
On this symbol and sing."

Pendragon:
"Sing, dost thou say!" crieth Uter in scorn:–
"Thinkest thou that thy Jesu hath valour to aid
Pendragon the king – Pendragon forlorn;
Thy cross is no cure for a heart over weighed.
And now get thee gone,
Or prithee anon,
My henchmen may make
Thy cross for thy stake;
And serve thee as He
Was hung on the tree."

Witches:
"Ho, ho!" cry the beldames, "Pendragon hath wit;
Beshrew us the king knoweth better his want;

Than presbyter's clerk, or starved Jesuit,
　　With a lay for a curse, and a cross for a taunt.
　　　　But hark ye great king,
　　　　If thou wilt now fling,
　　　　Thy purse as a dole,
　　　　For the ease of thy soul;
　　　　Or ten hides of land,
　　　　To Piran's poor band,
He'll absolve thee the lust now freighting thy mind,
　　And set thee no penance thy vice to defend;
For Satan our master made riches to bind,
　　A man to make pleasure his aim and his end!
　　　　Then toss him thy purse,
　　　'Twill stay him his curse;
　　　　He'll absolve thee thy lust,
　　　　As if it were just."

Jubelin:
"Beware, oh Pendragon!" cries young Jubelin;–
　"Beware of these hags with evil endowed;
Their sneers and their scoffs but burden thy sin,
　Look then to this cross with thy head duly bowed;
　　　And thank him great king,
　　　In fealty sing;
　　　Exalt him above,
　　　For all his great love."

Pendragon:
"Thank Him!" cries Pendragon, "Get hence, Jubelin;
　Take this bauble away; to Tintagel I hie;
And if there the devil will bid me come in?
　　On the name of the devil I vow I will cry;
　　　And own him as lord,
　　　By blood and by sword!"

Merlin:
"Who crieth for me?" sounds a voice from the gloom,

Ursan:
"What, Merlin!" cries Ursan all witless with fear;

Merlin:
"Aye, Ursan. I haste to put into the room,
　　Of Gothlois, Pendragon in Gothlois' brave gear;
　　　Then hail me great king,
　　　That thou long'st for I bring.
Thy starved desire shall no longer be lean;
　　Igerna shall greet thee with jest and with lay;

She'll dance to thee, Uter, like Egypt's dark queen;
    And this night of thy love shall be brighter than day,
        While Gothlois her lord,
        With spear and with sword;
        Shall hold Demeliock,
        'Gainst battering shock;
        Till the day dawneth red,
        Thou shalt lie in his bed!
        While he travails in toil,
        Thou his lady shall spoil!
        With thy jest and thy kiss,
        Thou shalt rob him his bliss!
        Thou shalt lust to thy fill
        By my magic's skill!"

Jubelin:
"Stay, stay, great Pendragon!" young Jubelin doth cry;

Pendragon:
"Away!" cries the king, "Away with the loon!"

Witches:
Ho, ho!" cry the witches, "Though dark be the sky,
Yet darker for Gothlois 'twill be ere the noon
        See the sun shine again,
        On Demeliock's plain;
        For there he will die!
        And there he will lie.
        Then shout mighty king,
        Tintagel shall ring,
        For to-night shall be got
        That prince without blot!"

Song of the Good Spirits:
    Dark though by the night of sin,
        Love with turn the gloom to day;
    Evil cloaked will wander in,
        Evil bared will flee away!

Song of the Witches:
    Whisper softly, winds above,
        Softly as the flight of owl;
    O'er Tintagel hovers love,
        To your caverns, sprite and ghoul!
    To your dread abodes be gone,
        Well your master's work have done;
    Stay your nightly toils anon,
        Fate has well her task begun.

Tintagel's lone keep is reared 'gainst a sky,
    All swollen with clouds rolling over the deep;
While birds of the darkness now echo the cry,
    Of the sad moaning sea by the lone castle's keep.
        Not a star or a light,
        Cheers the blackness of night;
        But Merlin's sage art,
        Makes Pendragon start!
        He opens his eyes,
        He stares with surprise;
        For gone is the night,
        All round him is light!

Merlin:
"Now gaze at the castle," cries Merlin, "awhile,
    Thy henchmen with sleep-dusted eyes lie around;
Through walls thou now seest Igerna's rare smile,
    While her chamber is ringing with twanging harp's
    sound.
        And now she doth chaff,
        Now with handmaid doth laugh;
        She thinks of her lord,
        Now fighting with sword;
        Now fighting to flee,
        From thy henchmen and thee.
Yet gaze thee, Pendragon, as woman she's fair,
    As ever was woman from the first woman Eve;
Or Helen of Troy – or the goddess who bare
    Ulysses the wanderer whom none could deceive.
        And not well her grace
        Her form and her face!
        Her white shining feet,
        So subtle and fleet;
        Her skin like the snow,
        Her hair flowing low;
        But witless is she,
        That peeping eyes see."
Pendragon is fuming for again it is dark,
    But burning is he with unquenchable fire;

Pendragon:
Then he crieth "O Merlin thou has not lit the spark,
    That fires my sad longings with maddened desire!
        Then Merlin I cry,
        With Igerna I'll lie;
        I'll lie in her bed,
        Or by her lie dead!"
'Tis bustle in hall as servitors all,

Of lonely Tintagel are rushing about;
For loud is the cry from a far reaching call,
And the rattling of armour and weapons without.

Alward:
"Who now cometh nie?"
The porter doth cry.
"What villainous wight,
Stirreth castle at night!"

Merlin:
"Lower drawbridge, good Alward," cries Merlin disguised; –
"Lower quickly for Gothlois the earl draweth near."

Alward:
"Be it Jordan who cries?" speaks the porter surprised;

Merlin:
"Aye and Bricot, with Gothlois, from Demeliock drear."
Crieth Merlin as lock,
And creaking of block;
And rattling of chain,
Are sounding again.
And now the three plotters are all housed within,
While dark is the sky by portcullis and keep;
But 'tis merry in hall with the merry tongues din,
And many door ope, and many eyes peep;
While Uter is led,
To Igerna's bed;
While Gothlois her lord,
With buckler and sword,
Is staying the shock,
Against Demeliock.

Song of the Witches:
Birds of night fly o'er the sea,
Singing songs of bliss or woe;
Bat and owl ope eyes and see,
What Tintagel hath to show.
Wind of night blow high, blow low,
Fan the flame of man's desire;
Blow ye mightily and glow
Into flame the smouldering fire.

Song of the Good Spirits:
When the heart no evil knows;
Evil ne'er will enter in;
But the guile that evil sows,
Soon will reap the tares of sin.

Igerna:

"Dear lord!" cries Igerna, "Now fain I would cry,
     For Bricot brought word that bold Uter the king
Had held thee in thrall, but now thou art nigh,
         In gladness I greet thee, good husband, and sing:–
             With love cometh light,
             No longer 'tis night;
             But list thee I pray,
             To my heartfelt lay:–
         The red lamps in the northern sky,
             Streamed fiercely yesternight;
         And then I keened by Bricot's sigh,
             That sorely waxed the fight.
         The lamps paled wan, and then he cried:–
             'My lord is held in thrall;'
         The darkness came and then he sighed:–
             'Sweet Mary save us all!'
         And then on her blest name I prayed;
             And prayed my lord for thee;
         And now sweet Mary – heavenly maid,
             Has sent my lord to me!
         And as I passed from tower to hall,
             Stars one by one did peep;
         When Bricot murmured, 'Save us all;
             God watch us while we sleep.'
         Then blithe in hall strove Jubelin,
             And to the henchmen cried;
         'A lord is come to drive out sin;
             His grace spans far and wide.'
         And as lamps flared and smoked in hall,
             And henchmen bowed their head;
         This blithesome clerk came to my call,
             And this is what he said:–
         'Our winsome Jesu high above,
             Kens well there be no sin,
         In bliss of holy-wedded love,
             Sore evil ne'er comes in.'
         Thus well it fares my welcome lord,
             But trow no ill of me;
         I've bared my heart by spoken word,
             That my dear lord may see."
Pendragon the fearless now faintly doth smile,
     As the voice of the porter is heard from afar;
Then he turns to Igerna and mutters in guile:–

Pendragon:

I come my beloved from sword-clashing war;
     But though lamps may light,

The northern sky bright;
Though billows may roar;
And fight waxeth sore;
Though flame smoke in hall,
And henchmen bow all;
While I live, till I die,
Got wot, well I cry:–
"My winsome blithe lady Igerna my queen,
Now long lag the hours ere the cock croweth day;
For to-night once again is our bridal I ween?
When love shall enthral us till dawn gleameth grey."

Song of the Witches:
Keeper of the midnight skies,
Put your stars out one by one;
Morn all blushing doth arise,
Merlin's magic work is done.
'Tis terror in hall as servitors all
Are snatching their weapons with faces severe;
For with coming of day there soundeth a call,
A call from the gate sore laden with fear:–

Bearer:
"Bold Gothlois is dead!
And Bricot is fled!
High placed Dameliock,
Lies low with the shock,
And now in the hands,
Of Uter's lewd bands!"

Pendragon:
"What news?" crieth Uter who cometh in sight,
"What news prithee bearer I ask thee again?"
But the bearer at Uter stares with affright,
For Gothlois his lord he saw lying slain!
But as he thus stares,
Bold Alward he dares,

Alward:
To thunder – "Close gate!"
But ere he could prate,
Merlin hammered his fist,

Merlin:
And cried, "Gentles, list:–
'Tis Merlin you see,
A prophet I be;
But list ye, good folk, before I pass by,

Look yonder, 'tis Uter, not Gothlois you see;
And gaze fair Igerna, sans dolour or sigh,
    'Tis Britain's great king, and his queen thou shalt be."

Igerna is staring while tears her eyes well,
    For Uter, and Merlin, and Ursan once more,
Are as they e'er were, before Merlin's spell,
    Gave Uter, Igerna to hold and adore.
        But as he comes by,
        And heareth her sigh;
        He taketh her hand:–

Pendragon:
    "Fair one of this land;
    By the sun and the moon,
    By this heyday of noon;
    By this Cornishland's sod,
    By the Christian man's God,
    Igerna I swear,
    Thy ring I will wear;
And when thy late lord is laid low in the grave,
    By this token of gold my queen thou shalt be;
Then dry thy blue een – in blithness be brave,
    For Britain shall offer proud homage to thee."

Song of the Witches:
    Sun shines bright on tower and keep,
        Wind blows softly over the sea;
    List our chant comes from the deep,
        List to lay from witches three.
    She shall long be Britain's queen,
        Uter's days the briefest time;
    From a fount by mosses green,
        Death shall take him in his prime.

Song of the Good Spirits:
    Sun shines over Pol and Pen,[2]
        Once again is summer's light;
    Fair Igerna smiles again,
        Tears are gone, and all is bright.
    Time for aye her beauty sing,
        And for Arthur thus begot;
    Laud for Britain's valiant king,
        Ne'er shall be his name forgot.

Thus in this castle by the Cornish sea,
    And in the fashion herein boldly told;
We thus begotten one whose fame shall be,

A song unending till the world be old.
He lived for Love, and e'er for Love would fight;
But if he loved, yet loved he Honour more;
Undaunted he, he fought the cause of Right;
For God, and land, his sword he ever bore.
And thus went Arthur o'er the sunlit sea,
Borne to a land of never ending day;
Where valiant hearts, their fighting o'er may be
Enshrined with those whose fame shall live for aye.

38 Anglice, a Patriotic Song of our Motherland[1] by Katharine Lee Jenner (1926)

Throned above the western sea,
  Battleground of forces grim,
Holy Motherland, for thee
  We thy children raise our hymn;
Scattered over all the earth
  Loving hearts we turn alway
To the Land that gave us birth,
  And for thee our voices pray.

On the billows wild and free,
  In the darkness of the mine,
Wheresoe'er thy children be
  Evermore they shall be thine;
Thine in thoughts of sounding seas,
  Downs with heath and furze aglow,
  Thine in glorious memories
  Of thy heroes long ago.

Thine was Arthur, thine his knights,
  Strong Geraint his admiral,
Lancelot of a hundred fights,
  Tristan, Gawain, Percival.
Thine were they in shining mail
  Through thy forest ways who trod,
Seeking for the Holy Grail,
  Mystery of the Faith of God.

To that Faith thy sons were true,
  In its hour of darkest night,
Dared to die, a faithful few,
  Worsted in that hopeless fight.
Sons of thine with Grenville fell
  For their King in Lansdown's[2] fray;
Let the Royal Letter tell
  How they failed him not that day.

Michael of the Guarded Mount,
    Saints before God's Face who stand,
Keyna of the hallowed fount,
    Piran of the drifting sand,
Petrock of the iron shore,
    Ruan of the southern strand,
Ia, Breage – a hundred more,[3]
        Watch and ward our native land!
        One and all, on you we call;
        Pray for Cornwall, One and All!

39   Tintagel Castle in History and Romance by Henry Jenner (1927)

There is very little to say about Tintagel in real authentic history. What is now the parish may have been a place of some importance during the Roman occupation of Britain, but the existence of two Roman milestones, one of 251–253 and the other of 313–323, show little more than that a Roman road ran through the district, the objective of which was perhaps the estuary of the Camel at Padstow. Most of the possible Roman roads in Cornwall led to seaports. The promontory of Tintagel may have been a cliff fortress in very early, even perhaps pre-Roman, times – the situation is too good to have been neglected – but of this no evidence remains. Such a fortress may have become a religious establishment of Celtic saints or monks at a later period, and the presence of the evidently Celtic chapel of St. Ulyst or Julitta and of Christian interments of perhaps the 5th or 6th century, and the fact that it came into the possession of the monks of St. Petrock's, Bodmin, seem to indicate something of the sort. There are several cases in which disused forts were taken over by monks. But all this must needs be pure conjecture. The evidence is very slight. There is nothing certain until the Domesday Survey of 1086. At that time the Church of St. Petrock owned a large number of manors, and one of these was that of Botcinnii, now Bossiney, in which was the headland now called Tintagel. Of this manor it is said: –

Ide(m) com(es) ten(et) de S. Petroc(o) Botcinnii. Eluui teneb(at) T(empore) R (egis) et n(on) poterat a S(ancto) sep(ar)ari. Ibi e(st) i hida. t(er)ra vi car(rucatae). Ibi e(st) i car(ruca) cu(m) i seruo et ui uill(an)i et iii bord(arii) et xxx ac(rae) pasturæ. Oli(m) xx solid (os) modo val(et) xu solid(os).

[The same Earl (i.e., Robert, Earl of Mortain, half-brother of William the Conqueror) holds of St. Petrock Botcinnii. Eluui held it in the time of King Edward, and it could not be alienated from the Saint. There is one hide (vaguely about 120 acres). The (arable) land is six carucates (or plough-lands, a carucate being originally the amount of land that could be managed with one plough and its oxen, but it was rather a vague measure). There is one plough with one serf and six villani (i.e., unfree tenants attached to the soil, but not saleable apart from it) and four bordarii (i.e., small tenants or cottagers, also unfree) and thirty acres of pasture. Formerly 20 shillings, now it is worth 15 shillings.]

Even if you take the present value of money at thirty times its value in 1086, it will appear that the rateable value of Bossiney has gone up considerably. Nothing is said of the existence of any castle in the manor then, but not long after that a castle was built in what is now the hamlet of Bossiney, where a great mound still marks its site.

Later, the manor becomes the property of the Earls of Cornwall, and some time in the reign of Henry II, certainly after the death in 1175 of Reginald FitzHenry, illegitimate son of Henry I, to whom King Stephen had granted the Earldom of Cornwall in 1140, Henry FitzCount, illegitimate son of Reginald, who farmed the Earldom on behalf of John, afterwards King, granted the manor of Bossiney and the Castle of Tintagel to Gervase de Hornacot (in Tamerton) who then called himself "Gervase de Tintajoel". There must have been a castle of Tintagel with that name to it as early as the publication in 1148 of Geoffrey of Monmouth's "Historia Regum Britanniae", and probably as early as the lost first recension of that history, which was seen by Henry of Huntingdon in the Abbey of Bec in Normandy in 1139. If, as I am inclined to believe, the so-called "Chronicle of Tysilio" is a Welsh translation of the now lost Latin of Geoffrey's first recension, Tintagel was certainly mentioned there. This puts the date of the building of the castle and the attaching of the name of Tintagel to it at some time between 1086 and 1139. What Geoffrey has to say about it belongs to romance rather than to history, but his mention of it is valuable as providing a *terminus ad quem* for its building and naming. There was a castle which was called Tintagel at least as early as 1139. How much earlier we have no means of knowing. The name has always been a puzzle. The form *Dundagel*, used by, among others, Tennyson and Hawker, is late – not earlier than the 14th century. The 12th century manuscripts of Geoffrey give it *Tintagel*, *Tingagol*, *Tintagaol*.[1] A very early documentary form is *Tintaiol*, the *i* representing a *j*, which is that of some French romances. It is evident that the *g* was always soft, a sound which does not come into Cornish until it appears as a corruption of *d* before a thin vowel in the quite late stages of the language. It is therefore very improbable that it is a Cornish name, and the only possible alternative is that it is Norman French. There is a rock called "Tente d'Agel" or "Tente d'Ageau" in the island of Sark, which is locally said to mean the "Castle of the Devil," and there is a hill nearly 4,000 feet in height called "Mont Angel", about six miles to the north-east of Monte Carlo. (There is a strong modern fort on the top of the latter and the golf-links are at the foot of it). What "agel" may mean I do not know. There is also a Val d'Ajol, near Plombières, on the edge of the Vosges mountains. It is just possible, since the castle of Tintagel was on occasions used as a prison, that the last syllable is the Norman French and old French *gaiole* or *jaiole*, modern French *geôle*, English *gaol* or *jail*, a prison. But I am not satisfied with that derivation.

The grant to Gervase de Hornacot was confirmed by King John in 1215, and the family of "de Hornacot" or "de Tintaioel" held the property until in 1235 it was acquired in exchange for other manors by Richard, Earl of Cornwall, afterwards King of the Romans, if not actually Emperor. Since then it has been in the possession of the Earls and Dukes of Cornwall. It is probable that Richard rebuilt the castle and that the present ruins are the remains of his building. He also gave its first borough-charter to Bossiney, and he gave the church of Tintagel to the Abbey of Fontevrault in Anjou, where so many of his relations, including his mother, Isabel of Angoulême, and his grandfather, Henry II, were buried. In 1245 Richard got into trouble with his brother, Henry III, for harbouring at Tintagel their nephew Dafydd ap Llywelyn, Prince of North Wales, whose mother was Joan, daughter of King John. Dafydd had made war upon his uncle and had got very much the worst of it. As he died at Aber Castle in Carnarvonshire in 1246, his stay at Tintagel was not very long.

Later the castle was held by constables appointed by the Earls, who were often Sheriffs of Cornwall, but in 1337, when John of Eltham, son of Edward II, the last Earl of Cornwall, died, the priest in charge of the chapel doubled the parts of chaplain and constable, the latter office evidently not amounting to much. At that time the castle was becoming ruinous and appears to have been of small extent, two rooms beyond two weak gates, a room with a small kitchen, stabling for eight horses, a cellar and a ruined bake-house.

In the time of Richard II the castle was sometimes used as a prison. Carew says that John Northampton, Lord Mayor of London, was imprisoned there – it was in 1385 – and in 1397 Thomas Beauchamp, Earl of Warwick, who had been one of the Regency Commission of the King's uncle, Thomas, Duke of Gloucester, was sent there as a prisoner, and remained there until Richard was deposed in 1399. Various constables were appointed from time to time by the Dukes of Cornwall or, when there was no Duke, by the Sovereign, but as the Castle become more and more ruinous the office became a sinecure.

Leland in about 1540 describes the ruins at some length and conjectures what it must have been in its best days. According to him there were originally three wards, of which two "be woren away with gulphyng yn of the se, insomuch that yt hath made there almost an isle and no way is to enter ynto hyt now but by long elme trees layde for a bryge". He says that "shepe now fede within the dungeon," as they still do, and that "the residew of the buildings of the castel be sore wether-beten and yn ruine". He mentions the chapel of St. Ulette alis Uliane as still standing and calls it later "a pretty chapel with a tumbe on the left side".

In 1583 Sir Richard Grenville reported on the condition of the castle, and found that some of the rooms might "be made fite to be dwelt in" with some small charge, but that a great deal had been under-mined by the sea. Richard Carew in 1602 gives a short description of of it as a complete ruin, though he says that the drawbridge to the island had existed "within men's remembrance", and Norden much about the same time made a drawing of much more extensive build-ings than the walls still remaining. Borlase's description and engrav-ing (1754) show that a great deal of destruction had happened since Norden's time, but that the remains were more extensive than now. In 1855 the chapel, which would seem to have been kept up and used for some time after the rest of the castle had been allowed to fall into ruin, probably down to the Reformation period, was excavated and found to be 54ft. by 12ft. The stone altar, a stone bench along the walls, and some graves lined with slate were discovered, and may now be seen. It is not quite clear that the chapel was visible in Borlase's time, for he only mentions it in a quotation from Leland.

This is all the known *history* of Tintagel Castle, and for a building so famous it is singularly little. One point with regard to it is worth mentioning. There are four Norman castles of importance in Cornwall, which belonged to the Earls, Dunheved or Launceston, Restormel, Trematon and Tintagel. Some years ago, Mr. Otho Peter pointed out that these four castles are at the angles of an almost exact square with sides of twenty miles. This may have been intentional. and certainly reminds one of the famous Austrian "Quadrilateral" of Verona, Mantua, Peschiera and Legnago, which was of such strategic importance in 1860. Dunheved and Trematon are mentioned as cas-tles of the Earl in Domesday Book. Restormel was built later, no doubt by the Cardinans, from whom it passed to Thomas de Tracy by his marriage with Ysolt de Cardinan in 1264. From him it pased almost immediately to Simon de Montford and very soon after to Earl Richard, so that Restormel was not actually built for the Earls. You have already heard the little that is known of the origin of Tintagel.

In romance Tintagel has an importance very much out of propor-tion to the curiously little that is said about it even there. The earliest mention of the castle known to exist anywhere is as I have said, in Geoffrey of Monmouth's "History of the King of Britain", of which the first recension, now lost, appeared in about 1139. If the Welsh Chronicle of Tysillio is, as I think probable, a translation of Geoffrey's lost first recension, it certainly contained the same story, though in different wording, as does the extant Latin second recension, which appeared in 1148. Once only is Tintagel mentioned by Geoffrey. He tells how Uther Pendragon, King of Britain, fell deeply in love with Igerna, the beautiful wife of Gorlois, Duke of Cornwall, who very nat-urally objecting to the King's marked attentions to her, took her away from the court and returned to Cornwall. Uther sent after him and ordered him to bring her back, and when he refused, invaded Cornwall with a large army. Gorlois put his wife for safety into the town (oppidum) of Tintagel, on the sea shore and himself entered the castle of Dimilioc, where Uther besieged him. While Gorlois was shut up in Dimilioc, Uther with the help of Merlin, devised a scheme by which he could get to Igerna. By magic, Merlin transformed the King into the likeness of Gorlois, Ulfin of Ricardoc, a personal attendant of Uther, into that of Jordan of Tintagel, and himself into that of one Bricel or Britel, as the French romances call him, these two being attendants of Gorlois. They rode to Tintagel, and were admitted to the castle, where everyone, including Igerna herself, believed them to be what they appeared to be. Meanwhile Gorlois made a sortie from Dimilioc and was slain. Later Uther, who had gone away in the morning, returned to Tintagel, took the castle, and eventually married Igerna. There is a little by-play of puzzle when in the morning messengers come to announce the death of Gorlois and find him apparently sitting there quite alive. But Uther keeps up the deception with some very unabashed lying and all goes well. Geoffrey does not say that Arthur, the son of Uther and Igerna, was born at Tintagel nor do the romances which follow him.

Arthur was no doubt a real historical character and there is no reason to disbelieve the statement that he was the son of Uther and Igerna; but Geoffrey's account of how it came about certainly, as Mr. Weller would say, "werges on the poetical" and must be counted as romance, not as history. Also I think that Geoffrey is wrong in placing the incident, even if it ever happened at all, at Tintagel. He claims to use as his authority an old book in the British tongue which Walter, the Archdeacon of Oxford, brought out of Brittany. There is no need to disbelieve in the existence of this book, for Archdeacon Walter was still living when Geoffrey's History appeared, and apparently never contradicted him. I think this book certainly mentioned Dimilioc, which is not a likely name for Geoffrey to have invented, and it is a real place, mentioned as *Dimelihoc* in Domesday, and still known as *Domellick* or *Dameliock*. It is in St. Dennis parish and the castle was probably the circular earthwork in which the church now stands. The old British book was not likely to mention a castle with a French name, which could not have been more than half a century old when Geoffrey wrote. I am inclined of think that if the book was in Cornish, Welsh or Breton it simply said the *Dinas* – it will be noted that Geoffrey calls Tintagel *oppidum* and *dinas* in Welsh certainly and probably in Cornish also, though it only occurs in place-names there, a city or fortified town. In Welsh it is the regular word for a city. And I believe that the book really meant Castle-an-Dinas in St. Columb, which is visible at a few miles distance from Dameliock, and that Tintagel, which is 25 miles off, had nothing to do with Uther, Igerna or Arthur. How and when it first got to be claimed as Arthur's *birthplace* also I do not know.

The French "Merlin", the first of the great cycle of the standard Arthurian romances, tells Geoffrey's story of Arthur's origin at great length, amplifying it considerably, but only by fanciful conversations, and adding little of importance, except that Gorlois was certainly killed *before* Uther got to Tintagel. Malory follows the French, but cuts it down a good deal, and he calls the other castle, which the French form does not name, "Terrabil". I do not know his authority for this name. The nearest Cornish name is *Treravel* in St. Ervan, also not very far from Castle-an-Dinas.

This is Geoffrey's only mention of Tintagel. The developed romances of the real Arthurian cycle mention it very little after this incident. Lancelot on one occasion came to a long bridge and, as Malory says, "there start upon him a passing foul churl", who smote his horse on the nose and tried to stop him. Lancelot, as was his usual practice in such cases, made short work of him, and split his head down. At the end of the bridge was a fair village, and beyond this was a castle, where Lancelot killed two giants and set the castle free. On enquiry he got for answer "Fair Sir, the name of this castle is Tintagel and a duke owned it some time that had wedded fair Igraine and after wedded her Uther Pendragon," and he goes on to say that they were the parents of Arthur. In the "Perceval" of Chrétien de Troyes, one of the earlier Grail romances, Gawain goes to a tournament at the castle of Tiebaut of Tingaguel, and there is a pretty incident of the child daughter of Tiebaut who claims him as her knight. But though the name is similar and is actually one of the misspellings of Tintagel in early MSS. of Geoffrey, there is nothing to identify it with the castle of Igerna. In Wolfram of Eschenbach's "Parzival" the same story is told, but the name of Tingaguel does not appear. In the "Perlesvaux" or "Perceval li Gallois", the Grail romance, of which my friend the late Dr. Sebastian Evans made a very fine translation under the title of "The High History of the Holy Grail," which I use in the following quotations, Arthur, Lancelot and Gawain riding together incogniti "come to a little castle in a combe. They came thitherward and saw that the enclosure of the castle was fallen down into an abysm, so that none might approach it on that side, but it had a right fair gateway and a door tall and wide." There was also a fair and rich chapel, and an old priest came out of the chapel and told them that this was the great Tintagel. They asked him why the ground was all caved in about the castle, and he told them the story of Gorlois, Uther, Igerna and Merlin's magic, "and," he ended, "for this sin hath the ground sunken in on this wise." This was the first that Arthur heard of it. "King Arthur hath heard this as concerning his birth that he knew not, and is a little shamed thereof and confounded on account of Messire Gawain and Lancelot, and much it misliketh him that the priest hath said so much." A little later Arthur at the tournament of the Golden Circlet is asked who he is, and answers "My name is Arthur and I am of Tincardoil," which seems to be a portmanteau word made up of "Tintagel" and "Carduel." And this is all about Tintagel in the true Arthurian and Grail Cycle. After the not altogether creditable incident Tintagel drops out of the story. Carleon-on-Usk, which, I think, ought really to be Carlyon in Kea, Camelot, Carduel, "Pannenoisance that is on the sea," which may be Penzance, Kelliwic in Cornwall, which Mr. Charles Henderson has rather convincingly identified with Kellybury in Egloshayle, Winchester, York, and even London are scenes of incidents in Arthur's career, but Tintagel is done with.

But there is one series of quasi-Arthurian romances in which it plays a very important part, not as King Arthur's, but as King Mark's Castle. In an early form of the Tristan romance, the French poem of Béroul, King Mark's residence is at Lancien, which M. Loth has identified with Lantine in Golant, and the whole topography of the poem is along the south coast of Cornwall. In the interesting English version by Thomas of Ercildoune, edited in 1821 by Sir Walter Scott, no name is given, but in the later poems, in the German version of Gottfried von Strassburg, and in the great prose romance followed by Malory, the greater part of the incident takes place at Tintagel. It is on an island in the sea by Tintagel, now invisible, that Tristan fights with the Irish champion Morholt or Morhaus. The various secret meetings with Queen Ysolt, narrow escapes and resourceful evasions, take place there. It was at Tintagel that Eliot the harper sang "the lay that Sir Dinadan made by King Mark, which was the worst lay that ever harper sang with harp or with any other instrument," and finally it was at Tintagel, according to the prose romance, that King Mark treacherously slew Tristan, or according to the poems, in which Mark is a much nicer person, it was to Tintagel that the King ordered the bodies of Tristan and Ysolt to be brought from Brittany and buried in fine tombs. The probably original Tristan story knew nothing of Tintagel, but before the later poems and the prose romances were written it had been, so to speak, "boomed" by Geoffrey, and the authors, who unlike the clerical writers of the standard Arthurian cycle, had no wish to point any moral, but only to write a good story – a "best-seller" of the period, as indeed it turned out to be – found in Tintagel a suitable atmosphere. When the clerical moralists captured the Arthurian cycle to serve a definite religous purpose, its scandalous associations – for the plea of magic, which perhaps was Igerna's attempt to save her reputation, was a little unconvincing even for the 12th century – rendered Tintagel an unsuitable place for the high ideals of the Knights of the Round Table, and so it was just dropped. The Tristan story was on a different plane.

Altogether, Tintagel Castle, considering how famous it is, especially in modern imitations of Arthurian romances, has singularly little history and not much romance attached to it, when one comes to sum it up, and it was probably not really the scene of the one incident that brought it into notice. Historically and romantically Tintagel Castle is rather a fraud.

40 *From* **Ceremonies of the Gorseth of the Bards of Cornwall (1928–present)**

XIII.   *The Sword of King Arthur*[1]

Deputy Grand Bard: Still Arthur watches our shore,
In guise of a Chough there flown;
His Kingdom he keep his own,
Once King, to be King once more.

All the Bards: King Arthur is not dead!

Grand Bard: Behold a Sword which represents Excalibur, the Sword of King Arthur, which came from the lake, and went to the Lake again. Will you swear upon it to be ever loyal to Cornwall, our Motherland?

All the Bards: We swear it!

XIV.   *Song: Old Land of our Sires*

Old country of our fathers thy children love thee,
Dear land of the west, what country is thy equal?
Over all the world we are scattered abroad,
But all our love is thine.

Chorus – Cornwall! Cornwall! we love Cornwall;
While the sea is around thee like a wall
We are one and all for Cornwall!

Kingdom of Arthur, the Saints and the Grail
Move loved by us is no other land
In thee every carn, valley, hill and house
Speaks in Cornish to us.

All Cry: Cornwall for ever!

41 *From* **King Arthur's Territory by J. Hambley Rowe (1929)**

Arthur's Twelve Battles:
    Much has been written about the sites of these battles and they have been located all over England. One writer has imagined them all to have been fought in Southern Scotland and Northumberland. Nennius,[1] who records them, says the first was at the mouth of a river which is called Glein, the next four were upon a river called Dubglas in the region of Linnuis, the sixth upon the river called Bassas, the seventh in the Wood of Celidon, the eighth on the Castles of

Guinnion, the ninth in the City of the Legion, the tenth on the bank of the river called Tribruit, the eleventh on the mount called Agned, the twelfth on the mount of Badon. In some manuscripts the battle of Mount Agned has the alternative name of the Cat (i.e. battle) Bregoin, Breguoin, or Bregomion.

As undoubtedly King Arthur was the son of a Cornish chieftain or sub-regulus, and presumably succeeded to the paternal kingdom, it is well within the bounds of possibility that some of these battles against the encroaching and raiding Saxons took place in the county.

It is a possibility that some, if not all of them, were in the nature of successful efforts to repel the landing of large bodies of Saxon raiders on the Cornish shores, as eight of them were fought on river banks.

Of the names given, the most Cornish are Guinnion, Tribruit and Mount Agned. Of these, Mr. Jenner has suggested that Guinnion is now Winnington, in Gunwalloe, near which is the headland of Penguinnion. There are earth-works at Winnington whose remains represent the type of a "castle" of King Arthur's day.

Mount Agned, Mr. Jenner has also pointed out, may well mean St. Agnes Beacon. The old name for St. Agnes was St. Agnet (1331), and there is a place-name Mount within the parish. There is also a place called Bryanick (Brieannoc 1201) and this may be a development of the alternative names Bregoin for the battle.

Tribruit, according to the same authority, may possibly be Truro, and not far from this town at Blanchland in Kea[2] we know that King Arthur presided over the trial of Iseult.

In regard to the other names, their location on Cornish soil is even more conjectural.

If Glein be in Cornwall it can only be the Gillan Creek at the mouth of the Helford River, a district which abounds in camps and earth-works. Four battles were fought be the River Dubglas, which may or may not refer to Duloe. The Dubglas, however, is said to be in the region of Linnius, and the nearest name to the latter is that of the River Luney (Lithney?) which flows into the sea near Carhayes. This river may have been called the Luney from the fact that in its upper reaches it bounds the Barton of Luney in St. Ewe. Mr. C.G. Henderson, however, considers that the barton rather received its name from the river.

The name Bassas does not appear to be Celtic, no river name approaching it in sound at all is to be met with in Ferguson's "River Names of Europe."

The City of the Legions is usually said to be Carleon-on-Usk, but in Cornwall, as already recorded, we have several such names, Carlion (Caerleghion 1287) in Kea, Carlean in Camborne, and Mawgan-in-Meneage, and Carleen in Breage.

For Celidon (which has been equated with Caledonia) the nearest aspirant in Cornwall is Callington, of which early spellings without the first n exist, Calwetone (1086), Kalwiton (1300). There is reason to suppose that in Arthurian days the Callington district was heavily wooded and it lies near the Tamar, thus offering a different approach for raiding sea rovers.

The Mount of Badon has generally been supposed to have been in the neighbourhood of Bath. Certain it is that no considerable hill in Cornwall bears a name in the faintest degree resembling Badon. The nearest place-name to it is that of two farms in Duloe known to-day and in 1564 as Badham.

42   *From* **King Arthur: His Symbolic Story in Verse by B. D. Vere (1930)**

PROLOGUE
SCENE 1

There is a legend that the merchant Joseph of Arimathea, came to Britain and brought the boy Jesus with him.

SYNOPSIS. – Jesus desires to go back home again. He feels He had been long enough in quiet. He wants to be amongst people and He also feels His destiny is in the East.

He has been copying in wood the scene which lies before Him. He compares the work He has been doing, the world within His vision, with the actual world; He likens the rugged land to the minds of men and the sea to peace. He cannot make one portion of His work harmonise with the other part.

He lays His work down unfinished and expresses the opinion that others may in the future come and complete it.

SCENE: *The Top of the Island, Tintagel*

JOSEPH *has brought Jesus from His home in Judea. During the time he had been conducting his business* JESUS *has been on the Island interesting Himself in various ways. It is the last night before they depart for home. The boy* JESUS *is sitting with the tools of a carpenter beside Him. He has copied in wood the sea portion of the view of the horizon which from this Island at Tintagel forms about three parts of a circle; the fourth part, that of the land, being rugged, spoils the completion of a perfect circle. The sun is setting. There is a strong light in the West; the East is in shadow. A SENTRY is passing to and fro during the time the action is taking place. There is a beacon fire ready to be lit. Soft music should be played throughout all this Scene.*

> **Jesus** (*sitting at His work, is looking towards the West*)
> I long for morn, when we shall be away
> From all this rugged beauty; where the birds
> And beasts in simple fearlessness do live
> Their joyous lives, unfettered and at peace.
> The call that fills my being is for home …
> For friends … for those I love … the haunts of men.

I love the rest and quiet of mountain top
Where I can see the grandeur of the world,
And sit alone and think ... and dream ... and plan ...
But these are fancies fit for sluggish minds
And not for those whom action calls ... who dare.
The busy world cries out to me to come
And live where men and women love and hate,
Where life is but a market-place for souls
And men are less than men, the slaves of those
Who steal their freedom, soul and body too.
There I can teach ... and learn also ... and live
In service for the world e'en though the price
I have to pay is that my life is given
To serve this purpose, or it is my fate.
(*He rises and points to the West with a sweep of His
    arm.*)
This is the world which lies within my range
Of vision as I look towards the West,
The great sweep of the sea, I know it well
In all its moods... I've made of wood, this world.
        (*He holds up His work.*)
See, here it is ... this represents the sea
That merges into sky and but for line
And cloud might pass as one.
Each night the sun,
Where firmament and sea begin and end,
Slips out of sight behind the waves to sleep.
        (*He sits and works again.*)
'Twas easy task to make the world that can
Be seen from this great height, a perfect curve
And it was done ... But this is but of wood. (*Pause.*)
It would be easy too, like setting sun,
To let the waves divide and in their breast
Be rocked to quiet sleep which leads to death. (*Pause.*)
(*Meditatively.*) This will not be to me like that, I shall
Not pass on bed of billows, nor in peace.
        (*He turns to the East.*)
The East doth call me now, not as the East
Calls to the world to seek for wealth and fame.
I go towards the East to face my task ...
The work my Soul tells me to do.
The East now calls ... The East now calls me ... home.
    (*He rises and looks towards the darkness of the East.*)
No sun in splendid death there greets mine eyes,
No easy sweep of water cool and clear;
The night comes quickly on, the clouds are dark,
Cov'ring the mountains as it were a pall.
What of my world of wood? The hardest part

Is yet for me to do. I shall not now
Complete it but for ever lay it down
And take the challenge up. (*Boldly*) Gone be the dark.
Let East now give us Light ... There let me go.

JOSEPH *enters with his* SERVANT. *He has heard the last
of the soliloquy of* JESUS.
Joseph
My son, art ready in the morn to leave?

Jesus
My preparations all completed are. I long to go.

Joseph
Hast thee finished all Thy work?

Jesus
The simple part is finished (*he turns to the West*) but the
sea
Means peace and quiet and rest. It is so smooth
And even that the plan is e'er the same.
(*He points to the East.*)
That of the land, with all its rugged rocks,
Its mountains steep, its hidden vales, its moors,
Which, windswept, hold the slimy bogs like traps,
And soft, enticingly attract and draw
The wanderer from the path where safety lies,
Is like the twistings of the minds of men.
'Tis hard to make a pleasing curve of these,
They will not with the sea make harmony.

Joseph
I heard Thee speak as I came up. Thou'rt full
Of Knowledge for Thine age ... but Thou art sad.

Jesus
Those who can see the end and who can read
The hearts of men, have much to make them sad.

Joseph (*to Servant*)
The night hath come. Make ready to depart.
(*Servant begins to gather up the things which are lying
about.*)

(*To JESUS*)
Dost thou fear the darkness?

Jesus
No the light is near.

Joseph
Leave now Thy work until again Thou com'st.

Jesus
I shall come here again but not in flesh,
My hands will never take my work again;
I lay it down. (*He lays it down.*) By others who will come
Some day the circle may be made complete.
God grant them hearts and hands to work and may
Their workmanship well stand the test of time.

Joseph
Thou'rt strange.

Jesus
'Tis as I feel.

Joseph (*to Sentry*)
All's well?

Sentry
All's well.

(*The sun sets ... The beacon is lit by the* SENTRY *...
    JOSEPH and his* SERVANT *leave with their
    belongings.* JESUS *sits looking towards the East,
    deep in thought. Darkness, except for the light from
    the beacon.*)
CURTAIN.

SCENE II
(*There is a lapse of twelve years since the last Scene.*)

Chorus
There is a legend that Joseph returned to Britain after the death of our
Lord, bringing with him the Holy Grail, the Dish wherefrom our Lord
ate the lamb on the Thursday before He died: that he built a small circular Church and placed therein a Table in remembrance of the Table
of the Passion of our Lord, upon which he deposited the Grail; that he
then decided he would journey the country taking the Grail with him
and would build other Churches; and that he built the small church
at Glastonbury and buried the Holy Grail there.

SYNOPSIS. – Joseph describes his previous visit to Britain, the
thoughts of Jesus when He was there with him and his present and
future plans.

SCENE: *The Top of the Island, Tintagel*

Soft music should be played throughout all this Scene.

Enter JOSEPH *and* FRIEND

Joseph
This is Tintagel … Many years ago
I came here. I have spoken of it oft
To thee.

Friend
Why hast thou come again for now
Thou hast no need to manage thine affairs?

Joseph
My journey was not made for worldly gain …
A mighty force which would not be denied
Drove me to seek this place to hide my grief.
Heartbroken, I desired to be alone.
'Twas here I spent some time with Him when He
Was but a lad. He made, in part, a world
Of wood but this He could not here complete.
I think I understand the thoughts which then
Were in His mind. Someone, He said, would come,
To carry on His work … It may be that
The force is His, which made me come again.
Friend
I feel as though I stand on hallowed ground.

Joseph
See here this Holy Dish *(shows it)* wherefrom He ate
The lamb the night before He died. The blood
Which fell as He was hanging on the Cross
I caught therein.[1] 'Tis ever sanctified.
Within this land, where still the people dwell
Unconquered by the hordes of Roman power,
Here shall this Grail remain. The Western world
Hath need of Light … here shall the seed be sown.

Friend
Hast thou a plan? Ask what thou wilt of me
And all the help that I can give is thine.

Joseph
Tomorrow we will build a Church wherein
This Sacred Vessel shall be placed. We'll make
Our Shrine for all the world to gather near

To listen to our message and to pray.
Round as the world shall be our little Church;
Within it, we will place a Table Round,
A symbol of that board around which sat
In Fellowship our Lord and those He loved.
'Twill mind us of the night this Grail was used
By Him Who is the Christ. Here will we sit,
Rememb'ring Him Who suffered for us all.
Here will we follow His command; here will
We break the bread; here will we drink the wine,
That we may think of Him and His great love.

Friend
And then, what work hast thou in mind to do?

Joseph
A little while and I will go and take
The Holy Vessel with me and will build
Me Churches where the people so desire.
Pray with me now that in this land, the Light
We bring shall e'er shine bright. Pray that from this
Our Church shall go the message that we bring
To all, that they must love the Lord their God,
Likewise their neighbour as they do themselves.
(*They pray*).

43   An Balores/The Chough by Robert Morton Nance (1932)

The folk, four men and two women, stand round a little bier with a dead chough on it under a pall. The justice, who is seated, speaks:

The Justice: This is a doleful thing, good folk, that has befallen among us, and must be faithfully judged by us. Behold here dead our hallowed bird – the Chough of Cornwall, the Chough of King Arthur.[1] Never any more will its voice be heard by us. Never any more will be seen by us its crooked bill nor its slender legs, red-hued like blood. Who is the rascal that slew her?

1st Man: It is some rough common daw, surely; for those wicked birds are ever building their nests in the crags of the cliff, where the poor chough lived. And every day they robbed it, thrusting it out of its own nest, even as the accursed Saxons did to our forefathers, driving them out of their country into the peninsula of Cornwall!

2nd Man: I will prove that to be false. We ourselves are to blame! We, the people of Cornwall, it is, who have killed it! It thought within itself, "What good is it for me to live, keeping the spirit of King Arthur alive in me, since the folk of Cornwall won't speak Cornish any more? What is the use of Arthur being alive, if his tongue is dead?" Then, doubtless, it lay down and gave up this spirit, and died, broken-hearted.

The Justice: Silence with thy stories, Bartholomew Battler,[2] and thou, Peter Grief, hold thy chatter! You do but talk beside the point! We haven't come here to listen to stuff like this. Truth has to be brought into this affair. This lovely innocent bird, that we loved so much is dead. Who has seen anyone kill it? If anyone knows, let him speak without fear.

1st Woman: I have heard one to say, sir justice, that if he would, he could lay hold of that same rogue by the ear.

The Justice: That's better. – Then, you know a man who could take by the ear the rogue that killed it. Is that the follow come here with you?

1st Woman: He is, sir justice, if it please you; it was Jack Smart, the man that stands there, that said so.

The Justice: How say'st thou, sir? Can'st thou do as thou said'st that it was in thy power to do?

3rd Man: In truth, lord justice, by your good will, I never said as much as that. This good woman is somewhat mistaken as to me, as it seems. But I told her, indeed, there was one of my neighbours saying he could do so.

The Justice: And where is that neighbour?

3rd Man: It is this man, Tom Hardhead, sir justice, that you see here before you.

The Justice: Since thou be he, then, say to me, good friend Hardhead; canst thou tell us who has killed this bird?

4th Man: No I cannot, in truth sir lord justice, nor did I ever say I could do such a thing of myself. There are folk in the world, long tongued, who exaggerate everything that's told them so much that it might never be recognised again by those who first told it. You can see me, what sort of fellow I am. I'm not one of those foolish boasters, saying what cannot be. But I said, verily, that one said to me that one could say and nothing more.

The Justice: And who is it, that said so to thee?

4th Man: Right truly, sir lord justice, it is Aunt Molly Thickhead, my neighbour here.

The Justice: Say, good mistress, is anyone known to you that might tell us who it was that killed King Arthur's bird?

2nd Woman: To speak without a lie, if it please you lord justice, never did I say that I knew anyone who would say surely who killed it; but I said indeed that one was known to me, as well I thought, who could discover who killed it, if anyone in the world could discover it.

The Justice: Now, then, though it is after much labour, we come at last to something of use. But, say, what makes thee believe that this man could discover the truth, good woman?

2nd Woman: I speak of no man, save thy grace, for it was a woman – an old woman and a monstrous wise one. Would that she were once here with you, sweet sir justice, so that she might speak to you with her own mouth.

The Justice: No matter whether it be a man or a woman: she can be fetched, no doubt, wherever she is.

2nd Woman: By my faith, good sir justice, if she were brought before you, she would tell you great marvels: for by my soul, I have heard her say many wonderful things ere now.

The Justice: What hast thou heard then, that was said by her?

2nd Woman: Right, verily sir, if anything on earth were stolen from the neighbours – though 'twere an egg, or a hen, or some clothes, or stockings, mayhap, that were drying on a furze bush on the common – anon she would tell where it were gone.

The Justice: Could she tell, too, since she is so wise, by what name the thief was called by whom they had been taken?

2nd Woman: That she could, sweet sir justice; and therefore, I know well enough *she* could tell who slew the chough – every bit as truly as she could tell who stole an egg!

The Justice: And so we think, everyone, as I believe. But, say, how could she divine these things so clearly? Is she a sorceress, who divines what is hidden by the Devil's help? We had better be careful of women of that sort!

2nd Woman: No, she's not, by my troth – God forbid! For never did I see her to use a worse way than to gaze earnestly on the hand of one that had a thing stolen from him.

The Justice: And who is this wise old woman, and where is she to be found?

2nd Woman: She's a gipsy, sir, verily and lately lived here in Cornwall, quite near my house; but more's the pity, she's now gone over sea. Still, she hasn't gone to her own country, I think; for 'tis said that Egypt is a long way from here, and she didn't take ship to go thither until but a month now past.

The Justice: All the same, Aunt Molly, I fear it would be of no earthly use for us to send another vessel after her with messengers of the law to bring her back! – Now, to start afresh, is there no man of you all that can give us better advice than that, to know who killed Arthur's bird? [*Here the eye of faith will see the chough come to life again.*]

1st Man: Here's a miracle! How good this is!

2nd Man: It opens its eyes!

1st Woman: It's spreading its wings!

3rd Man: It flies!

4th Man: It's alive! Hurrah!

2nd Woman: The chough's not dead!

The Justice: Come let us sing therefore sing all together merrily, THE SONG OF THE CHOUGH.

All: Ebon hued, with leg and bill
          Coral crimson, brightly planished,
       On the cliffs of Cornwall still
          Lives the chough they said had vanished.

       In a chough, as all men know,
          Arthur's spirit, too, unsleeping
       Round our isle while tides shall flow,
          Over us his watch is keeping.

       O, King Arthur, grant that all
          Who shall take thy chough as token,
       May upon thy spirit call
          To keep Cornwall's faith unbroken.

       So again our Cornish tongue

That has lain so long a-dying,
Shall rise up as strong and young
As is e'er a chough that's flying.

King Arthur is not dead!

44   *From* **Dawn in Lyonesse by Mary Ellen Chase (1938)**

From her bed [Ellen Pascoe] could see in the August darkness the flash of the great light on Trevose Head.[1] Its gleam was
already paling a little at the first early suggestion of the summer
dawn. She could hear, far below, the rhythmic thunder of gigantic
waves battering away at the shoulders of the cliffs beneath King
Arthur's Castle, the mighty surge of water, the roar of its impact, the
hoarse undertones of its recoil, the almost breathless gathering of
itself for another onrush. She knew that the tide was coming through
hearing at intervals of a few seconds the reverberating explosion of
monstrous breakers meeting each other at the height of their fury in
Merlin's Cave. And within all these more immediate and tangible
sounds as it was above, beneath, and beyond them was the almost
inperceptible and yet inescapable voice of the sea itself, of its
essence, its being, its length and breadth and depth – a murmur, an
undertone, a refrain, an unceasing harmony without beginning and
without an end.

Once Trevose Light had quite lost its whitening gleam and the gulls
screamed once more above the sea, her thoughts would again nag
her. King Mark would fade from his high throne, and the ship which
had borne his nephew Tristram to Ireland to seek the Fair Iseult to be
his uncle's bride would give place to Derek Tregonny's fishing boat, at
this very hour perhaps rocking on the seas above the lost and sunken
land of Lyonesse where Tristram had been reared.

Derek Tregonny, she knew, had never heard of the lost land of
Lyonesse. His thoughts were solely on his cork-strewn nets, his mind
intent only on sea and wind and weather. Nor did he know of this fair
Iseult, whose beauty, when she came into the hall amid the vassals
of King Mark, shone so that the walls were lit as they are lit at dawn.
Nor how, though she lived as a queen, she lived in sadness because
of her love for Tristram.

She had King Mark's tenderness and the barons' honour. The
people also loved her. She passed her days amid the frescos on the
walls and floors all strewn with flowers. Jewels had she, and purple
cloth and tapestry of Hungary and Thessaly, too, and songs of
harpers, and curtains upon which were worked leopards and eagles
and popinjayes and all the beasts of sea and field.

Derek, she felt sure, would have small patience with such goings-on, either then or now, even with a love-potion to explain or justify them. For within his heavily set body and his gruff, curt ways Derek was like Tristram, faithful in life and even unto death, although the death he would sometime die would never startle one as did that of Tristram by its tragic glory.

When she came down to the kitchen at half-past six, in a fresh cap and a clean apron over her black dress, a post-card was standing upright against the pile of plates ready for her tables. The postcard bore her name in cramped handwriting, framed laboriously and with obvious dislike of pen and ink.

Miss Ellen Pascoe, the post card said,
    King Arthur's Castle Hotel,
        Tintagel,
            Cornwall.

The writing was Susan's. Even before she turned the card to read what was written on its back, Ellen remembered how Susan hated to write anything at all.

"Writing's not for me," Susan was often saying. "It fair makes me ache in all my bone, that it do."

Even before she turned the card, Ellen knew that all the others in the kitchen had read it, the head-waiter with his oily hair, who was just now scrubbing some spots off his black coat in the pantry, the three other waitresses, who slept in their homes in Tintagel and whom she did not know much, the two cooks, the grubby kitchen girl. They had all stopped what they were doing and were staring at Ellen as she turned the card.

DEAR ELLEN (the stiff writing said), – I write to say that Derek was drowned on Monday. The burying is Wednesday. If you could come for it, it would be good.
    Susan.

45   *From* **Trystan hag Ysolt/Tristan and Isolt by A.S.D. Smith (1951) and D. H. Watkins (1962)**

King Mark reigned
in Cornwall, and lived
at his castle in Lantian.[1]
His enemies rose up
and waged war against him,
threatening both great and small.

From Lyonesse,[2] King Rivalen
came with great speed
to maintain Mark and his friends,
and with the aid of good counsel,

as well as through the strength of his sword,
he overcame his enemies.

Mark was greatly pleased with him,
and gave his sister
Blanchefleur to him as a reward.
She was greatly loved by Rivalen
and they were swiftly married
with much rejoicing.

Several months had passed
when news came to the court
that Duke Morgan had landed
in Lyonesse, ravaging
the towns of the country and hurting
the people on every side.

Immediately Rivalen
gathered his mighty men
and speedily sailed for home,
and Blanchefleur, his faithful wife
went with him in his ship,
and as it happened, she was with child.

He landed safely
in front of his stronghold of Canoel,[3]
and Blanchefleur he gave
into the hands of his seneschal,
Roald, a faithful knight,
to keep her safe both day and night.

In a great host lords
and their men-at-arms
came to him from every parish.
They all went straight into battle.
Rivalen led them,
as is the duty of a good king.

Blanchefleur waited a long time
to receive news of the battle;
great was her anxiety.
Rivalen was killed.
He never returned,
despite her prayers.

With her heart thus broken,
a child was born to her,
a little boy as fair as an angel.

As she was in her agony of death,
she took the child
in her arms, and said:

"My son, I have longed grievously
to see you. I cannot thank God too much,
I swear it.
You are the fairest
little boy ever born
to womankind in this world.

"I have brought you to life,
but sadly I see my own death
coming before long,
even though I have no wish to leave you.
Now your father is dead,
and your mother is in atrocious pain.
Because of so much suffering,
Tristan[4] will be your name."

———————————

Behind the castle of Tintagel
there was a hidden garden:
about it was a palisade of stakes,
sharp and straight like spears,
enclosing an orchard
and many kinds of sweet fruits.

In the place farthest from the castle,
near these high stakes,
a tree was growing,
a great pine with many branches.

Beneath it, a stream rises from a spring,
and the water runs through the garden.
Between banks of marble
it runs into the castle
by the women's chambers.

Here, then, is the stratagem
that Brangyen taught him,
so that unimpeded, Tristan
could meet his Isolt.

Every night Tristan would go
boldly to climb the palisade
into the garden, and stand
beneath the high pine tree.

Then he cut little twigs,
each one as big as his finger,
and threw them into the stream
that flows to the castle.

When she saw the twigs floating past,
Isolt knew Tristan
was waiting for her in the garden,
under cover of the night.

Often, through the help of Brangyen
she avoided the scoundrels
and slipped out of the court
to most beloved Tristan.

———————————

When Tristan leaped over the cliff
(and that through false hope),
a poor man, spying
around, saw him fleeing.
He went surreptitiously
and reported it to the Queen
that Tristan had escaped on the beach
without a sword or armour.

"I thank God," said she,
"that from now on I shall not heed at all
what wickedness they[5] may do,
binding me or unbinding me,
or setting me free.
Let them do exactly as they will.
Tristan is safe! They will never kill him,
and his enemies will rue it."

Her wrists were fastened tightly together
with a rope
which drew blood.
But, laughing, she said, "If I were to shed tears
when Tristan is safe,
through the grace of God
I should not be worthy to be loved."

———————————

A bright beam of sunlight
    came over the shelter.
It was falling on Isolt's face
    for a short while.

Isolt's face was pale and very thin,
as God is witness.

King Mark placed
   (and it was regret to him)
a pair of gloves close to her,
   adorned with precious ermine.
He remembered that these were the same ones
that she had brought from Ireland to him.

Next, he took
   the splendid emerald ring
and with great care placed
   another ring there instead
– the ring that Isolt gave him for good fortune
when they were married.

Also between the two fugitives
   he took away
the unsheathed sword
   that once killed Morholt,
and he placed his own sword
exactly between them.

He went out of the shelter
and leaped onto the back of his horse
and said in a low voice
to the forest guard,
"Flee, lest you be killed,
and escape as quickly as you can."

———————————

On the appointed judgment day
the King and the Queen
went riding
to the White Land on the bank of the stream,
with the lords accompanying them,
and the three villains amongst them.

On the bank opposite
there was another great host.
King Arthur of great renown
and his knights, indeed
saluted them.

The Cornish came rowing
in swift boats

before the knights
standing on the beach.

When they were ready to land,
Isolt said to the barons,
"How can I reach land
without dirtying my long clothes?
One of the people ought
to bring me to the bank over the mud."

Stretched out on the ground
by the stream was a certain pilgrim –
pitiful to see, in truth,
and his dirty cloak all around him.
He was holding out his wooden bowl,
asking for alms
with a pitiful trembling voice.

To him a certain knight
shouted, "Friend, take off your cloak
and descend to the water. Go,
carry the Queen to her place
– unless you are too weak
and fall before you reach the bank!"

Tristan took the Queen
in his strong arms
and to her, in a low voice,
whispered: "My love!"

"Make sure to fall on the shore!"
Isolt whispered to him,
and when he came to the bank,
Tristan stumbled and fell.
The squires and oarsmen
heartily attacked him
with boathooks and oars.
He almost died because of their attack.

Isolt said, "Leave
the poor man in peace, for in truth
he was feeble and weakened
from walking many miles."
She threw her ring of fine gold
to the pilgrim.

After a long and bloody fight
the mighty giant was killed.
Tristan cut off his right hand,
and brought it as a gift to the Duke.

"Sire," said Tristan to him,
"remember the promise.
Give me the reward I have earned:
your enchanted dog named Pettygrew."

"My friend – what? You will not
separate me from my dog?
You can take half of my land,
and my sister with it. Think and look!"

"Sire, your sister is fair in truth.
Nor have I seen a fairer land,
but it was so that I could win the dog
that I overcame Urgan!"

"Then take him as you must,
but know that you have taken
my heart's delight clean away from me.
Remember that Tristan."

The dog was entrusted
to a shrewd Welsh minstrel.
Through his cunning,
he brought him to Tintagel.

The Queen was joyful
at receiving so sweet a gift.
She gave ten gold marks to the man
for the trouble that he had.

When the King saw the dog,
the Queen said
that her greatly-loved mother
had sent it to her.

She ordered that the goldsmith
should make a box for the dog,
so that he could be taken
with her wherever she might go.

She took no more account of her troubles.
She did not understand the miracle.

Every time she looked at the dog,
her sadness went away from her.

Undoubtedly the cause of it
was the gift sent to her
by her beloved Tristan
that drew her from her despondency.

But one day she recognised
that it was the little bell and its magic
that tinkled delight to her heart
when she heard it ringing.

"Alas," said she, "I should not
live in such delight
while Tristan is bearing
every hardship of this world.
He could have kept the dog
and forgot his trouble,
but through courtliness
he sent it to me.

"By giving up this thing
to me he gave up all his happiness,
but I know what I will do.
I will not hesitate any longer.

"It is not fitting for me dear Tristan,
to be so comfortable and in good spirits,
while you are mournful without your dog.
I will suffer with you."

She opened the window,
and she took the little bell
and threw it far into the great sea.

Dinas the Seneschal
went back to Tintagel.
Going up into the hall,
he went to the Queen.

The King and Queen
were playing chess
under a high canopy.
They spoke not a word.

Dinas sat
between them on a footstool
as if he wished
to follow closely every move.

He left his hands
plainly to be seen
so that Isolt noticed
Tristan's ring on his finger.

She accidentally knocked Dinas' arm,
and some of the pieces
immediately fell to the floor,
and the game was overturned.

"Ah! Seneschal," she said,
"my game has been spoilt
so that I cannot
take it up again."

Mark withdrew from the hall
and Isolt went to her room
to speak with Dinas.

"My friend, have you come
as an envoy from Tristan?"

"Queen, he is hidden
in my Castle of de Liden."

"Is it true that he is married
to a woman of Brittany?"

"Queen, woe is the hour,
but he is indeed married.
But he affirms to you that he has
never betrayed you,
and that you are held by him
above all the women of the world.
He prays you to grant him
that he may see you once again
according to the promise between you
when you spoke directly to him.
If you will not see him,
he will die, O Queen."
Thinking deeply,
Isolt was silent for a while.

She doubtless thought
of the other Isolt, the wife of her lover.

"Truly you say, as I know,
concerning that promise between us.
To Tristan I said,
"When I see the green ring,
there is no power in the world,
or royal prohibition, believe me,
that will prevent me from doing your desire".

"Madam, for certain in two days' time,
you will leave Tintagel
to go the White Land,
you and the King and all the Court.
Tristan will send a message,
and will seek your leave,
for he will hide
close to the road to the White Land.
It is for your pity that he asks."

"By my father, the promise
that was made will stand, as I said.
Neither royal prohibition nor strong castle
shall prevent me from doing his will."

_____

When Mark heard of the death
of the lovers, immediately
he crossed the broad sea
and went to Brittany.

There he ordered two coffins
of great value to be made,
one of chalcedony
for Isolt, in memory of her,
and the other of bright beryl[6]
in kind respect to Tristan.
Mark sadly brought them
in his ship to Tintagel,
and by the apse of the chapel
on either side
the two of them were buried.

During that night, a green
and leafy thorn tree grew big
out of worthy Tristan's grave,
having many sweet flowers of the Spring,

climbing over the roof ridge
of the apse and then coming down onto the bright grave
of Isolt and taking root in it.
How firmly is the bond of love
united again in death!
In the midst of its strength the great thorn tree
was cut down by the people of the country.
But the next day, I confess,
swiftly reviving,
the thorn tree grew so mighty again
and so full of flowers, as green as before.
It came down immediately
to the grave of Iseult and wrapped
itself round it, taking root,
covering it over entirely.

Three times the people of the country cut it
and three times it grew big.
At last, word was sent
to the King about the miracle.
He forbade the people
to cut down the thorn tree any more.

46   *From* **Mines and Miners of Cornwall by A.K. Hamilton Jenkin (1970)**

To many people it will come as a surprise, and perhaps to the more romantically-minded as a shock, to learn that mining has taken place on the Island of Tintagel and beneath the very precincts of its far-famed castle. Yet, in truth, the history of King Arthur Mine is a good deal more authentic than the legendary associations of the old British hero with the spot. Although there is evidence to show that the lodes which traverse the headland were recognised in Elizabethan times, the earliest recorded proposal for working them is found in an announcement in the Royal Cornwall Gazette, 12 July 1806, that "persons wishing to Adventure in Wheal Heart Copper and Lead Work, in King Arthur's Castle and Island may apply to Thomas Baker (owner), at the Castle Inn, Trevena. There is a good prospect of four courses of ore in the above work, with a good stream of water for Engines and Stamps".

Whether anything came of this invitation to the investing public is not known, but in 1852 a company prospectus was issued in which it was claimed that two silver-lead lodes and three copper lodes had been discovered in the elevated tract of Tintagel Head, and that a sett had been granted for mining purposes by H.R.H. the Duke of Cornwall. The Prince's Lode was said to be about 15 feet wide in the back and producing stones of copper ore, whilst at low tide it could be seen for a length of 30 fathoms on the foreshore. Assays made by John Harvey of Liskeard showed in one case 14 in 20 for lead and 32 ounces of silver to the ton; and in another 25³/₄ per cent for copper. There was a waterfall on the property and a shipping cave adjoining.[1] A year later is was announced that King Arthur Consols had three men driving the adit on the lode, and six others sinking the engine shaft. One of the miners had recently brought in "a solid nugget of malleable silver-lead ore, weighing nearly 10lbs., such as had never been produced from any mine in Cornwall. It was so ductile that it could be cut with a chisel. It is to be sent to the offices in London". Twenty tons of ore were sampled and ready for sale in June 1853, but by the following January operations appear to have ceased.

As King Arthur Mine the property was again being worked in the 1870s when the lode in the adit was reported to be 3 feet wide, and containing a leader of silver-lead 6 inches in width. The gossan was then selling at £3 a ton for its silver content, and "the lead ore, just as it is found without any dressing, fetches £16.5.0 a ton". A report by George Henwood in 1872 refers to five roughly parallel lodes in the cliff, all of which contained small quantities of silver-lead ore, copper and zinc. Under the terms of the Duchy lease no breaking of the surface was permitted within the precincts of the Castle, and in order to develop the principal or northernmost lode a 10 H.P. portable steam engine for pumping and winding was erected in the adit some 200 feet below the site of the "supposed Great Hall of King Arthur". The engine was hoisted from the beach to the level in the presence of several hundred spectators and by its aid a subterranean shaft or winze was sunk to a depth of 15 or 16 fathoms. After working for a few months the steam engine was replaced by a 30 H.P. turbine, to drive which water was brought through glazed pipes for a distance of a quarter of a mile. Although a number of later reports were issued, they amount to very little in substance. The mine was evidently poor and struggling, and in 1873 the company was subject to a winding-up order and the machinery and materials were advertised for sale. In addition to the steam engine and turbine, these included 70 fathoms of 10 inch pumps, 18 fathoms of pumps in the shaft, 18 fathoms of ladders and two timber bridges, each about 40 feet long. Notwithstanding this, another four years seem to have elapsed before the plant was finally disposed of, the address of the then liquidators being the Government and Emigration Offices, Camelford.

In his History of Tintagel (1927) Mr. William Taylor adds some further notes to the above: "Just beyond Merlin's Cave (in the Island) is a bricked-up entrance of a silver-lead mine which was worked about 50 years ago. Inside is a shaft sunk to below the level of the beach and continued under it. A pipe line from the pond in the valley conveyed water to work a turbine to pump the shaft, and at one time a wooden bridge crossed the mouth of Merlin's Cave to convey the men to their work. The turbine pipe also crossed the Cave. The pipe line is now a pathway to the Castle Keep. The cottage on the north side of the stream was formerly an office, carpenter's and blacksmith's shop belonging to the mine".[2]

47 From **Geraint: Last of the Arthurians by Donald R. Rawe (1972)**

They enter the chamber. Jowanet finishes her washing, still singing, and exits. Elbryn emerges from the King's chamber to find himself confronted by Jestyn, Selyf an Merouda.

Jestyn: Ah, there you are, Elbryn. How is our gracious Lord the King?

Elbryn: As well as most days, sir.

Jestyn: Will he see the Queen? Or myself?

Elbryn: He still refuses, sir.

Jestyn: Pah! This old man's obstinacy will be the ruin of the kingdom. It must be overcome somehow.

Elbryn: Today he insisted on going out onto the battlements.[1]

Selyf: What, in this wind? It'll hasten his end.

Jestyn: Don't pretend concern, brother. I know what is in your heart.

Selyf: And in yours too, Jestyn, despite your pious utterances. I am anxious for the kingdom, not for myself: the Saxons have been reported west of the Parrett[2] – inside Dumnonia itself.

Merouda: If Geraint would only hand over to Selyf as Commander in Chief, he'd be on his way with an army tomorrow.

Jestyn: And grab the kingdom in the process? Geraint knows very well what you're up to, Selyf. The Saxons have been drifting west for years – it's hardly a planned invasion. In any case, we must learn to live at peace with our neighbours.

Selyf: A vain and pious hope if ever I heard one. The Saxons are savages who live by fire and the sword: as Arthur and our father both knew when they fought and beat them. And we can beat them also if we strike now, instead of waiting, and waiting.

Jestyn: Mere war-talk, brother. Of course you generals have to invent something to fight for, to justify your existence.

Merouda: Elbryn is appears you're the only person Geraint confides in these days. What does he say about the Saxons?

Elbryn: He doesn't talk to me about such things, Madam. Only about hunting and fishing and the old days ...

Jestyn: (*wearily*) You needn't tell us. The last of the Arthurians, and so on...

Elbryn: That's what they call him, sir.

Jestyn: A bloodthirsty race if ever there was one. All that delight in battle and fighting ... it sickens me.

Elbryn: Yes: Geraint is of sterner metal than those that come after him. Now I must go and service my armoury... (*Goes*)

Jestyn: Insolent herdsman! Jumped up swineherd! Just because he has a reputation as a marksman...

Selyf: (*laughs*) The best in all Cornwall. And he could break both our heads for us, despite his sixty years.

Jestyn: When Geraint dies, he goes. I shall have none of you war-mongers about me. A peaceful Christian kingdom, that's my aim.

Merouda: Naturally, there will be many changes. More than you anticipate, perhaps, brother Jestyn.

Selyf: (*displeased*) Merouda: leave this to me. You never could handle Jestyn, or anyone else in our family, for that matter.

Jestyn: I warn you, Selyf, and you too Merouda; I am the eldest son of Geraint Map Erbyn and heir to the Kingdom. You two play politics at your peril. The Lord is my guide and counsellor, and he will not see his servant maligned.

Selyf: Some day soon, brother, you'll find out that God is on the side of those who fight for Christian kingdoms against the heathen hordes.

Merouda: Yes: you think that because you've done a bit of fasting and founded a church or two, that you've got the Almighty in your pocket ...

Enid: (*approaching with Ladies in Waiting*) My sons, my sons, must you forever argue? Our state will fall into dissension even as our family disintegrates. You fight like dogs over the body of your dying father.

Jestyn: (*sententiously*) Mother ... my deepest apologies. I forgot myself; and may the Lord forgive me.

Merouda: Aaaagh! You disgust me.

Enid: Selyf: you too were brought up as a Christian. It is a religion of gentleness and joy. I see little of it in either you or Merouda these days. Has ambition eaten you up my son?

Selyf: Not quite, Mother. It seems that I alone can see what Cornwall needs if it is to be saved: a strong man at the head of a strong army: to awake from her long sleep and defend herself, or all will be lost between the Saxons on the one hand and mealy-mouthed altar-grovellers on the other.

48   Arthur by Tim Saunders (1990)

Austere my world, dark my lineage[1]
dire need and terror my destiny
for my rights I shall pay with my blood,
my kingdom, whatever touches my feet.
The crown of the tribes I shall not have
until I lay hand on a sword.
Arthur I have been, a man at arms:
my fame has gone through the world.

My horse's hooves constantly on the road,

gaps frequently recurring in my retinue,
a rough stone over whoever falls
cross on shield, burden on shoulder,
my wealth consisting of memory and song,
stale bread, scarce salt.
Arthur I have been, a mighty man:
who will place a stone on my cairn?

Tamar waters and Land's End,
greenness that pleases the eye,
damp breeze that sings of sea
whispers of Scilly through its moisture,
year, month, week and day
thousand voices through the tops of the withered trees.
Arthur I have been, an undefeated man:
from that, for a while, I shall retreat.

49 *From* **Nativitas Christi/The Nativity by Alan M. Kent (2000)**

THE DEVILS *leave the Spoon.*[1] JESUS, JOSEPH OF ARIMATHEA, THE SAILORS *and* THE TINNERS *wake.*

Jesus
In truth, I've never slept so well.
I was tired out I can tell.
And yet, this place gave me great dreams.
I know not whether 'tis sea air,
but for this land's a future fair.
Much was told under the mine beams.

I've a notion it was Father's voice.
At His words, all should rejoice.
He is glad my feet walk here
– a piece of stone set in the sea.
As my coming others did see,
the dream gave me visions most clear.

Joseph of Arimathea
Now, sleep from my eyes I've rubbed,
yet fore-telling on you God's dubbed.
'Tis more miracles I am sure.
Proceed, tell us all you saw.
What does the future have in store?
Come lad, don't keep it obscure.

Jesus
Three things God revealed to me.
Locked doors He opened with a key.
First, at Tintagel in the north,
a British king shall be born.
To God's word he will be drawn,
and challenge unbelievers forth.
To many battles he will ride,
but my mother shall be his guide.
To one great contest he will trek,
and on his shoulder he'll carry
an image of dear Mary,
a cross of tin around his neck.

My own death I know about.
Thus of salvation have no doubt.
Upon the cross I shall bleed,
but you Joseph, shall catch the blood.
In a cup, stem the red flood.
By the Rood,[2] do this I plead.
To this same Cornish king's court,
twelve brave knights shall be brought.
Twelve shall match each apostle.
They shall seek this famed grail.
Each will go beyond the pale,
and make sacrifice colossal.

Lastly here, where we now stand,
shall become a Christian land.
This horn of strangers around
shall nurse many a saintly life.
Holy men crossing shall be rife,
and women saints shall abound.
Their parish shall go past Land's End.
On this, you may depend.
Along lonely ways they'll plod.
Persecution they shall know too,
but to My word they'll be true.
In Heaven, these saints shall join God.

Joseph of Arimathea
Such marvels then are to be seen!
Fine future people God did glean.
You Emmanuel we shall call.
All of us know You are God's son,
the Messiah, the Chosen One.
Down to our knees we all fall.

Appendix: texts in Cornish

12 *From* **Beunans Meriasek by Radolphus Ton (1504)**

[*Hic Dux Cornubie pompabit dicens*]

Me yv duk in oll kernow
  indella ytho ov thays
hag vhel arluth in pov
  a tamer the pen an vlays
tregys off lemen heb wov
  berth in castel an dynas
    sur in peddre
ha war an tyreth vhel
thym yma castel arel
a veth gelwys tyndagyel
    henna yv ovfen tregse

40 *From* **Ceremonies of the Gorseth of the Bards of Cornwall (1928–present)**

XIII. *Cledha Myghtern Arthur*

Cannas Barth Mur: An als whath Arthur a wyth,
                           Yn corf Palores yn few:
                           Y Wlas whath Arthur a bew,
                           Myghtern a ve hag a vyth.

An Vyrth Oll: Nyns yu marow Myghtern Arthur!

Barth Mur: Otomma Cledha us yn le Calespulgh, Cledha Myghtern Arthur, a dheth dyworth an Logh, ha dhe'n Logh eth arta. A vynnough-why ty warnodho bynytha bos lel dhe Gernow, agan Mamvro?

An Vyrth Oll: Ny a'n te!

XIV. *Can: Bro Goth Agan Tasow*

Bro goth again Tasow, dha fleghes a'th car
Gwlas ker an Howlsedhas, pan vro yu dha bar?
War oll an norvys 'th on-ny scullyes ales,
Mes agan kerensa yu dhys.

Kescan – Kernow! Kernow! Y keryn Kernow;
    An mor hedra vo yn fos dhys adro
        'Th on "Onen hag Oll" rag Kernow.

Gwlascor Myghtern Arthur, an Syns kens, ha'n Gral
Moy kerys genen nyns yu tyreth aral,
Ynnos-sy pup carn, nans, meneth ha chy
A gows yn Kernewek dhyn-ny.

Pup A Gry: Kernow bys vyken!

43   An Balores/The Chough by Robert Morton Nance (1932)

An bobel, peswar den ha dyw venen, a-sef adro dhe un vasken vyghan, warnedhy palores varow, yn-dan elerlen. An Justys, yu esed-hes, a-lavar.

An Justys: Hem yu tra druesy, a dus vas, es wharfedhys y'gan mesk, hag a-res bos brusys yn-lel genen. Otomma marow agan edhen sacrys - Palores Kernow, Palores Myghtern Arthur. Nefra na-moy ny-vyth clewys genen hy lef. Nefra na-moy ny-vyth gwelys genen hy gelvyn cam na'y garow mon, ruth aga lyu avel gos. Py yu an gal re wruk hy ladha?

An Kensa Den: Nep choca keth garow yu, yn-sur; rag an ydhyn drok-na prest ymons ow-cul aga nythow yn clegrow an als, le mayth esa trygys an balores voghosak. Ha pupteth-oll y a-wre hy ladra, orth-hy-herdhya mes a'y nyth hy-honen, kepar del wruk an Sawson dh'agan hendasow, orth-aga-helghya mes a'ga fow bys y'n cona tyr Kernow-ma!

An Nessa Den: My a-bref bos henna gow – Ny agan-honen yu dhe vlamya! Ny, an dus Kernow, yu, re-s-ladhas! Hy res-ombrederas, "Pandr' a-dal dhem bewa, ynnof ow-quytha yn-few spyrys Myghtern Arthur, aban na-vyn tus Kernow kewsel Kernewek na-moy? – Pandr' a-dal bos Arthur bew, marow mar pe y davas?" Ena, hep mar, hy a-wrowedhas a-hes, has dascor an spyrys-na, ha merwel, terrys hy holon-hy!

An Justys: Taw gans dha whethlow, Bertyl Breseler, ha ty, Peder Dughan, syns dha glap! Why a-gows a-drus, agas deu! Nyns-on-ny devedhys omma rak golsow dhe ufereth a'n par-na. Res yu dry lendury aberth y'n cas-ma. An edhen dek gwyryon-ma, kemmys a-garsyn, marow yu. Pyu re-welas onen dh'y ladha? Den mar cor, ef kewsens hep own.

An Kensa Benen: My re-glewas den dhe leverel, syr justys, mara mynna, y-halsa settya dalghen yn scovarn an keth cam na.

An Justys: Hem yu gwell. – Ytho, why a-wor den a-alsa kemeres er y scovarn an cam re-s-ladhas. Es devedhys genough omma an gwas-na?

An Kensa Benen: Es, syr justys, mara plek dheugh; Jowan Connek, an den es ow-sevel ena, o, yndella a-gowsas.

An Justys: Fatel leverta, Syra? – A ylta-sy gul kepar del leversys y vos y'th hallos dh'y wul?

An Tressa Den: Yn gwyryoneth, arluth justys, dre 'gas both da-why, byth ny-leverys kemmys ha henna. Yma'n venen-vas-ma nebes tullys y'm kever, del hevel. Saw my a-lavaras dedhy, yn-tefry, yth-esa onen a'm kentrevogyon ow-leverel y-halsa gul yndella.

An Justys: Ha py le yma'n kentrevak-na?

An Tressa Den: An den-ma yu, Tubby Pencales, syr justys, omma a-n-gwelough-why arag dheugh.

An Justys: Pan vy-sy ef, ytho, cows dhem, a goweth Pencales mas; a-ylta-sy deryvas dhen pyu re-ladhas an edhen-ma?

An Peswara Den: Na-allaf, yn gwyryoneth, syr arluth justys, na nefra ny-wruga leverel y-halsen-vy gul tra a'n par-na a'm honen. Yma tus y'n bys, hyr aga thavas, kemmys a-vyn cressya pup-oll es deryvys dhedha, nefra na-ve aswonys arta an dra gans nep a-n-lavaras kensa. Why a-yl ow gweles, py par gwas of. Nyns-oma onen a'n vosteryon fol-na, ow-leverel an pyth na-yl bos. Mes y-leverys yn-tefry, onen dhe leverel dhem y-halsa onen y leverel, ha tra na hen.

An Justys: Ha pyu yua, yndella a-lavaras dhes?

An Peswara Den: Yn pur wyryoneth, syr arluth justys, Modryp Mally Pentew, ow hentrevoges omma, yu.

An Justys: Lavar, a vestres vas; es godhvedhys genes onen a-alla deryvas dhen pyu o a-ladhas edhen Myghtern Arthur?

An Nessa Benen: Rag leverel hep wow, mara plek dheugh, arluth justys, byth ny-wruga leverel y-whodhfen-vy nep a-wrussa leverel yn-sur pyu a-s-ladhsa: mes y-leverys yn-tyogel bos aswonys genef onen, yn-ta del brederys, a-alsa desmygy pyu a-s-ladhas, mar calsa onen y'n bys y dhesmygy.

An Justys: Lemmyn, ytho, kynth yu wosa mur lafuryans, y-teffen y'n deweth bys yn neppyth 'vas. Mes, lavar, pandr 'a-wra gul dhes crysy y-halsa an den-ma desmygy an gwyryoneth, ben 'vas?

An Nessa Benen: Byth ny-wraf cows a dhen, saw dha ras, rag un venen o – benen goth, ha fest onen fur. Y-fensen a-pe-hy unwyth omma genough, syr justys whek, may halsa kewsel dheugh a'y ganow hy-honen.

An Justys: Na fors bo den bo benen kyn fo: y-hyller hy herghes, hep mar, py le pynag-oll a-vo-hy.

An Nessa Benen: Re'm crysyans, syr justys da, mara pe-hy dres adherag dheugh-why, hy a-lavarsa dheugh marthusyon vras; rag, re'm ena, my re-s-clewys dhe leverel lyes tra varthus kens lemmyn.

An Justys: Pandr' us genes clewys, ytho, bos leverys gensy?

An Nessa Benen: Yn pur dhefry, syra, mar pe ledrys neppyth y'n bys dyworth an gentrevogyon – oy kyn fe, na yar, na nep lyennow na lodrow, martesen, esa ow-tesegha war vagas-eythyn y'n pras – ware hy a-wrella leverel py tyller yth-o gyllys!

An Justys: A-alsa-hy leverel ynweth, aban yu mar fur, py hanow a-ve gylwys an lader ganso a-vyens-y gyllys?

An Nessa Benen: Galsa yn-ta, syr justys whek; ha rag henna, y whon lour, y-halsa-hyhy leverel pyu a-ladhas an balores maga whyr yn-tyen es del lavara pyu a ladra oy!

An Justys: Hag yndella ny a-dyp pup-huny, del gresaf. Mes, lavar, fatel alsa-hy desmygy an traow-ma mar dhyblans? Yu-hy pystryores, a-dhesmyk an pyth es cudhys dre weres an jowl? Gwell vya dhen bos war a venenes an par-na!

An Nessa Benen: Nag-yu, re'm lelder, po Dew defen, rag nefra ny-s-gwelys dhe usya gweth forth es whythra glew yn luf a nep a-ve ledrys dyworto un dra.

An Justys: Ha pyu yu an venen goth fur-ma, ha py fyth-hy kefys?

An Nessa Benen: Un Ejyptyones yu, syra, yn-tyogel, ha trygys o agensow omma dhe Gernow, pur oges dhe'm chy; mes, syweth, gal-las-hy lemmyn dres mor Retegens, nyns-yu-hy whath devedhys bys yn hy fow hy-honen, del dybyaf; rag y-leverer bos pow Ejyp pell bras alemma, ha nyns-o-hy gyllys y'n gorghel rag mos dy kens es nans-yu mes un mys tremenys.

An Justys: Ha whath, Modryp Mally, own a-m-bus na-dalvya travyth y'n bys dhen danvon lester aral war-hy-lergh, ynno cannasow an lagha, rag hy herghes tre! – Lemmyn, rak dalleth arta, a nyns-us den vyth-oll ahanough-why a-yl ry dhen gwell cusul ages honna, rak godhvos pyu a-ladhas edhen Arthur? [*Lemmyn lagas fydhyans a wel an balores dhe dhasvewa.*]

An Kensa Den: Otomma marthus! Ass-yu hemma da!

An Nessa Den: Hy a-agor hy deulagas!

An Kensa Den: Yma-hy ow-lesa hy dywaskel!

An Tressa Den: Hy a-nyj!

An Peswara Den: Hy a-vew!

An Nessa Benen: Nyns-yu marow an balores!

An Justys: Dun, canen oll warbarth yn-lowenak, raghenna, CAN PALORES.

Pup Oll: An balores, du hy lyu,
       Ruth ha'y gelvyn cam ha'y garrow,
    War als Kernow whath a-vew,
       Kyn leverer hy bos marow.

    Yn palores, ny a-wor,
       Spyrys Arthur, mo ha myttyn,
    Whath a-dryk, ha ryp an mor
       A-wra gwytha Enys Breten.

    Myghtern Arthur, dre dha voth,
       Pan us gansa dha balores,
    Re bo gans tus Kernow Goth
       Bys vynytha bew dha spyrys.

    Yeth Kernow, re-be hyrneth
       A'y groweth yn enewores,
    Ena a-dhassergh ynweth
       Maga few avel palores.

    Nyns-yu marow Myghtern Arthur!

45 *From* **Trystan hag Ysolt/Tristan and Isolt by A.S.D. Smith (1951) and D. H. Watkins (1962)**

An myghtern Mark o regnys
yn Kernow, hag ef trygys
dh'y gastel yn Lantyan.
Y yskerens a sordyas
hag er y byn a werryas,
ow codros bras ha byan.

A Lyonesse, Rivalen
an myghtern a dheth toth men
dhe wytha Mark ha'y gerens,
ha dre weres cusul dha
kefrys dre nerth y gledha
y fethas an yskerens.

Pys da o Mark anodho,
hag y ros y whoer dhodho,
Blanchefleur, yn weryson.
Gans Rivalen murgerys
hy o, ha scon demedhys
y fons 'mysk jubylasyon.

Nebes mysyow o passys
may teth newodhow dhe'n lys
bos tyrys an Duk Morgan
yn Lyonesse, ha pylla
trevow an pow ha shyndya
an dus a bup tenewan.

Adhesempys Rivalen
a guntellas y dus ven
ha golya toth bras dhe dre,
ha Blanchefleur y wrek lel
eth ganso yn y worhel
ha hy gans flogh, del wharfe.

Ef a dyras dyogel
arak y Ger Canoel,
ha Blanchefleur ef a ros
ynter dywla y seneschal
Roald, marrak len, a dal
hy gwytha saw deth ha nos.

Arlydhy mur aga lu
a dheth dhodho a bup plu
ha'ga thus ervys gansa.

Oll y eth poran dhe'n gas.
Rivalen a's hembrynkyas,
del yu devar myghtern da.

Pell Blanchefleur a wortas
cafos newodhow a'n gas:
mur o hy fyenasow.
Rivalen a vu ledhys:
byth namoy ny dhewhelys
yn despyt dh'y fysadow.

Yndelma, ha'y holon trogh,
y fu genys dhedhy flogh,
meppyk tek kepar hag el.
Ha hy yn enewores
an flogh y whruk kemeres
yn hy dywvregh ha kewsel:

"Ow map, hyreth tyn re'm be
dhe'th weles: ny allaf re
grassa dhe Dhew, my a'n te.
Tecca meppyk yth osta
es del vu genys nefra
dhe venenryth y'n bys-ma.

"Tryst my a'th tuk dhe vewnans:
tryst my a wel ow mernans
ow tos dhymmo adhewhans,
rak dha asa ny'm bus whans.
Lemmyn dha das yu marow
ha'th vam yn paynys garow:
awos kemmys galarow
Trystan a vyth dha hanow.

———————————

Adref an castel Tyntagel
yth esa lowarth mes a wel:
adro dhodho ke stykennow
lym ha compes avel guyow
ow tegea avallennek
ha lyes eghen frutys whek.

Y'n tyller pella a'n castel
ogas dhe'n stykennow ughel
yth esa ow tevy gwedhen:
saben vras gans lyes scoren.

Yndanny gover-fenten a darth
ha'n dowr a res dre an lowarth.
Ynter glannow a varbel gwres
aberth y'n castel ef a res
ryp stevelyow an benenes.

Awotta'n coyntys, ytho,
a dhyscas Brangyen dhodho
may halla Trystan metya
gans y Ysolt hep lettya:

Pup nos Trystan mos a wre
harth dhe grambla dres an ke
bys y'n lowarth, ha sevel
yndan an saben ughel.

Ena barennow munys
pup onen kemmys ha'y vys
y's troghas ha'ga thewlel
y'n streth a res dhe'n castel.

Pan y's gwelas ow nyja
Ysolt a wodhya yn ta
bos Trystan dywor' an nos
y'n lowarth orth hy gortos.

Menough dre weres Brangyen
goheles an dus-vylen
a wre ha scapya a'n lys
rag metya Trystan kerys.

───────────────

Pan lammas Trystan dres an als
(ha henna dre wovenek fals)
den boghosek, owth aspya
adro, a'n gwelas-ef ow fya.
Yn un slynkya henna eth
ha deryvas dhe'n vyghternes
Trystan dhe dhyank war an treth
hep cledha ganso na hernes.

"Dhe Dhew y whon gras," yn meth-hy
"alemma rak fors ny wraf-vy
pana sherewneth a wrellons:
ow helmy py ow dygelmy,
py ow delyfrya dhe wary:
gwrens poran kepar del vynnons.

Tryslan yu saw! Ny'n ladhons byth,
ha'y yskerens cuth a's tevyth."

Hy deu gonna-bregh warbarth o
fast kelmys gans lovan adro
may tardhas an gos warnodho.
Mes ow mynwherthyn, yn meth-hy:
"Scullya dagrow mar qurussen-vy
ha Trystan saw dre weres Dew,
dhe vos kerys ny vyen gwyw."

———————

A'n howl adrus dhe'n scovva
    y teth golowyn cler:
was fas Ysolt ow codha
    yth esa termyn ber.
Gwyn y lyw kefrys tanow fest
yth o fas Ysolt, Dew yn test.

An myghtern Mark a worras
    (ha ganso yth o cuth)
dyw vanek yn hy ogas
    tekhes a ermyn druth.
Otta'n keth re, cof o ganso,
a dhros-hy a 'Werdhon dhodho.

Nessa, ef a gemeras
    an bysow-emrod gay
ha gans mur rach a worras
    ken bysow yn y le
a ros Ysolt rag goda chons
dhodho-ef demedhys pan vons.

An cledha noth kekefrys
    ynter an dheu dhyvres
a ladhas Morholt solabrys
    ef a gemerras mes:
hag ef a worras y gledha
y honen poran yntredha.

Ef eth yn mes a'n scovva
bys yn y vargh ha lamma
war y geyn, ha leverel
dhe'n gwythyas cos yn ysel:
"Ty omsaw, ledhys na vy,
ha dyank sconna gylly."

———————

War an jeth-brus appoyntyes
yn un varogeth yth eth
an myghtern ha'n vyghternes
dre'n Tyr Gwyn dhe lan an streth,
ha gansa an arlydhy,
a 'ga mysk an bylens try.

War an lan a dal dhedha
lu mur aral yth esa;
Myghtern Arthur mur y vry
ha'y varogyon, yredy,
a wruk aga salujy.

Ow revya, an Gernowyon
yn scathow scon a dheth
adherak an varogyon
ow sevel war an treth.

Parys dhe dyra pan vons,
yn meth Ysolt dhe'n barons:
"Fatel allaf hedhes tyr
hep mostya ow dyllas hyr?
Y coth dhe onen a'n dus
ow don dhe'n lan dres an lys."

Plattyes ryp an streth war lur
yth esa un pryeryn:
trueth y weles, dhe wyr,
ha'y huk plos yn y gerghyn:
owth ystyn y volla pren
ef a bys rag alusen
gans lef truethek a gren.

Dhodho un marrek a wruk
garma: "Coweth, dysk dha huk,
ha dhe'n dowr dyeskytn, ke,
dok an vyghternes dh'y le
marnas ty a vo re wan,
ha codha kens dos dhe'n lan!"

Trystan yn y dhywvregh gref
a gemer an vyghternes
ha dhedhy, ysel y lef,
ef a whyster: "Ow hares!"

"Byth sur a godha war an treth!"
Ysolt dhodho a whystras;

Ha Trystan, dhe'n lan pan dheth,
ow trebuchya a godhas.

Squyerryon ha revyoryon
gans hygow-scath ha revow
a set warnodho gans colon:
namna gafas y ancow.

Yn meth Ysolt: "Geseugh cres
dhe'n boghosek, rak dhe wyr
ef o dyfreth ha gwanhes
ow kerdhes lyes myldyr."
Hy a dewl dhe'n pryeryn
hy modrewy a owr fyn.

———————————

Wosa omlath hyr ha gosek
ledhys vu an cawr gallosek.
Treghy y luf dhyghow a wruk
Trystan, ha'y dry yn ro dhe'n Duk.

"Syra," yn meth Trystan dhodho,
"An ambos porth cof anodho.
Ro dhym ow weryson prenys:
Pettygrew dha gy gorhenys."

"Ow howeth, dar! my vynta-jy
gul dybarth ynter my ha'm ky?
Ty degemer hanter ow thyr
ha'm whoer ganso, preder ha myr!"

"Syra, dha whoer yu tek, dhe wyr,
na ny welys byth tecca tyr;
mes may hallen dyndyl an ky
y fethys Urgan, yredy!"

"Ytho, kemer ef dhys del res,
mes gothfyth ty dhe gemeres
joy ow holon dhe ves glan,
Porth cof a henna, Trystan."

An ky a vu kemynnys
dhe venstrel Kembrek fel:
henna dre y ynjynnys
a'n duk dhe Dyntajel.

An vyghternes o lowen
ow cafos whecca ro:

dek mark owr y ros dhe'n den
rak an ponvos a'n jevo.

Dhe'n myghtern y leverys,
pan welas-ef an ky,
y whruk hy mam murgerys
y dhanvon dhedhy-hy.

Dhe'n owror hy a erghys
kysten dhe'n ky may whrella:
gensy may feva kerghys
yn pup tyller mayth ella.

A'y gref namoy ny wre vry:
an marthus ny gonvedhy:
pup prys pan vyra orth an ky
hy thrystyns eth anedhy.

Preder a Drystan hy har
ha'n ro ganso danvenys
o an skyla hep nep mar
hy bos a'y thrystyns tennys.

Mes un jeth hy wruk aswon
bos an cleghyk ha'y bystry
ow tynkyal joy dh'y holon
pan y'n clewo ow seny.

"Ogh," yn meth-hy, "dhym ny goth
bewa yn joy a'n par ma
ha Trystan ow ton, forsoth,
pup cales ran an bys-ma.
"Ef a alsa gwytha'n ky
ha'y bonvos y ankevy,
mes y dhanvon dhymmo-vy
ef a wruk dre gortesy.

"Ow tascor dhym an dra-ma
y tascoras oll y joy,
mes gon yn ta pandwrama:
ny vynnaf hokkya namoy.

"Dhymmo ny dheseth, Trystan ker
bys mur attes ha da ow cher,
ha ty morethek hep dha gy.
My a vyn godhaf genes-sy."

An fen'ster yth ygoras.
ha'n cleghyk y kemeras
ha'y dewlel pell dhe'n mor bras.

Wardhelergh dhe Dyntajel
Dinas an Seneschal eth:
owth yskynna bys y'n hel
dhe'n vyghternes ef a dheth.

An myghtern ha'n vyghternes
yn dan un tylda ughel
yth esens y ow quary chess:
gervyth ny wrussons kewsel.

Dinas a wruk esedha
yntredha war scavel-dros
kepar ha pan vynna'n ta
sewya pup mevyans yn clos.

Ef a asas y dhywla
yn apert dhe vos gwelys
may whruk Ysolt aspya
bysow Trystan war y vys.

Bregh Dinas hy a gnoukyas
dre wall, ha ran a'n pysys
dhe'n lur war nuk a godhas
ha'n gwary o domhelys.

"A! Seneschal" yn meth-hy,
"Ow gwary why re shyndyas
ma na allaf, yredy,
y dhaskemeres yn fas."

Mark a omdennas a'n hel
hag Ysolt eth dh'y stevel
gans Dinas rak keskewsel.

"Ow har, why yu devedhys
yn cannas dhyworth Trystan?"

"Myghternes, ef yu cudhys
yn ow Hastel de Lidan."

"Yu gwyr y vos demedhys
gans gwrek a Vreten Vyghan?"

"Myghternes, soweth an prys,
demedhys yu, yn certan.
Mes ef a'n afyth dheugh nefra
na wruga agas trayta,
ha ganso why yu synsys
dres oll benenes an bys.
Ef a'gas pys a wrontya
ma'gas gwello unwyth arta
warlergh an ambos yntredhough
orth y anow pan gowssough.
Mar ny vynnough y weles,
merwel a wra, myghternes."
Down yn prederow gyllys,
Ysolt a dewy un spys.
Hy a bredery, hep mar,
a'n Ysolt aral, gwrek hy har.

"Gwyr a leverough, del won,
a'n ambos-na yntredhon.
Dhe Drystan y leverys:
'Pan welaf an bysow gwyr,
nyns us gallos war an bys
na dyfen ryal, dhym crys,
a'm let a wul dha dhesyr'."

"Madama, deu dheth alemma
gasa Tyntajel why a wra
rak mos dhe'n Tyr Gwyn, yn sur,
why ha'n myghtern hag oll an Cur.
Trystan a dhanvon negys,
ha'gas cumyas ef a bys,
rag omgudha ef a vyn
ogas dhe'n forth dhe'n Tyr Gwyn.
Agas pyta ef a wovyn."

"An ambos o gwres a sef,
del leverys, ren ow thas:
dyfen ryal na castel cref
ny'm let a wul y vynnas."

Mark pan glewas a'n mernans
an garoryon, adhewhans
y trethas an mor efan
ha mos dhe Vreten Vyhan.

Ena bos gwryys yth erghys
dyw eler mur aga prys:

an yl a galsydony
dhe Ysolt er cof anedhy,
ha 'y gyla a veryl splan
er revrons cuf orth Trystan.

Mark a's duk yn y worhel
yn tryst bys yn Tyntajel
ha ryp aps an chapel
y fons, onen a bup tu
eno encledhys aga deu.

Dres an nos-na dreysen las
ha delek a devys bras
mes a veth Trystan wordhy
mur scorennow cref dhedhy
ha blejyow whek an Gwaynten,
oll a gramblas dres cryben
an aps hag ena poran
dyeskynna dhe veth splan
Ysolt hag ynno gwrydhya.
Ass yu fast colm kerensa
Y'n mernans unyys arta!

Yn cres hy nerth an dhreysen vras
a vu treghys gans tus an wlas.
Mes ternos freth ow tasvewa
tevys ve'n dhreysen gref arta
mar ven ha mar lun a vlejyow
gwer avel kens my a'n avow.
Y tyeskynnas desempys
dhe veth Ysolt hag yn serghys
owth omwrydhya yn y gerghyn
orth y worhery yn tyen.

Tergwyth y's troghsons tus an wlas
ha tergwyth hy a devys bras.
Dhe hes ger a vu danvenys
dhe'n myghtern adro dhe'n marthus.
Orth an dus ef a wruk dyfen
namoy na droghens an dhreysen.

48 Arthur by Tim Saunders (1990)

lomm ow byz tywl ow ac'h
dhÿ'w rann anken ha' brawac'h
ow c'herth y'n paeav a'w gwoez
gwlazgordh a'dav ow dywdroez
kurun ann kordhow ny'm bydh
bÿz gworra dorn war gledhydh
Arthur rÿ'vuv, gwwr ervyz:
rÿz aeth ow c'hadhl dre'nn byz.

karnow ow marc'h prêst war fordh
mynoc'h azvwlc'h y'm koskordh
maen garw war neb a'goedh
krows war skoez beic'h war dhywskoedh
ow c'hÿvoeth yn kov ha' kan
lyst bara tânow holan
Arthur rÿ'vuv, gwwr kadarn:
pyw a'worr maen war ow c'harn?

dowr tammar ha' penn ann wlaz
glasnedh a'bleg dhÿ'nn lagaz
awel leith a'gan a'nn mor
c'hwystrow syllan dr'y gwlybor
bledhenn mis seîthenn ha'dydh
mîl lev dre varrow'nn gwywwydh
Arthur rÿ'vuv, gwwr didrec'h:
a hÿnna, tro, my a'dec'h.

List of primary characters

This list is not comprehensive but aims to provide the reader with a brief roster of the central characters in the Cornish Arthurian corpus and their relationships. We have taken the most common spelling for the names, though there are often variations.

Arthur – Son of Uther and Igraine, leader of the Britons.
Anna – Arthur's sister.
Bedivere – The knight who returns Excalibur to Dozmary Pool.
Bricelm – A retainer of Gorlois.
Ector – Arthur's foster father.
Galahad – Knight of the Round Table, key knight in the Grail quest.
Geraint – High King of Dumnonia.
Gorlois – The Duke of Cornwall, married to Igraine.
Governal – A retainer and travelling companion of Tristan.
Guenever – Arthur's wife, and lover of Lancelot.
Howell – The Duke of Brittany.
Igraine – The wife of the Duke of Cornwall, mother of Arthur.
Iseult of the White Hands – The Breton Iseult who marries Tristan.
Iseult the Fair – The Queen Iseult, married to King Mark.
Jordan – A retainer of Gorlois.
Kay – Arthur's foster brother, son of Ector, knight of the Round Table.
Launcelot – Knight of the Round Table, lover of Guenever.
Lady of the Lake – An otherworldly woman, keeper of Arthur's sword Excalibur.
Languis – A King of Ireland in Tristan narratives.
Mark – King of Cornwall, married to Iseult the Fair. Uncle of Tristan.
Meliodas – King of Lyonesse, and Tristan's father.
Merlin – Prophet, magician and advisor to Uther and Arthur.
Mordred – Son of Arthur and Morgan le Fay, killer of Arthur.
Morgan le Fay – Half-sister of Arthur, mother of Mordred.
Nimue – Merlin's lover, one of the damsels of the Lake.
Perceval – Knight of the Round Table, key knight in the Grail quest.
The Morold Marhaus – Languis' champion, brother to the Queen of Ireland.
Tristan – Son of Meliodas, lover of Iseult the Fair, nephew of Mark.
Ulfin of Ricaradoch – A knight and retainer of Uther Pendragon.
Uther Pendragon – King of Britain, lover of Igraine, father of Arthur.

Bibliography and sources

1   Stone Inscriptions of Cornwall (500–800AD)

The so-called 'Arthur Stone' was discovered on Tintagel Island in 1998. Any connection with a historical Arthur is tenuous; nevertheless, the find led to a re-examination of the historical and mythological connection between Arthur and Tintagel. The inscription at Slaughter Bridge is a different case; it has been associated with King Arthur for centuries. A misreading of the last word as MACATRY suggested that Arthur's name had been contracted to Atry. The stone is also known as King Arthur's Tomb. The Selus Stone may refer to Selyf, brother of Yestin and son of the High King of Dumnonia, Geraint. The names on the Tristan Stone have been related to Tristan himself and to King Mark of Cornwall. A ninth century manuscript mentions 'Marcus, also named Quonomorius (Cunomorus)'. Cunomorus is cognate with modern Welsh cynfawr meaning 'great prince'. The stone's location certainly fits the geographical setting of much of the Tristan literature.

The 'Arthur' Stone is displayed in the Royal Institution of Cornwall Museum, Truro. For other stones, see Ordnance Survey Grid references, SX 109857, SW 372315 and SX 110524. Translation by the editors.

2   The Dialogue of Arthur and Eliud by Taliesin (c.550)

Taliesin was a Welsh poet associated with the territories of the Britons in the 'Old North'. He immortalised in poetry his most generous patron Urien of Rheged, an area probably corresponding with modern Cumbria. In later ages prophetic poetry was often ascribed to him. This extract is from a dialogue in which Arthur questions his dead nephew Eliud, in the form of an eagle, about the elements of Christian doctrine. Arthur here is explicitly identified with the land of Cornwall, and is portrayed not only as a soldier, but as a man unacquainted with the fundamentals of Christianity. The theme of a man transformed into a bird is common in post-Roman Celtic texts, especially in prophetic literature.

Jesus College, Oxford, MSS 3, 1–3a. Translation by the editors.

3   *From* How Culhwch Won Olwen (c.1000)

Culhwch and Olwen is probably the oldest of the collection of Welsh medieval tales known as the Mabinogi. This section portrays a Celtic-speaking Britain in which even the Romans have not yet arrived. In order to marry Olwen, the giant's daughter, Culhwch has to obtain the magical razor, shears and comb from the Twrch Trwyth, a giant boar. Arthur and his men help him, and during the chase pursue the boar to Cornwall where Arthur has a residence. Kelli Wig is traditionally identified as Callington.

J. Gwenogvryn Evans (1907) *White Book of the Mabinogion*, Pwllheli: Privately published. Translation by the editors.

4   *From* The History of the Kings of Britain by Geoffrey of Monmouth (1136)

Geoffrey of Monmouth (d. 1155) was an Augustinian canon from Wales who spent most of his life at Oxford. His 'History', which he claimed was based on an ancient book, is a massive compendium of historical and mythological material imaginatively blended into a continuous narrative. It displays the glory of the Britons from their first arrival as refugees from Troy and culminates in the reign of Arthur. There are indications that some of his sources were in Brythonic languages, possibly Cornish.

San-Marte (ed.) (1854) Historia Regum Britanniae, Halle: Edward Anton, pp. 112–13, pp.114–15, pp.116–18 and pp.156–7. Translation by the editors.

5   Concerning the Miracles of St Mary of Laudun by Hermann of Tournai (1146)

This incident at Bodmin (probably around 1113), recorded by the Trappist monk Hermann of Tournai (d.1147), concerns a tour by the canons of Laon in France through Cornwall to collect money for their cathedral. This text offers us an important picture of a strong Cornish association with, and belief in, King Arthur. Not only does the observer note that the territory had been Arthur's Land, but also that he is still alive and waiting to return. Twentieth-century Cornish revivalists drew on this as an important Cornish ideological construct.

E. K. Chambers and R.D. White (ed. and tr.) (1927) *Arthur of Britain*, London: Sidgwick & Jackson.

6   The Prophecy of Merlin by John of Cornwall (c.1150)

John of Cornwall, probably born in St Germans in the early twelfth century, studied in Paris and died sometime around 1199. This text belongs to the widespread medieval tradition of expressing political and religious propaganda in the guise of ancient prophecy and draws heavily on Cornish and Celtic mythology. Many of the references – necessarily cryptic at the time —are now obscure beyond recovery, but clearly the text calls upon the House of Arthur to unite against incursions by other territories and peoples into the islands of the Britons. Cornwall in particular is asked to respond to the invasion.

John of Cornwall, *Prophetia Merlini* (Cod. Ottobonianus Lat. 1474, Vatican). Translation by the editors.

7   *From* The Cornish Glosses of the Prophecy of Merlin by John of Cornwall (c.1150)

John of Cornwall's notes reveal that his sources included documents in Old Cornish, so demonstrating that the Cornish literary tradition was thriving despite the loss of noble patronage. The reference to the castle at Piriron is interesting, for it would appear to be an earlier Cornish name for the area now known as Tintagel. Brentigia (present-day Bodmin Moor) has several Arthurian sites, including Dozmary Pool.

John of Cornwall, *Prophetia Merlini* (Cod. Ottobonianus Lat. 1474, Vatican). Translation by the editors.

8   *From* The Romance of Tristan by Béroul (c.1150)

Little is known about Béroul. What is certain, however, is that he had an intimate knowledge of Cornwall which he used as the setting for his re-telling of Tristan and Isolde story. The two sequences here are Tristan and Isolde in the forest of Moresk, and the crossing made at Malpas. All the evidence suggests that there must have been a Cornish provenance for the Tristan and Isolde narratives which emerged in continental Europe.

Ernest Muret (ed.) (1903), *Le Roman de Tristan par Béroul*, Paris: Firmin Didot et Compagnie.

9   The Sicilian Coverlet (c.1400)

This quilted linen coverlet was produced in Sicily around the start of the fifteenth century and is now kept in the Victoria and Albert Museum, London. It is a striking example of how the popularity of Cornish narratives spread across Europe during this period of the middle ages. The fourteen extant panels contain scenes from the early part of the Tristan narrative: the oppression of Cornwall by King Langius of Ireland and his champion the Morold, and Tristan's battle with the latter on behalf of his uncle King Mark. The story is probably taken from chapters seventeen to nineteen of the fourteenth century novella *La Tavola Ritonda o l'istoria di Tristano*. The text on the embroidery is in Sicilian dialect. Fragment 14 is incomplete.

Thurstan C. Peter (1907) 'Tristan and Iseult' in *Journal of the Royal Institution of Cornwall* VolsXVII Part one.

10   *From* Arthur, a short sketch of his life and history in English verse by the Marquis of Bath (c.1428)

This little known English poem shows the importance of Cornwall within an Arthurian narrative, perhaps because the English author knew the territory. It establishes three core motifs which later become part of Cornish Arthurian belief. First, it stresses that Arthur died in Cornwall and was only later taken to Glastonbury. Second, the narrative indicates that both the Cornish and the Bretons believed that Arthur would return to rule. Third, the text shows the continuing tension between Britons and Saxons at what some would consider a relatively late date. The author explains that the Saxon term 'Welsh' also includes Bretons and Cornish.

Frederick J. Furnivall (ed.) (1889) *Arthur, a short sketch of his life and history in Engish verse* London: Trübner and Co.

11   *From* Le Morte D'Arthur by Thomas Malory (1485)

The exact identity of Sir Thomas Malory (d.1471) has always been a mystery, but most scholars agree on Malory of Newbold Revel who after 1450 was imprisoned on several charges. In 1485 William Caxton printed the text, reshaping the work and giving it the title by which it is known. The version uses modernised spelling but otherwise is in accordance with Caxton. Our selection encompasses Cornish material: Arthur's procreation and birth, his pulling of the sword from the stone, Merlin's death (linking tenuously but interestingly to Merlin's cave and the Merlin Rock off Mousehole), a sequence set in Brittany (yet having Cornish equivalents – St Michael's Mount and its legends of giants), as well as sections depicting the deeds of Tristan. Malory makes Cornwall and Lyonesse two separate countries.

A. W. Pollard (ed.) (1900) *Thomas Malory: Le Morte D'Arthur*, London: Macmillan.

12   *From* Beunans Meriasek by Radolphus Ton (1504)

Radolphus Ton, the likely author of Beunans Meriasek, was a clergyman. The Cornish play *The Life of Saint Meriasek* contains many veiled topical political allusions. This is particularly obvious in the character of Teudar, the Duke of Cornwall, a broad theatrical personification of Henry Tudor. In the play Arthurian geographical associations remain strong. Cornish dukes or kings ruled from Castle-an-Dinas and Tintagel, notably called the 'chief dwelling-seat'. The original Cornish text can be found in the appendix.

Whitley Stokes (ed. and tr.) (1972) *The Life of Saint Meriasek: Bishop and Confessor, a Cornish Drama*, London: Trübner and Co.

13   *From* Itinerary by John Leland (c.1540)

John Leland (1503–52) was one of Britain's first antiquarians. This extract gives an interesting account of the state of Tintagel castle and of the battle of Camlan.

John Leland, 'The Itinerary: So far as it relates to Cornwall' in Davies Gilbert (ed) (1838) *The Parochial History of Cornwall*, Vol 4, London: J. B. Nichols and Son.

14   *From* A Herring's Tail by Richard Carew (1598)

Richard Carew (1555–1620) is one of the first writers to fully embrace 'English culture' in Cornwall, though he had a residual knowledge of Cornish matters. He saw English as a modernising force. *A Herring's Tail* is a much neglected piece of Anglo-Cornish literature which satirises the medieval Arthur as a great British leader. Carew achieves this by showing the progress of a snail called Sir Lymazon (Greek for a snail) who is climbing the steeple of a mausoleum at Tintagel castle. The snail has lofty dreams of chivalry but the wind eventually knocks him off.

Richard Carew (1598) *A Herrings Tayle: Containing a Poeticall Fiction of Divers Matters Worthie of Reading*, London: Matthew Lownes.

15   *From* The Survey of Cornwall by Richard Carew (1602)

Tintagel also features in Carew's survey. Most of the work for his volume had been completed in the previous decade, and the text was constantly revised right until its eventual publication. Carew situates himself within the trend of Cornish Arthurian writing of this period, so the quest to climb the dangerous cliffs to the castle somehow parallels the activities of Arthur's knights. To this Carew adds a brief poem – interestingly still recalling Cornwall's relationship with Brittany. Also included in Carew's *Survey* is the prophecy in Cornish regarding the Spanish attack on Cornwall in 1595, which mentions the Merlin Rock, just outside Mousehole harbour.

Richard Carew (1769 [1602]) *The Survey of Cornwall, and an Epistle concerning the Excellencies of the English Tongue*, Penzance: J. Hewlett.

16   *From* The Lives of the Saints by Nicholas Roscarrock (c.1620)

Roscarrock (c.1548–1634) was from North Cornwall and spent four years in the Tower of London, imprisoned for his Catholic beliefs. His greatest work was his lives of the British and Irish saints. In the Life of Saint Piran, he alludes to King Arthur. Roscarrock would have known the Tintagel area well.

Nicholas Roscarrock, *Lives of the Saints* (MS Add. 3041, Cambridge).

17   *From* Merlin's Prophecies and Predictions by Thomas Heywood (1651)

Thomas Heywood (c.1574–1641) is known primarily as a dramatist, but he was also interested in the folklore of Britain. In this posthumous collection he considers the role of Merlin as a prophet. In the first and second sections here, he writes a history in the style of the Prophecies of Merlin and interprets them much as one would the verses of Nostradamus. In the third section, Heywood embellishes an incident involving the Earl of Cornwall during the reign of Edward II (c.1307). Pierce Gavestone from Gascony was given the Earldom of Cornwall, but he seemed to be a rather unpopular man, stealing and generally irritating other royal peers. He was banished to Ireland but returned to steal jewels and a gold table reputed to have belonged to King Arthur and shipped them to France to have them sold. Eventually he was besieged at Warwick and beheaded by Thomas, Earl of Lancaster, whom Heywood interprets as 'the Bear' of the verse.

Thomas Heywood (1651) *Merlin's Prophecies and Predictions*. London: Paul's Churchyard.

18 *From* **The Dutchesse of Cornwall's progresse to see the Land's end & to visit the mount by Nicholas Boson (c.1665)**

Nicholas Boson (c.1624–1703) was one of several patriotic gentry from this period who learnt Cornish from his neighbours and servants. This children's tale combines folklore, classical learning, mythology, invention and satire. At this point the story of Harry the Hermitt collides head on with Arthuriana; one of the few incorporations of the motif into seventeenth-century Anglo-Cornish/Cornish literature. Presumably Boson sees Harry's witchery as being somehow connected to the magic of the Arthurian era.

Writings of the Boson Family (BL Add, MS 28 554 = Gwavas Papers plus Gatley MS, Truro, RIC and Tonkin MS B, Truro).

19 The History of King Arthur, and his Progenitors by William Hals (c.1736)

Hals (1655–c.1737) was a scholar and historian of Cornwall. He claimed one of his sources of his *History* was John Trevisa's now lost *Book of the Acts of Arthur*. Trevisa (c.1342–1402) was a Cornish-speaking scholar, and so it is possible that there was once more Arthurian material in Cornish which has not survived.

William Hals (c.1736) *The Complete History of Cornwall*, Truro.

20 *From* **Cornubia: A Poem in Five Cantos by George Woodley (1819)**

In his epic tribute to Cornwall, George Woodley (1786–1846) takes the reader on a journey to the different coastlines of Cornwall. Here in the 'Northern' section he deals with Tintagel and King Arthur. Like the Thomas Hogg text which follows it is interesting to see how central Arthur was to the Cornish self-image at the very beginning of the nineteenth century, long before Tennyson sparked a revival of interest elsewhere.

George Woodley (1819) *Cornubia: A Poem in Five Cantos*, Truro: Mitchell and Co.

21 *From* **The Fabulous History of Cornwall by Thomas Hogg (1827)**

Thomas Hogg (1777–1835) has received little attention from Cornish scholars, even though his fantastical history of Cornwall has much to tell us about conceptualisations of Cornwall from ancient druids and goddess worshippers to the folklore of mining. Like Woodley, he provides a complete Arthurian sequence within his history. Here, we have chosen three sections: Prince Arthur – with its early reference to Merlin's cave; Sir Tristrem – with its reference to Restormel Castle; and Merlin and the Woodcutter – a story ancillary to the central corpus.

Thomas Hogg (1827) *The Fabulous History of Cornwall*, Truro: E. Heard.

22 The Sisters of Glen Nectan by Robert Stephen Hawker (c.1831)

Vicar of Morwenstow in North Cornwall, Robert Stephen Hawker (1803–75) was an eccentric poet and mystic. His 'The Song of the Western Men' is better known as the Cornish anthem 'Trelawny'. St Nectan's Glen and its waters were an important Arthurian theme for later writers. The Kieve is just a few miles from Tintagel. In legend the site is imagined as the secluded place where Arthurian knights bowed their heads in prayer before setting out upon their Grail quest. Here, Hawker tells the story of the tragic sisters.

C.E. Byles (ed.) (1904) *R.S. Hawker: Cornish Ballads and Other Poems*. London: The Bodley Head.

23   *From* Scilly and its Legends by H.J. Whitfeld (1852)

The Rev Henry John Whitfeld (1808–55) was educated at Shrewsbury and Downing College, Cambridge. His visit to the Isles of Scilly as a folklore collector was inspirational for this re-telling of the last days of Arthur and his battle with Mordred. The creation of Scilly as well as the destruction of Lyonesse is depicted as the result of Merlin the Enchanter's revenge on Mordred. The second section is a piece of topographical folklore concerning the Arthur rocks of the Eastern Isles. In this, Whitfeld draws the connection between his narrative and the Scillonian environment.

Whitfeld, H.J. (1852) *Scilly and Its Legends*, London: Timpkin, Marshall and Co.

24   *From* Idylls of the King by Alfred, Lord Tennyson (1856–74)

Tennyson (1809–92) first came to Cornwall in June 1848, and met Robert Stephen Hawker. He recorded in his journal: 'Coldest manner of Vicar till I told him my name, then all heartiness. Walk on cliff with him, told of shipwreck'. Perhaps more than any other epic nineteenth-century Arthurian work, 'Idylls of the King' has had a tremendous influence on poets in Cornwall and elsewhere. Seeking inspiration, Tennyson toured Cornwall again in August–September 1860, allowing him to add further sequences. Here we include four key sections of the work: Arthur's birth, the finding of Excalibur, the final battle with Mordred, and Arthur's journey to Avalon. The poem is dedicated to Queen Victoria, Tennyson feeling that she exchanged the 'darkness of the battle in the west' for 'ever-broadening England'. The first two extracts are taken from *The Coming of Arthur*, the third and fourth from *The Passing of Arthur.*

Hallam (ed.) (1908, 1913) *Idylls of the King, annotated by Alfred, Lord Tennyson (the Eversley Edition)* London: Macmillan.

25   The Quest of the Sangraal by Robert Stephen Hawker (1863)

'The Quest of the Sangraal' is an Arthurian masterpiece, written at the height of Victorian interest in such matters. Biographical evidence has shown that the poem was written just after the death of Hawker's wife, Charlotte, while he was taking opium. Longfellow said, 'I have read Tennyson's 'Holy Grail' and Mr. Hawker's 'Quest', and I think the latter poem far superior to the Laureate's.' Tennyson commented, 'Hawker has beaten me on my own ground.' High praise indeed for Hawker, though there is a sense that both Longfellow and Tennyson are slightly dismissive. It is shameful that many collections of Arthurian verse choose to ignore Hawker's epic.

C.E. Byles (ed.) (1904) *R.S. Hawker: Cornish Ballads and Other Poems*. London: The Bodley Head.

26   *From* Popular Romances of the West of England: The Drolls, Traditions, and Superstitions of Old Cornwall by Robert Hunt (1865)

Robert Hunt (1807–87) was born in Plymouth and was Keeper of the Mining Record Office in Cornwall, as well as being an important early collector of Cornish folklore. Here, one senses some of Hunt's desperation to find more Arthurian material in Cornwall whilst he was collecting. In comparison to other legends and narratives, he was to find little, and had to put together a kind of 'hotch-potch' of material to deal with the subject. Elsewhere we see typical mid-nineteenth-century Cornish Arthuriana, much of it collected from earlier writers. The possiblity of a Knights Templar settlement at Temple Moors suggests a potential Cornish association with the controversial theory that the Templars were the guardians of the blood-line of Christ, symbolised in the Holy Grail, which was taken to Britain by Joseph of Arimathea.

Robert Hunt (ed.) (1865) *The Drolls, Traditions and Superstitions of Old Cornwall: Popular Romances of the West of England (First and Second Series)*, London: John Camden Hotten.

27   The Buried City by John Harris (1868)

John Harris (1820–84) was an Anglo-Cornish poet from Bolenowe near Camborne. Although he is most well-known for his adept poetic depiction of the industrialisation of Cornwall, he was also interested in shaping the image of Cornwall in other ways. His collection *Luda: A Lay of the Druids* was inspired by Carn Brea and other 'druidic' monuments of Cornwall. It also contains a number of poems based on Cornish legends. Here we see Harris' re-telling of the drowning of Lyonesse.

John Harris (1886) *Luda: A Lay of the Druids London*, Hamilton, Adams and Co.

28   Dozmare Pool, Cornwall by John Brent (1880)

It is difficult to date the association between Dozmare (or Dozmary) Pool and Arthur's sword Excalibur. However, the proximity of the pool to Camelford and North Cornwall is perhaps one contributing factor to its incorporation into the narratives, as is the subsequent romanticisation of Bodmin Moor. Here, the antiquarian and novelist from Kent, John Brent (1808–82) makes his observations on the landscape, heavily inspired by the poetry of Tennyson. During various periods of drought, the Pool's bottom has been searched for the sword, but only flint arrowheads have been found. Another possible contender for the final resting place of Excalibur is Loe Pool, near Porthleven in south Cornwall.

John Brent (1880) *Dozmare Pool*, Cornwall: n.p.

29   *From* Tristram of Lyonesse by A.C. Swinburne (1882)

Swinburne (1837–1909) turned to this Arthurian theme after he had broken away from the Pre-Raphaelites, and claimed Wagner's opera as a major influence. He may have been inspired by his visit to Tintagel in 1864; the sea looms over everything in this poem.

A.C. Swinburne (1899) *Tristram of Lyonesse and Other Poems*, London: Chatto &Windus.

30   *From* An Unsentimental Journey through Cornwall by Dinah Craik (1884)

This sequence is from the diary of Dinah Craik (1826–87), novelist, writer of short stories and fairly tales. Her diary is one of the finest nineteenth-century travelogues to have been written about Cornwall. In this rather sentimental section about Tintagel she cannot resist re-telling the legend of Arthur. King Arthur appears often in her journal as a metaphor.

Dinah Craik (1884) *An Unsentimental Journey through Cornwall*, London: Macmillan.

31   *From* Cornish Feasts and Folklore by Margaret A. Courtney (1890)

Margaret Courtney (1834–1920) was a Cornish folklore collector. Her contribution shows the early effects of tourism on the corpus of Arthurian material derived from Tintagel. She suggests that the labelling of the stone features known as 'King Arthur's cups and saucers' was an invention of tour guides rather than a continuation of local tradition. Interestingly, she also refers to Arthur as King of Cornwall rather than of England – a view against the grain at this period.

Margaret A. Courtney (1890) *Cornish Feasts and Folklore*, Penzance: Beary and Son.

32   *From* The Arthurian Legend by John Rhys (1890)

The Welshman John Rhys (1840–1915) was a pioneering Celtic scholar who had studied at the universities of Heidelberg, Leipzig and Göttingen. He became the first Professor of Celtic Studies at the University of Oxford. Unlike many scholars throughout the nineteenth and twentieth centuries who have minimised the importance of the Cornish elements of Arthurian literature, Rhys considered the cultural geography of North Cornwall central to the development of the Arthur corpus.

John Rhys (1890) *The Arthurian Legend*, Oxford: Oxford University Press.

33   Lyonesse by James Dryden Hosken (1902)

Hosken (1861–1963) is a much underrated Anglo-Cornish poet. Here he presents a poetic construction of Lyonesse, embedded with images of courtly love and chivalry. By Hosken's time, Lyonesse was becoming a key imaginative element of Cornish Arthuriana.

James Dryden Hosken (1902) *Poems and Songs of Cornwall*, Plymouth: Mitchell, Burt & Co.

34   *From* Some Possible Arthurian Place-Names in West Penwith by Henry Jenner (1912)

Henry Jenner (1893–1934), born in St Columb, is widely regarded as one of the founding figures of the early twentieth-century 'revival' in Cornish language, literature and culture. For much of his life, he was a keeper of manuscripts at the British Museum. Here, he offers an insight into the relationship between history, romance and real place-names. It is perhaps one of the first Arthurian critiques to be made from a Cornish point of view. Jenner's scholarly conclusions are cautious, yet it was arguably Jenner's personal belief and interest in Arthur as a Cornish symbol which helped establish the figure's centrality in the Cornish Revival.

Henry Jenner (1912) 'Some Possible Arthurian Place-Names in West Penwith' in *Journal of the Royal Institution of Cornwall*. Volume XIX.

35   *From* Legend Land by 'Lyonesse' (1922)

The story of Lyonesse continued to fascinate travellers in the 1920s. Here, 'Lyonesse' (relying heavily on the work of Robert Hunt) offers a re-telling for passengers using the Great Western Railway. The Great Western Railway did much to publicise Cornwall's legendary past, publishing this and several other similar booklets. The company also gave several locomotives names with Arthurian associations – *Duke of Cornwall*, *Tintagel Castle* and *Chough*. The London and South Western Railway, whose line served North Cornwall, had engines with names such as *Excalibur*, *Iseult*, *Lyonesse*, *Pendragon* and *Merlin*.

Lyonesse (1922) *Legend Land: Being a collection of some of the old tales told in Cornwall once, served by the Great Western Railway, now retold by Lyonesse*, London: The Great Western Railway.

36   The Famous Tragedy of the Queen of Cornwall at Tintagel in Lyonesse by Thomas Hardy (1923)

Although Hardy (1840–1928) is most associated with Dorset, he had close connections with North Cornwall. In 1870 he was sent to St Juliot's church, near Boscastle, to commence work on its restoration. While there, he met his first wife, Emma Gifford, who died in 1912. Hardy later returned to the area with his second wife, Florence Dugdale, recalling his earlier love, and immersing himself in Arthuriana. He already had constructed his own vision of Cornwall – which he renamed Lyonesse and used as the background for the novel *A Pair of Blue Eyes* (1873) and the short story *A Mere Interlude* (1885). Some commentators have suggested that his re-telling of Tristram and Iseult – with its two Iseults – may be a psychological study of his two wives. The play is reproduced in full here and demonstrates the fashion for Arthurian drama in this period.

Thomas Hardy (1923) *The Famous Tragedy of the Queen of Cornwall at Tintagel in Lyonesse*, London: Macmillan.

37   The Coming of Arthur by John Baragwanath King (1925)

John Baragwanath King (1864–1939) was born in Penzance and worked as a painter, satirist and poet. He appears to draw heavily on Hals' eighteenth-century version of the Arthur story, though the verse itself is beautifully rendered, incorporating figures such as Jubelin, a disciple of St Piran, and pagan elements – the witches and the good spirits.

John Baragwanath King (1925) *Arthur and Others in Cornwall*, London: Erskine Macdonald.

38   Anglice, a Patriotic Song our Motherland by Katharine Lee Jenner (1926)

Katharine Lee Jenner (1854–1936), a well-known poet in her time, was the wife of Henry Jenner. This poem not only celebrates the Cornish conceptualisation of King Arthur in the post-World War One era, but also anticipates the way in which the revival would reconstruct him. It is one of several poems where Katharine Lee wrote the English text and her husband the Cornish.

Katharine Lee Jenner (1926) *Songs of the Stars and the Sea*, London: Erskine MacDonald.

39   Tintagel Castle in History and Romance by Henry Jenner (1927)

In essence, this article follows up Jenner's earlier paper with the focus this time on the specific role of Tintagel. Drawing on his wealth of manuscript knowledge, his conclusions were dismissive, and hardly likely to encourage tourism. That, however, was Jenner's point. On the whole he felt the development of tourism at Tintagel during the early part of the twentieth century was founded on dubious associations, and failed to celebrate what he considered what was of real interest in Cornwall – Cornish language and literature.

Henry Jenner (1927) 'Tintagel Castle in History and Romance' in *Journal of the Royal Institution of Cornwall* No. 74.

40   *From* Ceremonies of the Gorseth of the Bards of Cornwall (1928–Present)

The Arthur material was not included in the first two Cornish Gorsethow. Most probably Jenner and Nance added the Arthurian allusions after the 1930 Arthurian Congress which was held in Cornwall. Today, the Arthurian portions of the ritual differentiate the Cornish Gorseth from its Welsh and Breton counterparts. Allusions to the Holy Grail in the ceremonial demonstrate the ties between the Gorseth, the Revival and Christianity – particularly, and paradoxically, the Church of England. The role of Anglo-Catholicism in the early revival was strong. The sword-bearer remains a mythic – if somewhat tenuous – link to the Celtic 'heroic' age of Arthur. The original Cornish text can be found in the appendix.

'Ceremonies of the Gorseth of the Bards of Cornwall' (n.d.) Cornwall. Leaflet handed out at the Annual Gorseth.

41   *From* King Arthur's Territory by J. Hambley Rowe (1929)

The Cornish Revivalist J. Hambley Rowe (1870–1937), founder of the Arthurian Congress, was born in Hayle but practised medicine in Yorkshire for much of his life. Here he offers an argument for the possibility of some of Arthur's twelve battles having a Cornish context. There is some convincing place-name evidence, which is often overlooked.

J. Hambley Rowe (1929) 'King Arthur's Territory' in *Journal of the Royal Institution of Cornwall* No. 76.

42 *From* King Arthur: His Symbolic Story in Verse by B. D. Vere (1930)

The shadowy B.D. Vere (perhaps a pen-name pun on Bedivere) wrote this verse drama for King Arthur's Halls of Chivalry. The opening sequence shows the boy Jesus completing a wood-carving on Tintagel Island as well as setting the Grail quest in motion. Vere's is one of the finest modern re-tellings of the story of Christ and Joseph of Arimathea in Cornwall.

B.D. Vere (1930) *King Arthur: His Symbolic Story in Verse*, Tintagel: King Arthur's Halls.

43 An Balores/The Chough by Robert Morton Nance (1932)

Nance (1873–1959) was a leading Cornish revivalist and language activist. He started the Old Cornwall Societies, developed a system of standardised Cornish (Unified) and was the key figure behind the Cornish Gorseth. One of the most important strands of Cornish identity, as Nance perceived it, was King Arthur and his presence in the form of a chough. If Arthur might one day return and lead a reconstructed Cornwall, then there was at least hope for a Cornwall in industrial, economic and cultural turmoil. This allegorical drama was written to entertain the delegates of the first Celtic Congress held in Cornwall in 1932. This Congress gave Cornish activists an opportunity to share development in the Cornish language with an international audience. Interestingly, Nance promotes a vision of a Cornish-speaking Arthur – something rarely conceived of outside Cornwall. The play's structure would seem to be based on elements of Cornish liturgical drama. The original Cornish text can be found in the appendix.

Robert Morton Nance (1932) *An Balores*, St Ives: James Lanham.

44 *From* Dawn in Lyonesse by Mary Ellen Chase (1938)

Mary Ellen Chase (1887–1973) was an American scholar and author who spent time in Cornwall from 1934–1936. At the end of nineteenth century, William Taylor had built his King Arthur Castle Hotel. Mary Ellen Chase set her novel in that hotel just as the revival in Arthuriana in Cornwall was coming to an end. Filled with romantic depictions of the Cornish landscape, the text is akin to a magic realist re-telling of 'Tristan' laced with other Arthuriana, and retains the original's tragic ending. At the time it was described curiously as 'a story of the fishing folk of Cornwall'. Her heroine (or rather Yseult) bears the identifiably Cornish name of Ellen Pascoe.

Mary Ellen Chase (1938) *Dawn in Lyonesse*, London and Glasgow: Collins.

45 *From* Trystan hag Ysolt/Tristan and Isolt by A.S.D. Smith (1951) and D. H. Watkins (1962)

A.S.D Smith (1883–1950) came from Sussex. He was a language teacher, author of popular textbooks of both Cornish and Welsh and editor of *Kernow* (1933–4), the first all-Cornish periodical. Well-known for his popular *Welsh Made Easy*, he adapted similar methods for *Cornish Made Easy*, which is still in print. His 8,000 line poem on Tristan and Isolt is perhaps the most important early twentieth-century work in Cornish. It was written while Smith was on Air Raid Warden duty during the latter part of the Second World War and remains incomplete. We only have the notes for Part 18 and the last part, the death of Tristan, was never written. The poem was then edited by E.G. Retallack Hooper and published in 1951. The unfinished part of the story was completed by D. H. Watkins in 1962. Watkins (1892–1969) came from the Rhondda Valley in South Wales. He taught for many years in Cornwall and finally settled here. Both Smith and Watkins follow Joseph Bédier's compilation of the various versions, *La Légende de Tristan*, fairly closely. They also display influences from the Arthurian revival in contemporary Welsh literature. A few small emendations to the text have been made here. The sections are from 1:1, 1–77, 6:6, 1–31, 8:4, 1–23, 9:8,

139–168, 12:1, 228–89, 14:1, 94–160 and 17:1, 1–69. The final section here is from D. H. Watkins, 19:5, 1–42. The original Cornish text can be found in the appendix.

A.S.D. Smith (1951) *Trystan & Ysolt*, Redruth: J. & M. Roberts; D. H. Watkins (1973) *Trystan & Ysolt*, Camborne: An Lef Kernewek. Translation by the editors.

46 *From* Mines and Miners of Cornwall by A.K. Hamilton Jenkin (1970)

The historian Dr Alfred Kenneth Hamilton Jenkin (1900–80) was born of a Quaker family in Camborne and is best known for *The Cornish Miner: An Account of his Life Above and Underground from Early Times* (1927) and *The Story of Cornwall* (1934). He was President of the Royal Institution of Cornwall from 1958–9 and President of the Federation of Old Cornwall Societies from 1959–60. He was one of the first bards of the Cornish Gorseth admitted in 1928. Here, in his survey of north Cornwall's mining history, he reviews the considerable amount of mining activity surrounding the island at Tintagel. Vestiges of mining equipment can still be observed, despite considerable effort by the heritage industry to 'cleanse' the site.

A. K. Hamilton Jenkin (1970) *Mines and Miners of Cornwall: Part XVI, Wadebridge, Camelford and Bude*, Cornwall: Old Cornwall Societies.

47 *From* Geraint: Last of the Arthurians by Donald R. Rawe (1972)

Donald R. Rawe was born in Padstow in 1930. A historian, folklorist, novelist and poet, he has been enormously influential in shaping modern Anglo-Cornish drama. In the early 1970s, as well as *Geraint: Last of the Arthurians*, he completed two other plays, *Petroc of Cornwall* and *The Trial of St Piran*, for performance at the open-air theatre-in-the round known as 'Piran Round'. Geraint was a reputed King of Cornwall (and Dumnonia), who as a young man fought alongside King Arthur. Rawe's version of the story follows the Welsh *Life of St Cybi* in making Jestyn (St Just) and Selyf (St Selevan) sons of Geraint.

Donald R. Rawe (1972) *Geraint: Last of the Arthurians*, Padstow: Lodenek Press.

48 Arthur by Tim Saunders (1990)

The Cornish language poet Tim Saunders (b.1952) here uses the symbol of Arthur to point out the dangers of forcing others to bear the actual as well as symbolic weight of people's aspirations. The original Cornish text can be found in the appendix.

Tim Saunders (1990) *Arthur*, Collection of the author.

49 *From* Nativitas Christi/The Nativity by Alan M. Kent (2000)

Several commentators on Cornish literature have remarked on the possibility that a now-lost Nativity text was part of the original *Ordinalia* cycle. The extant trilogy jumps from Solomon (in *Origo Mundi*) to the temptation of Jesus (*Passio Christi*). The Anglo-Cornish poet Kent (b.1967) supplies part of the 'missing' nativity narrative – running from the Annunciation to Christ's visit to Cornwall with Joseph of Arimathea. In Cornwall, the child Jesus predicts the coming of Arthur, the search for the Grail and the saints.

Alan M. Kent (2000) *Nativitas Christi*, Collection of the author.

8. Britain.

Notes

1   Stone Inscriptions of Cornwall (500–800AD)

1. Claimed as a possible early form of 'Arthur'.
2. Equated with Tristan.
3. Some sources identify him as King Mark.

2   The Dialogue of Arthur and Eliud by Taliesin (c.550)

1. Eliud is one of the names given to the wild man figure. Later re-tellings of the Merlin story cast Merlin as a prophetic poet/outcast of this type. Wild men figures occur in all branches of early and medieval Celtic literature.
2. Arthur is derived from the word for a bear.
3. Uther Pendragon.

3   *From* How Culhwch Won Olwen (c.1000)

1. Welsh: Mel y cavas Kulhwch Olwen.
2. The river Tawe which flows into the sea at Swansea.
3. In Herefordshire.

4   *From* The History of the Kings of Britain by Geoffrey of Monmouth (1136)

1. Cadwaladr, a descendent of Brutus, lost the dominion of Britain to the Saxons.
2. The constellation.
3. Two Saxon leaders.
4. Demeliock is a crucial Arthurian site in Cornwall. It lies between St Dennis and Castle-an-Dinas (mid-Cornwall), making both of them and the present-day Goss Moor potential battle sites. A farm in the area retains the name Demeliock.
5. This place-name is of Brythonic origin, but can no longer be identified.
6. In Geoffrey's time the ruler of Cornwall bore the title of Count.
7. Mordred.

5   Concerning the Miracles of St Mary of Laudun by Hermann of Tournai (1146)

1. Cornwall and Devon, the ancient land of the Dumnonii, the people inhabiting the territory from Land's End to the approximate area of the Rivers Parret and Stour at the time of the Roman conquest. In the Roman period Dumnonia became a typical self-governing territory of the empire. The name (Cornish *Dewnans*, Welsh *Dyfnaint*) could be interpreted as 'Land of Deep Valleys'. When the Britons were expelled from the land to the east of the Tamar, the name was preserved as 'Devon'. Hermann of Tournai uses the name to denote Cornwall, the legal and cultural continuation of ancient Dumnonia.
2. This seems to indicate a shared interest in Arthur among Bretons and the Cornish.

6   The Prophecy of Merlin by John of Cornwall (c.1150)

1. The constellation.
2. The first King of Brittany.
3. Probably the river Teifi in west Wales.
4. North-west Wales.
5. Caerleon in South Wales.
6. Snowdonia.

7   *From* The Cornish Glosses of the Prophecy of Merlin by John of Cornwall (c.1150)

1. The numbers here refer to the line numbers of the text.
2. Counting by scores has all but disappeared from most European languages, but still persists in Cornish.
3. King Arthur.
4. This is possibly a place in west Devon.

8   *From* The Romance of Tristan by Béroul (c.1150)

1. Moresk is a wooded area on the south-coast of Cornwall near Truro.
2. Cornish prowess at archery has been long acknowledged. Richard Carew in his *Survey of Cornwall* (1602) discusses the skills of Cornish archers.
3. The name of a retainer.
4. Strikingly similar to Periron, though the element *inis* (island) makes more sense

as a description of Tintagel.

5. Malpas is near Truro on the River Fal. The name is of Norman French origin, meaning 'bad step'.

6. Opinion varies on the meaning of this place-name. It probably means 'white heath'.

7. Here, this possibly means somebody named after the castle.

9   The Sicilian Coverlet (c.1400)

1. In Irish, the word *mór* means 'great'. The fact that the name is usually preceded by the definite article suggests that it may be a title.

2. This could be understood as the Irish name *Aonghus*, preceded by the Sicilian definite article.

10   *From* Arthur, a short sketch of his life and history in English verse by the Marquis of Bath (c.1428)

1. Brittany. Armorica means 'the land by the sea'.

2. Marcus Valerius Maximianus who lived in the late third and early fourth century AD. He was co-emperor with Diocletian, ruling the western part of the Roman Empire. He failed to suppress revolts in Gaul and Britain.

3. Great Britain.

4. Welshmen. This appears to refer inclusively to all Brythonic-speaking groups, the Welsh, Cornish and Bretons.

5. This suggests the Welsh *saeson*, rather than the Cornish *sawson*; both meaning 'Saxon'.

6. This appears to be 'Shut up dirty Saxons!' in slightly garbled middle Welsh.

7. A reference to Hengist and Horsa, the legendary leaders of the first Saxons to land in Britain.

8. A reference to the legendary Treason of the Long Knives when the Saxons treacherously murdered the leaders of the Britons.

9. Our Father.

10. Arthur's son by his half-sister, Morgan Le Fay.

11. Possibly Gawain.

12. Caerleon.

13. The Island of Avalon.

14. Here lies Arthur, King Once, and King to Be.

15. The year 542AD falls between the end of Roman power in Britain and the consolidation of the Saxon kingdoms. There is no reference to this date in the Anglo-Saxon Chronicle.

16. Ave.

11   *From* Le Morte D'Arthur by Thomas Malory (1485)

1. For Malory, who used French and English sources, Arthur was unequivocally an 'English' king.

2. Called.

3. Put.

4. Corresponding with Ulfin in Geoffrey of Monmouth's version of events.

5. Malory gives no clue to the location.

6. This system of fostering is familiar from a number of Welsh and especially Irish sources.

7. A possible explanation for the 'sword in the stone' motif could be a minute scribal error, confusing a Latin abbreviation for Saxon with the oblique form of the Latin word for a stone – *saxo*.

8. Merlin's lover.

9. Mont St Michel.

10. Sometimes spelt in other texts as Governal.

11. Where, in earlier versions, Tristan was brought up in Brittany, for safety's sake, here he is sent to France to learn French language and customs.

12. England: from the Welsh *Lloegr*.

13. In Cornish, the word *Dinas* means a fortress.

12   *From* Beunans Meriasek by Radolphus Ton (1504)

1. When *Beunans Meriasek* was written the Duke of Cornwall was named Arthur, the son of Henry Tudor, who may have used the name to gain political legitimacy among the British.

2. One of the middle shires of Cornwall.

13   *From* Itinerary by John Leland (c.1540)

1. In a place unassailable.

2. Cornish: 'Great Fortress'.

3. The name of the reputed site of Arthur's last battle.

14   *From* A Herring's Tail by Richard Carew (1598)

1. Cackling.

2. The cockerel of medieval romance.

3. Apollo, the sun god.

4. Malory argues that Merlin was the son of the devil.
5. Magic.

15   From **The Survey of Cornwall by Richard Carew (1602)**
1. Rabbits

16   From **The Lives of the Saints by Nicholas Roscarrock (c.1620)**
1. Dol, in Brittany.

17   From **Merlin's Prophecies and Predictions by Thomas Heywood (1651)**
1. A very early appearance of the word Celtic in English.

18   From **The Dutchesse of Cornwall's progresse to see the Land's end & to visit the mount by Nicholas Boson (c.1665)**
1. Part of the conceit is that Boson has taken the Cornish texts from an ancient script, rather as Geoffrey of Monmouth asserts that he has translated his story from a book in the British tongue.

19   **The History of King Arthur, and his Progenitors by William Hals (c.1736)**
1. In contrast to Geoffrey of Monmouth, Hals labels Gorthlois a prince.
2. Hals clearly appears to have come to interesting and correct conclusions about the etymology of the River Exe and its relationship to the original Celtic word for fish.
3. Hals offers an alternative site for Demeliock. He spells it two different ways.
4. Anna, in earlier versions of the story.
5. Geoffrey of Monmouth.
6. Excalibur.
7. In the Bible this was part of the priest's vestments.
8. Vandals, a Germanic tribe who invaded the Roman Empire and set up kingdoms in Spain and North Africa.
9. This use of Roman allusions may reveal an earlier stratum of historical memory referring to some fourth-century usurper such as Maxentius or Magnus Maximus.
10. *Aval* is the Cornish for 'apple'. *Avallan* means orchard.

20   From **Cornubia. A Poem in Five Cantos by George Woodley (1819)**
1. Camlan.
3. Cornwall.

21   From **The Fabulous History of Cornwall by Thomas Hogg (1827)**
1. One of the earliest references to Merlin's Cave in nineteenth-century literature.
2. A piece of armour.
3. Lanhydrock House, near Bodmin.
4. The River Fowey.
5. Healing ointments.
6. Restormel Castle, the former seat of the Dukes of Cornwall. Some evidence suggests that the medieval French poet Béroul wrote his Tristan and Iseult for the Cardinham family who first built Restormel Castle. This is consistent with the cultural geography of the story.
7. The moon.
8. An alternative for Nimue.
9. Possibly the forest of Moresk, near Truro.
10. After being betrayed, Merlin assists the woodcutter. However, as the Arthurian corpus shows, there are inherent dangers in accepting magical aid. The woodcutter is evidently a Cornishman.

22   **The Sisters of Glen Nectan by Robert Stephen Hawker (c.1831)**
1. Glen Nectan lies between Tintagel and Boscastle. It is more usually called St Nectan's Kieve, Kieve being Cornish for 'bowl'. Its waterfall and lake are contained in a steep wooded valley.
2. According to the legend, when St Nectan died, two mysterious sisters occupied his home and buried him and his silver bell. When they in turn died, people consistently failed to recover the treasured bell whose sound can be heard from time to time.

23   From **Scilly and its Legends by H.J. Whitfeld (1852)**
1. Cornish for Lyonesse.
2. The origin of these two verses is unclear. They may well have been written by Whitfeld himself.
3. On an equal engagement with Achilles.
4. Saracen, perhaps used here as 'unbeliever'.

5. Here the creation of Scilly is enacted cataclysmically. However, as Charles Thomas has demonstrated, Scilly is the remaining portion of a larger landmass which has gradually sunk during historic times.
6. Mentioned by the Greek historian Herodotus as a source of tin.

24   *From* Idylls of the King by Alfred, Lord Tennyson (1856–74)

1. Fine linen.
2. Part of the regalia of the high priests of the Bible.

25   The Quest of the Sangraal by Robert Stephen Hawker (1863)

1. The poem was dedicated to his first wife Charlotte: 'To a Vacant Chair: and an added stone: I chant these solitary sounds.'
2. The Holy Grail.
3. A measure for the wine of the sacrifice.
4. Tintagel. Hawker's revival of the old Cornish form is evidence of his interest in the Cornish language: 'As in the title, so in the Knightly Names, I have preferred the Keltic to other sources of spelling and sound.'
5. Chanted prayers.
6. Joseph of Arimathea, according to the Biblical account, took responsibility for the burial of Jesus. Later legend, however, made Joseph his uncle, a tin trader who visited Cornwall. It was also believed that Jesus as a boy visited Cornwall in his company.
7. The Passover. In Hebrew *Pesach*, in Greek and Latin *Pascha*, in Cornish *Pask*.
8. According to legend, the thorn tree in Glastonbury Abbey had sprung up from Joseph's staff.
9. An attempt by Hawker to produce a Hebrew-like utterance. This was a fashionable poetic device and was supposed to be impenetrable and mysterious.
10. A curse.
11. Caradon Hill above Liskeard.
12. Hawker notes that 'the city of "Sarras in the spiritual place" is the scene of many a legend of mediæval times'. It is sometimes identified as a mythic city near Stonehenge.
13. In his notes on the poem, Hawker philosophises on this subject at length. He appeared to be trying to express an integral vision of life, time and space.
14. The Disciples.
15. Hawker notes that in the 'Sign of the Son of Man' is a belief that a vision of the cross in the sky would be a sign of the end of the world.
16. Japhat or Japheth was believed to be the son of Noah from whom the western peoples were descended. His son Gomer was the ancestor of the British peoples – including the Cornish.
17. Hawker's notes on this reflect contemporary controversies over which way priests should be facing when celebrating the mass.
18. In the medieval Cornish drama the *Ordinalia* the devil and his associates are positioned on the northern side of the amphitheatre. Hawker here may be grounding his work in historical precedents.
19. The Southern Cross would not, of course, have been visible to the Wise Men. Nevertheless, Hawker finds its symbolism irresistible because of the symbolism of a cross in the sky. See note 15.
20. The hand would have been red because of the wound. Hawker notes that 'Our Lord was laid in His sepulchre with His head towards the west: His right hand therefore gave symbolic greeting to the region of the south: as his left hand reproached and gave a fatal aspect to the north'.
21. The archangel, regarding by many people, especially Henry Jenner, as the patron saint of Cornwall.
22. Hawker interprets this as 'golden hill'. While this is not entirely accurate, this is typical of his interest in Cornish. Its actual meaning is 'swallow hill' and is known more commonly as Brown Willy.
23. Brocelian is the forest in Brittany associated with Merlin. In his notes, Hawker refers to Hersart de La Villemarqué, author of the *Barzaz Breiz*, an Ossianesque compilation of supposedly ancient Breton poetry.
24. Assistant to the priests in the Jewish Temple.
25. The Maccabees were four brothers who led the Jewish resistance to a Greek king in 167 BC and stemmed the threat to Judaism from the advance of Hellenism.
26. This stanza is an early expression of the vision of the Cornish landscape as a sacred land inherently inhospitable to

the forces of industrialism and modernity.

27. 'Son of Amram': Moses, Numbers 20. II
28. An incorporation of Norse mythology. This is the tree on which the world rests.
29. The Sea of Galilee.
30. Aramaic: 'You have come'.

26   *From* **Popular Romances of the West of England: The Drolls, Traditions, and Superstitions of Old Cornwall by Robert Hunt (1865)**

1. If Hunt is here referring to prophecy regarding the Merlin rock, then this statement is incorrect. The Spanish landed in west Cornwall in 1595. However, the prophecy may well have been made known after the event to justify a retreat from a superior Spanish force.
2. John Francis Campbell of Islay, a mid nineteenth-century pioneer of Gaelic and Celtic folklore collecting.
3. Gildas was a 6th century Brythonic monk. In his *De Excidio Britanniae* (*On the Downfall of Britain*), he denounced the Britons and their leaders for their moral failure, and asserted that God sent the Saxons as a punishment.
4. This shows that the Cornish pronunciation has survived the shift to English.
5. Cornish: 'Fulling mill'.
6. Vikings. Arthur's enemies are diplomatically, though anachronistically, transformed from Saxons into Vikings. Ironically the Vikings sometimes fought as allies of the Cornish.
7. This verse was probably composed by Hunt himself.
8. It is a pity Hunt does not record more of this. There is clearly an echo of Gogmagog's battle with Corineus, as recounted by Geoffrey of Monmouth.
9. Hunt's etymology is wrong, Dinas has nothing to do with Danes. It may relect a folk belief in Danish settlements.

27   **The Buried City by John Harris (1868)**

1. In most stories, this is Trevilian, riding on a white horse. Maybe Harris was confusing the two, Trelawny being a more common motif of Cornish power and identity.

28   **Dozmare Pool, Cornwall by John Brent (1880)**

1. Brown Willy. Dozmare is actually quite a distance away from this tor.
2. From Tennyson.

29   *From* **Tristram of Lyonesse by A.C. Swinburne (1882)**

1. Iseult's serving maid.
2. A retainer.

30   *From* **An Unsentimental Journey through Cornwall by Dinah Craik (1884)**

1. Clearly, Craik is drawing heavily on Malory.
2. Another example of the Victorian blurring of the distinction between 'Britain' and 'England'.

31   *From* **Cornish Feasts and Folklore by Margaret A. Courtney (1890)**

1. These can still be seen.

32   *From* **The Arthurian Legend by John Rhys (1890)**

1. Galahad.

33   **Lyonesse by James Dryden Hosken (1902)**

1. Decorated with coats of arms.

34   *From* **Some Possible Arthurian Place-Names in West Penwith by Henry Jenner (1912)**

1. This literally means 'covered lane'. It appears to refer to the fogous in these locations.
2. This became the site of the first modern Gorseth in 1928, presided over by Jenner himself.
3. Here, Jenner is repeating the received wisdom which viewed the material assembled by Welsh antiquary and poet Iolo Morganwg (Edward Williams 1747–1826) as fabrication from start to finish. Despite mounting evidence to the contrary, this view persists in certain quarters.
4. This Tremodrett is not far from Roche Rock (interpreted by some as the hermitage of Tristan and Iseult) and Castle-an-Dinas.
5. Urien was Taliesin's patron.

35 *From* **Legend Land by 'Lyonesse' (1922)**

1. The provenance or an alternative source for this rhyme has not been found. It may not be of any great antiquity.

36 **The Famous Tragedy of the Queen of Cornwall at Tintagel in Lyonesse by Thomas Hardy (1923)**

1. The Breton Iseult is known as Iseult of the Whitehands in many of the versions. The Queen here is Iseult the Fair.
2. A hunting dog.
3. Tristan.
4. Puffin.
5. This was a Roman post meaning 'commander-in-chief'.
6. St Nectan's Kieve.

37 **The Coming of Arthur by John Baragwanath King (1925)**

1. Priest.
2. A shortened use of 'Tre, Pol and Pen' to symbolise Cornwall.

38 **Anglice, a Patriotic Song of our Motherland by Katharine Lee Jenner (1926)**

1. Cornish: Can Gwlasol, Agan Mam-vro.
2. The Civil War battle at Lansdown near Bristol in July 1643. Charles I's letter thanking the Cornish for their support in the victory is still displayed in some churches in Cornwall.
3. Cornish saints.

39 **Tintagel Castle in History and Romance by Henry Jenner (1927)**

1. Recent scholarship interprets this name as *Din Tagell*, meaning 'fortress at a constriction'.

40 *From* **'Ceremonies of the Gorseth of the Bards of Cornwall' (1928–present)**

1. At this point in the ceremony the bards have moved inside the circle to touch the sword. If they cannot reach it they place a hand on the shoulder of a bard in contact with it.

41 *From* **King Arthur's Territory by J. Hambley Rowe (1929)**

1. Arthur's battles are listed in the ninth century *Historia Brittonum*, formerly ascribed to 'Nennius'.
2. Near Truro.

42 *From* **King Arthur: His Symbolic Story in Verse by B.D. Vere (1930)**

1. Compare the portrayal of Joseph of Arimathea here with his depiction in the Cornish Mystery Play trilogy known as the *Ordinalia*. See in particular, Joseph at the beginning of the third play, *Resurrexio Domini*.

43 **An Balores/The Chough by Robert Morton Nance (1932)**

1. The chough was still being used as a symbol at the Celtic Congress 2000 held in Bude, Cornwall.
2. Nance uses a similar method of characterisation as in his *Cledry Plays*.

44 *From* **Dawn in Lyonesse by Mary Ellen Chase (1938)**

1. The lighthouse at Trevose Head, to the north-west of Padstow.

45 *From* **Trystan hag Ysolt/Tristan and Isolt by A.S.D. Smith (1951) and D.H. Watkins (1962)**

1. Near Fowey.
2. This Lyonesse is more probably Leon, the north-western province of Brittany.
3. Despite much searching, we have been unable to ascertain where this is.
4. *Trist* in Cornish means 'sad'.
5. Her enemies at court.
6. Chalcedony and beryl are precious stones.

46 *From* **Mines and Miners of Cornwall by A.K. Hamilton Jenkin (1970)**

1. The waterfall is still there. Various studies have shown that the beach was used as a harbour from ancient times.
2. These buildings were later used for selling pasties and ice creams to tourists.

47 *From* **Geraint: Last of the Arthurians by Donald R. Rawe (1972)**

1. The circumference of the Round forms the battlements in the drama.
2. The River Parrett.

48   Arthur by Tim Saunders (1990)

1. The poem was originally written in rhyming couplets in Cornish. See appendix for the original.

49   *From* Nativitas Christi/The Nativity by Alan M. Kent (2000)

1. The Devil's Spoon —the name given to a device found in Piran Round, probably once used to disguise and conceal actors.
2. According to the apocryphal legend of the Rood the seeds planted in Adam's mouth became the wood of the true cross.

Further reading

Ashe, Geoffrey (1960) *From Caesar to Arthur*, London: Collins.
    (1971) *The Quest for Arthur's Britain*, London: Paladin.
Alcock, Leslie (1971) *Arthur's Britain*, Harmondsworth: Penguin.
Barber, Chris and Pykitt, David (1993) *Journey to Avalon: The Final Discovery of King Arthur*, Abergavenny: Blorenge.
Brendon, Piers (1975) *Hawker of Morwenstow*, London: Jonathan Cape.
Cavendish, Richard (1978) *King Arthur and the Grail*, London: Weidenfeld & Nicholson.
Cope, Julian (1998) *The Modern Antiquarian*, London: Fontana.
Darrah, John (1981) *The Real Camelot: Paganism and the Arthurian Romances*, New York and London: Thames and Hudson.
Doel, Fran, Doel, Geoff and Lloyd, Terry (1998) *Worlds of Arthur: King Arthur in History Legend and Culture*, Stroud: Tempus.
Harvey, Graham and Hardman, Charlotte (1996) *Paganism Today*, London: Thorsons.
Holmes, Julyan (ed.) (1998) *An Dhargan a Verdhin/ The Prophecy of Merlin*, Hayle: Kesva an Taves Kernewek/Cornish Language Board.
Hutchinson, Don *et. al.* (1999) *One Man's Dream: The Story of King Arthur's Great Halls*. Tintagel: Sword in the Stone.
Koch, John T. and Carey, John (1994) *The Celtic Heroic Age: Literary Sources for Ancient Celtic Europe and Early Ireland and Wales*, Malden, Massachusetts: Celtic Studies Publications.
Loomis, Roger Sherman (ed.) (1959) A*rthurian Literature in the Middle Ages: A Collaborative History*, Oxford: Clarendon Press.
Miles, Dillwyn (1992) *The Secret of the Bards of the Isle of Britain*, Llandybie: Gwasg Dinefwr.
Moffat, Alistair (1999) *Arthur and the Lost Kingdoms*, London: Weidenfeld & Nicholson.
Murdoch, Brian (1993) *Cornish Literature*, Cambridge: D.S. Brewer.
Phelps, Kenneth (1975) *The Wormwood Cup: Thomas Hardy in Cornwall*, Padstow: Lodenek Press.
Phillips, Graham (1995) *The Search for the Grail*, London: Century.
Robins, Colin and Deacon, Bernard (1992) *Merlin's Diner*, Tiverton: Cornwall Books.
Symons, Andrew C., (November 2000) 'Aspects of the Mermaid', *An Baner Kernewek*, No. 102.
Tasker Grimbert, Joan (ed.) *Tristan and Isolde: A Casebook*, New York and London: Garland.
Thomas, Charles (1986) *Celtic Britain*, London: Thames and Hudson.
    (1998) *Christian Celts: Messages and Images*, Stroud: Tempus.
Tolstoy, Nikolai (1985) *The Quest for Merlin*, London: Hamish Hamilton.
Trezise, Simon (2000) *The West Country as a Literary Invention: Putting Fiction in its Place*, Exeter: University of Exeter Press.
Weatherhill, Craig (1985) *Cornovia: Ancient Sites of Cornwall and Scilly*, Penzance: Alison Hodge.